THE COMPLETE

TRACKER

THE COMPLETE
TRACKER

TRACKS, SIGNS, AND HABITS
OF NORTH AMERICAN WILDLIFE

LEN MCDOUGALL

Lyons & Burford, Publishers

Printed in the United States of America

Design and composition by Rohani Design, Edmonds, WA

10 9 8 7 6 5 4 3 2 1

Library of Congress Cataloging-in-Publication Data

McDougall, Len.
    The complete tracker: tracks, signs, and habits of North American wildlife / Len McDougall.
        p. cm.
    Includes index.
    ISBN 1-55821-458-5
    1. Animal tracks—North America. 2. Mammals—North America.
I. Title.
QL768.M43 1997
599'.097—dc21   96-37815
                                                              CIP

*For my nephew Josh, already
one of the best woodsmen I know.*

CONTENTS

TRACK FAMILIES

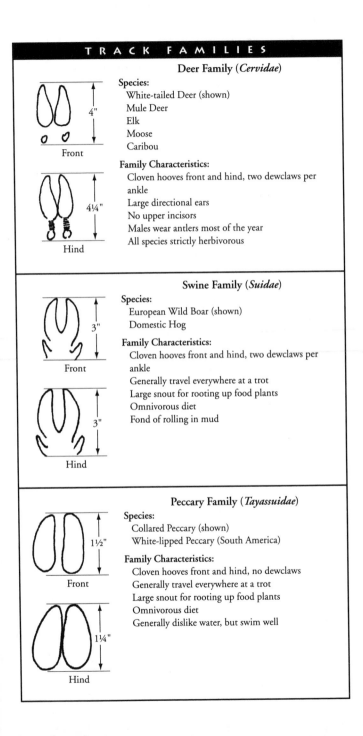

Deer Family (*Cervidae*)

Species:
White-tailed Deer (shown)
Mule Deer
Elk
Moose
Caribou

Family Characteristics:
Cloven hooves front and hind, two dewclaws per ankle
Large directional ears
No upper incisors
Males wear antlers most of the year
All species strictly herbivorous

Front — 4"
Hind — 4¼"

Swine Family (*Suidae*)

Species:
European Wild Boar (shown)
Domestic Hog

Family Characteristics:
Cloven hooves front and hind, two dewclaws per ankle
Generally travel everywhere at a trot
Large snout for rooting up food plants
Omnivorous diet
Fond of rolling in mud

Front — 3"
Hind — 3"

Peccary Family (*Tayassuidae*)

Species:
Collared Peccary (shown)
White-lipped Peccary (South America)

Family Characteristics:
Cloven hooves front and hind, no dewclaws
Generally travel everywhere at a trot
Large snout for rooting up food plants
Omnivorous diet
Generally dislike water, but swim well

Front — 1½"
Hind — 1¼"

American Antelope Family (*Antilocapridae*)

Front

Hind

Species:
Pronghorn Antelope

Family Characteristics:
Cloven hooves resemble those of deer species
No dewclaws streamlines legs for faster running speed
Good vision
Herbivorous diet of ground plants and prairie grasses
Social, travel in herds of mostly relatives
70-mph running speed, fastest animal in North America
Black marks on bucks' muzzles lacking on does
Buck and does grow horns, does usually lack prongs

Bear Family (*Ursidae*)

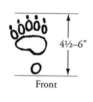

Front

Hind

Species:
Brown or Grizzly Bear
Black Bear (shown)
Polar Bear

Family Characteristics:
Five toes front and hind feet, small toes innermost
Plantigrade (flat-footed) walk, shuffling gait
Excellent sense of smell, fair hearing, poor vision
Omnivorous diet includes carrion, fish, fruit
Sleep through winter months, but none hibernates
All species superb swimmers

Wild Dog Family (*Canidae*)

Front

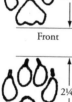

Hind

Species:
Gray or Timber Wolf
Coyote (shown)
Gray Fox
Red Fox

Family Characteristics:
Four toes front and hind feet, claws show in tracks
Pointed ears, excellent sense of smell, good vision
Lithe bodies, long furry tails
Both parents take part in rearing young
Pair believed to mate for life
Mostly carnivorous diet includes carrion, fruit

Wild Cat Family (*Felidae*)

Species:
- Puma or Mountain Lion
- Bobcat (shown)
- Lynx
- Jaguar

Family Characteristics:
- Four toes front and hind feet, retractable claws
- Lithe, muscular bodies, tail length varies
- Excellent sense of smell, fair hearing, good vision
- Omnivorous diet includes fish, mammals, fruit
- Solitary except when mating, only females rear young
- Rarely eat carrion unless starving, prefer to hunt
- All cats strong swimmers, but only jaguars like water

Front — 1¾"

Hind — 1¾"

Weasel Family (*Mustelidae*)

Species:
- Wolverine
- Badger
- River Otter
- Mink (shown)
- Ermine
- Striped Skunk

Family Characteristics:
- Five toes front and hind feet, claws show in tracks
- Small toes innermost, may not register in tracks
- Perineal (anal) scent glands
- Excellent sense of smell, fair hearing, fair vision
- Carnivorous diet includes fish, mammals, insects
- Slow runners, fierce and willing fighters

Front — 1½"

Hind — 1½"

Raccoon Family (*Procyonidae*)

Species:
- Raccoon (shown)
- Ringtail
- Coatimundi

Family Characteristics:
- Five toes front and hind feet, small toes innermost
- Plantigrade (flat-footed) walk
- Long, ringed tail
- Omnivorous diet includes meat, fish, insects, fruit
- Solitary, mostly nocturnal
- Good senses of smell and vision, fair hearing
- All species good climbers, ferocious when cornered

Front — 2¼"

Hind — 3⅛"

Opossum Family (*Didelphidae*)

Front

Hind

Species:
Virginia Opossum

Family Characteristics:
Five toes front and hind feet, thumblike toe on hind feet
Poor vision, fair hearing, excellent sense of smell
Carnivorous diet of mostly carrion, some plants
Solitary except when mating, only females rear young
Mostly nocturnal, sometimes active by day
Often play dead when threatened, prefer to tree

Beaver Family (*Castoridae*)

Front

Hind

Species:
Beaver

Family Characteristics:
Five toes front and hind feet
Poor vision, fair hearing, excellent sense of smell
Perineal (anal) sweat glands, obvious scent mounds
Strictly herbivorous, eat bark of aspen, willow
Slow runners, very strong and capable swimmers
Always live on flowing freshwater streams
Social, family colonies of up to 18 animals

Porcupine Family (*Erethizonidae*)

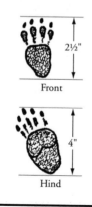

Front

Hind

Species:
Porcupine

Family Characteristics:
Four toes front, five toes hind, unique pebbled soles
Plantigrade (flat-footed) walk
Long, heavily quilled tail
Coarse fur with 30,000 quills on back
Solitary, mostly nocturnal
Good sense of smell, poor vision, fair hearing
Always found in forested areas, cedar swamps

Hare and Rabbit Families (*Leporidae*)

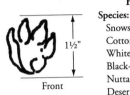

1½"

Front

Species:
Snowshoe Hare (shown)
Cottontail Rabbit
White-tailed Jack Rabbit
Black-tailed Jack Rabbit
Nuttall's Cottontail
Desert Cottontail

5"

Hind

Family Characteristics:
Four toes front and hind feet
Poor vision, excellent senses of smell and hearing
Fast runners, but only for short distances
Herbivorous diet of ground plants, buds, some bark
Solitary, mostly nocturnal
No fixed mating season

Squirrel Family (*Sciuridae*)

1½"

Front

Species:
Fox Squirrel
Gray Squirrel (shown)
Red Squirrel
Eastern Woodchuck
Yellow-bellied Marmot

2"

Hind

Family Characteristics:
Four toes front, five toes hind, elongated hind feet
Good vision, fair hearing, excellent sense of smell
Tree squirrels build cup-shaped nests high in trees
Ground squirrels dig burrows, most hibernate
Herbivorous diet of mostly nuts, some eat insects

Muskrat Family (*Zibethicidae*)

1"

Front

Species:
Common Muskrat

Family Characteristics:
Five toes front and hind, vestigial inner toe
Good sense of smell, poor vision, fair hearing
Black, scaly, ratlike tail
Much larger than rat species
Herbivorous diet also includes crustaceans, insects
Solitary, mostly nocturnal

2"

Hind

INTRODUCTION

FEW EXPERIENCES ARE MORE thrilling than watching unsuspecting wild animals go about their business in a natural environment. The ultimate triumph comes when you've tracked down an animal on its own terms, on its own turf. Most experienced animal watchers feel a soul-deep sense of accomplishment from executing a successful stalk against creatures with senses so acute we can scarcely comprehend them. Whether you take an animal as meat, as an image on film or videotape, or simply as a treasured memory, pressing the trigger—literally or figuratively—is the anticlimax of a successful stalk.

As modern society drives a wedge ever deeper between humans and nature, the ancient art of tracking has assumed an almost supernatural status in novels and movies. Fiction writers imbue characters with supernormal skills, glossing over details of the tracking process as simply unexplainable mysteries, and thereby creating an erroneous frame of reference for many. That mystical image has been supported and sometimes exaggerated by some outdoorsmen, who for one reason or another enjoy perpetuating it. But Hollywood's portrayal of trackers, hunters, and woodsmen in general is about as accurate as its portrayal of cops, doctors, and reporters, and tales spun around the campfire must be taken with a grain of salt.

There is indeed a kind of spiritual exhilaration associated with tracking down a canny denizen of the wild, but the ability to find and trail any animal is pure mechanics, not magic. One trait common to all accomplished trackers is a solid knowledge of the animals they pursue. Knowing a species' seasonal habitats and foods helps to narrow the search area, and a solid understanding of specific habits is invaluable for finding individuals within their own territories. A tracker is a detective, gleaning facts from minute details and assembling them into a cohesive picture of what went on before.

The goal of this book is to make you competent in the art of finding and observing wild animals in their natural environments, no matter how much actual experience you've had in the wilderness. In its pages you'll find the finer points of tracking, modern tools that can make finding an animal more certain, and an encyclopedia of pertinent information about the most prominent members of each family.

If you enjoy a good puzzle, you'll love tracking. The work is often tedious and seldom glamorous, but success is a heady reward that makes almost any effort worthwhile.

PART

1

TRACKING

TOOLS AND METHODS

TRACK
IDENTIFICATION
1

WATCHING A GOOD TRACKER at work can be pretty amazing. Making sense of scratches and impressions left in the earth, bent grasses, and shed hairs is a skill few folks ever need to learn. It wasn't always that way. Tracking and hunting skills were once the equivalent of today's college degree, and they were passed on to every youngster from early childhood. But like tanning hides and making soap, these skills long ago became obsolete in a world increasingly dominated by technology. The finer points of tracking became blurred with time and, as is always the case, myths sprouted up like toadstools on a fallen tree.

The chapters in part one will help dispel those myths. Here we'll learn the nuts and bolts of locating a species of animal by environment, learning its routines by interpreting the sign it leaves, and tracking it to a feeding, watering, or denning area where it can be observed. Also covered are the tricks and tools most valuable for avoiding being yourself detected as you stalk within visual range. The information is largely generic, making it applicable to species not covered in this book, to diverse types of terrain, and even to exotic species on other continents.

A warning is in order at this point: Trailing wild animals is a fascinating pastime, but their meandering paths can lead to remote country. Tracking yourself back out is never a good gamble; get a quality map compass, an area map, and a solid working knowledge of both before embarking on any tracking exercise. *Always* carry these items with you in the woods.

♣ READING TRACKS

Reading tracks accurately requires a trained eye. An expert tracker can detect and identify tracks invisible to most outdoorsmen by knowing what to look for and, equally important, knowing how to interpret what he sees. He knows what species are likely to inhabit an area, and his eyes automatically search for spoor. An obscure crescent-shaped impression in the ground in a field of tall grass is read as a whitetail's hoofprint. The sharpness of the corners in the print, along with the color, shape, and moisture content of any crushed vegetation within it, reveal the age of the track with sometimes surprising accuracy.

While this book is designed to be carried afield as a reference, there are many small pieces of information the beginning tracker will find helpful to carry in his head. All cats, for example, have four toes on each foot. So do canines, but cats have retractable claws that seldom print, while members of the dog family have fixed claws that print with every track. Bears have five toes with fixed claws on each foot, but their front paws are nearly doglike while the rear paws are shaped much like our own feet, only with the big and little toes reversed. All weasels, including skunks, badgers, and wolverines, have five toes on front and back paws, but the size and other characteristics of their tracks make it possible to identify individual species. Rabbits and hares have four toes on each foot, but their distinctive track patterns are similar only to those of squirrel family members, which have four toes on the front feet and five on the back. You'll still need a reference, however, because for every rule there are exceptions. The common muskrat, for instance, has five toes on each foot, while the closely related round-tailed muskrat has four on the front and five on the rear. As you become more practiced, certain facts are sure to be memorized. But if you can at least identify the family of animal whose tracks are before you, the species can be narrowed down and ultimately identified by referring to this book.

TRACKS IN MUD

Trackers are seldom fortunate enough to find an obvious trail of perfect prints, but wet sand, clay, or mud along the banks of lakes and streams will nearly always provide a few tracks distinct enough to take a plaster cast. Almost every animal in an area will visit low-lying shorelines to drink, to feed, or sometimes to escape predators (rabbits, for example, freely take to the water when pursued). Birds, reptiles, and even bats are among regular visitors to watering holes, while other animals, such as the beaver and the muskrat, live there full time. Careful survey of a muddy bank can provide an accurate roster of almost every species within a mile or more.

However, in a few instances animals walking through mud leave a clear yet abnormal print. White-tailed deer normally leave split, heart-shaped prints on solid ground, but on slippery mud and snow, the animals tend to splay their hooves into a plowlike V to protect against sliding. Cats also display a certain insecurity when crossing mud, and often partially extend their retractable claws, as if ready to scramble for solid footing. These tracks can be differentiated from the similar pawprints of the canine family by claw marks: Cat claws curve sharply downward and terminate in a very sharp point, while the nonretractable claws of canines are thicker, are blunt, and have a less pronounced curvature.

TRACKS IN SAND

Wet sand is a very good tracking medium, but dry sand can make track identification nearly impossible. Its powdery nature causes impressions partially to fill in as soon as an animal raises its foot, obscuring the details needed to make a positive identification. In beach sand, prints are likely to be no more than bowl-shaped depressions, with the tracks of a deer being indistinguishable from those of a large dog, goat, or llama. In these cases you can get some type of idea as to an animal's species by gauging its stride, straddle, and gait; these will be explained in greater detail later.

TRACKS IN SNOW

Snow is usually a good tracking medium, but the "tracking snow" so many deer hunters wish for can work for or against them. Light, wet snow in temperatures just below freezing can yield ideal prints—although, again, deer tend to splay their hooves in it. But warm snow, further heated by compression and an animal's own body heat, tends to melt rapidly outward from a print. This phenomenon is responsible for reports of giant tracks belonging to gargantuan animals that no one ever sees.

Hardpack snow in temperatures below 20°F is another matter entirely. Hoofed animals passing over it during warmer daylight hours may sink in more than a foot, leaving prints at the bottom of a deep hole. Lighter, wide-pawed species, such as bobcats and lynx, may leave distinct prints during daylight but they will begin to expand quickly, especially if the sun is shining. During the coldest hours, from about 12 midnight to 4 A.M., pawed animals can travel along a frozen surface and hardly leave a mark; even the tracks of a large deer or elk may be faint, with only a dusting of crushed crystalline snow to tell of its passing. Cutting the trail of a walking cat under such frozen conditions is nearly impossible, but this is where tracking devices and an ability to read sign come into play.

Tracking conditions may also vary a great deal from one snowfall to the next. Warm, fluffy snow will hold a print well for a time, depending on ambient temperature, but warm snowfalls are frequently heavy and may obliterate a trail completely in less than an hour. Conversely, cold, high-altitude snow—known as "powder" to skiers (it looks like laundry detergent to me)—comes to earth as tiny balls of ice in which tracks are frequently unrecognizable or at least badly distorted.

TRACKS IN VEGETATION

It's vegetation that defeats most would-be trackers. Leaf-strewn hardwoods, grassy fields, and thick swamps pose a real challenge, because prints there—especially those of pawed animals—are seldom distinct. In these environments, tracking consists mainly of looking for minor disturbances that couldn't have occurred naturally. Every creature that moves on the earth leaves a mark of its passing, and it's when a trail seems to just disappear that your entire arsenal of tracking techniques will come into play.

Areas of open grass are a pretty good bet for anyone looking for herbivores and omnivores, as well as many of the carnivores that prey upon them. The grasses, clovers, and plantains that thrive in open spaces are favorites with many plant eaters. Sunny, open areas also provide space for wild cherries, strawberries, serviceberries, and, of course, the ubiquitous black and red raspberries, all of which are irresistible attractions to many birds and mammals.

Tracking is difficult in tall grass because ground vegetation cushions each step, distributing an animal's weight over a greater area (as a snow-shoe would), and also obscures any impressions made in the earth. There may be no real tracks to follow, but with patience, you can follow almost anything with enough body weight to break grass stems or press a plant to the ground. You just need to break the mindset of looking for tracks and instead look for footprints—visible evidence that a paw or hoof was pressed downward. Twisted, broken grass stems and torn plant leaves at the bottom of a track impression in the grass indicate a change in direc-tion, made as the animal turned with weight on its foot. A furrow of grasses pushed forward and aside by an animal's passing will remain obvious for half a day, particularly when the plants are weighted with morning dew.

Tracking can also be tough over the leafy floor of a hardwood forest, where years of dead leaves form a cushion of loose humus. Fresh trails left by hoofed mammals are fairly easy to follow because these animals leave sharp impressions; prints from pawed animals are less obvious. And the smaller the animal, the less noticeable its tracks.

In this environment, tracking consists of looking very closely at the forest floor for unusual disturbances. You'll see for yourself that leaves are a slippery walking surface, and dry upper layers tend to slide over one another. Small disturbances at regular intervals tell of an animal passing through on its way to a feeding, sleeping, or mating area. If such a regu-lar trail can be found, the species of animal can often be determined, or at least narrowed down, by comparing to existing data its stride and strad-dle and the placement of its feet. A trail that looks as if the top leaves have been brushed forward and to either side, for instance, indicates that a porcupine passed through, sweeping the forest floor with its heavy tail as it lumbered along. Small sections of leaves pushed upward at short inter-vals denote the leaping gait of a squirrel.

Swamps are always interesting places to put your tracking skills to the test. Not only are they generally inhabited by an abundance of wild crea-tures but their terrain is also so variable that you can expect to encounter almost every type of tracking problem imaginable. One moment you're in water to your knees; a few minutes later you're on solid ground, or in shoulder-high sawgrass, or in a deadfall area so thick with fallen trees that normal walking is impossible.

There are several reasons that so many species inhabit swamps. The most obvious is that human beings avoid such places, which makes them wilder and thus more attractive to animals—and people seeking to observe them. Another reason is safety; a typical cedar swamp is so thick with brush and foliage that anything more than 50 feet away may be out of sight. Animals whose principal sense is eyesight (like people) prefer to avoid places that defeat their main advantage, while those with keen hearing and an acute sense of smell can often locate and slip past would-be predators undetected. The pronghorn antelope, for example, is a creature of the open plains, where its sharp eyesight allows it to detect enemies at a distance; the white-tailed deer inhabits thick cover, where its poor eyesight is more than offset by a keen nose. Swamps offer plenty of secluded spots to sleep in peace and, of course, also contain a wide variety of food plants.

The dense foliage of a swamp is both an advantage and a disadvantage for a tracker. Animals living there tend to follow regular, packed trails that allow swift, quiet travel; a patient observer can use this to good advantage. Any number of different animals from different species may use the same trail. Porcupines, raccoons, and bobcats use trails created by deer, and coyote packs patrol them routinely in search of carrion, fawns, or sickly adults. Bears also frequent deer trails in spring, hoping to catch a newborn fawn or a winter-weakened adult. Each of these creatures leaves its own spoor on the same trail, making any tracking exercise difficult. The advantage of walking such a trail, however, is that many kinds of tracks lead to it, and if you can see where a certain species joined or left the deer trail, chances are that the animal will return there.

TRACKS ON ROCK

The last and perhaps hardest medium to track over is rock (no pun intended), including asphalt road surfaces. Obviously no animals will leave footprints in stone—although I've seen ancient bear trails worn several inches into solid granite—but they will leave marks that can be followed. As any raw-fingered rock climber will attest, stone is very abrasive. Hooves, claws, and paws scraping over its surfaces will leave faint marks, like that on a piece of wood rubbed against sandpaper. Faint scrape marks and light disturbances in the dusting of sand that invariably covers rocky areas also provide trails that can be followed, albeit painstakingly, while patches of moss and lichen along the way may yield identifiable prints.

Roadways offer many of the same obstacles to trailing an animal as bare rock, but they do offer a few advantages. First, rural highways always have gravel shoulders alongside the pavement. This loose stone and sand is easily disturbed by even a mouse or a sparrow, so almost any animal will leave a conspicuous trail. By simply walking the edges of a road on each side you can determine whether an animal crossed straight over, turned back the way it came, or traveled down the road a way before heading into the bush.

Ironically, asphalt roads sometimes register near-perfect tracks on their surfaces, especially during early morning. Since most mammals are nocturnal, the hours just before dawn are busy with animals returning to their dens after a night of foraging or hunting. If an animal crosses a road during that commute, chances are it's walked through grass heavily laden with dew. As it then walks across the loose sand and gravel of the shoulder, its wet feet pick up small particles, leaving behind an outline in the shape of its paw or hoof. As it crosses over the paved surface, these particles fall away, leaving a kind of negative print in the shape of its paw or hoof.

The most common reason for losing a trail is simply a lack of patience. If you find just one track of any animal that can't fly, there must be more. In the case of leapers such as the whitetail, the next track may be as much as 20 feet from the first, but never doubt that it will be there; careful study of the last track will point you toward it. A change of direction is represented by a spiral twist against the earth, made as the animal spun on its foot. A sudden leap is indicated by hind-foot tracks that are abnormally deep, especially at the toes, sometimes with a spray of debris behind them. You may have to drop to hands and knees to decipher what made the trail seem to disappear, but always remember that a trail doesn't actually simply disappear. It continues on, and all you have to do is find it.

☙ STRIDE, STRADDLE, AND GAIT

When tracks are present but undefined, as they might be in loose sand, gravel, or thick grass, you can get a good idea of an animal's species by measuring its stride, straddle, and gait. *Stride* is the distance one foot travels in a single step. *Straddle* is the distance between an animal's feet on either side, which is sometimes, but not always, determined by its body width. *Gait* is the pace an animal was traveling when it made the tracks. Of course, there are times when these three factors overlap among species, and gait varies depending on whether an animal is walking, trotting, or running. But so many species have a distinctive track pattern that knowing the average distance of each one's stride, straddle, and gait can be critical to making a positive identification. These measurements are included in later chapters dealing with individual species.

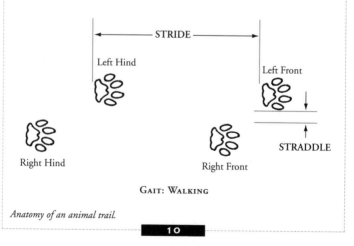

Anatomy of an animal trail.

❦ ESTIMATING WEIGHT

Estimating an animal's size and weight from track impressions is an important skill for all trackers, especially guides and hunters. Knowing a given species' average weight and size can help you, but probably the easiest method of gauging weight is to compare a print with the impression left by your own foot in the same terrain. For hoofed animals, I step down hard alongside the track with just the heel of my boot, imitating the force and area covered by the existing print. The greater area covered by your boot heel roughly compensates for the fact that a hoofed animal normally carries its weight on at least three feet. By knowing your own weight and comparing the maximum depth of your own print to the maximum depth of the hoofprint, you can make a close estimation of an animal's weight.

For larger pawed animals, such as bears or puma, I exert my full weight downward on just the ball of one foot. Most animals tend to walk on their toes, and the objective here is to mimic the animal's print as closely as possible. In this case, use a two-to-one ratio to make your weight estimations: A cougar print registering 1 inch deep in mud, for example, indicates an approximate weight of 100 pounds if the toeprint of a 200-pound man also sinks 1 inch.

❦ AGING TRACKS

In most instances, the tracks that most interest a hunter are the most recent, so knowing how to distinguish these from older tracks is a big plus. Aging tracks can also provide important background information about an animal's habits. Comparing the time interval between each set of prints can tell you how frequently a trail is used, and this can cut the amount of time you spend waiting for an animal to appear. Remember, most wild animals are creatures of habit unless pressured. With a comprehensive timetable of its comings and goings in hand, you can position yourself in a nearby hide literally within minutes of an animal's appearance.

The two factors that most affect tracks are temperature and humidity. Heavy rain can wash away a trail in minutes, and a hard snowstorm will erase the best trail. On the other hand, a track left in permanently wet swamp mud may stay sharp and fresh looking for weeks, while a pawprint made in wet sand crumbles quickly away under a hot sun. Sometimes you have to look closely to see everything a track has to tell.

All tracks become less well defined with continued exposure to the elements; the fresher a track, the sharper its features. Summer grass still pressed flat against the ground by a bear's foot means you should keep your eyes open lest you run into the animal. An hour later, that same print's grass stems will be slowly rising back to their upright positions. A day later, only a few broken, yellowed stems will mark the bear's passing.

Whenever possible, I like to hedge my bets by sweeping clean a sandy area where animal traffic appears regularly, in effect creating a clean slate on which fresh tracks will be conspicuous because there are no others. Surprisingly, wild animals seem almost oblivious to tracks—or lack of them—and even suspicious species will cross this prepared "litmus field" without apparent concern, so long as you take care not to disturb its surroundings or deposit foreign scent; never touch anything with bare hands if you can avoid it. By monitoring the swept area in the morning and afternoon and sweeping it clean again after each check, you can work out an individual animal's timetable precisely and quickly. In no more than a day or so, you'll probably be able to time your own arrival to within minutes of the animal's.

READING SIGN

2

AS WE SAW IN CHAPTER 1, reading tracks is only part of tracking. In most cases, following a set of prints alone ranges from fairly difficult to darned near impossible. Fortunately, much of the information about any animal can be garnered from other marks left by its passing, known collectively as *sign*. We've all seen Hollywood movie trackers who can determine whether a fellow is wearing boxers or briefs from a blade of bent grass, but cinematic license aside, interpreting sign is among the most important skills any tracker can possess.

❀ ENVIRONMENT

One fact about wild animals is true everywhere: If you find a species' preferred foods and environment, you'll probably find the animals somewhere nearby. It's senseless to look for river otters in a dry hardwood forest or fox squirrels in the middle of a cedar swamp. These animals have each adapted to a specific environment and to the foods available within it. Some animals—bears, for instance—may wander 50 miles or more following seasonal foods, while others such as the white-tailed deer spend their entire lives within a square mile or so.

Vegetation is the most important factor in locating any species, whether predator or prey. If you're looking for bobcats, begin by finding the grasses, willows, and other vegetation preferred by its primary foods, rabbits and hares. If there are any bears in an area (reclusive black bears are more numerous than most folks realize), probably the best place to find one is along a remote power line or meadow where raspberries, serviceberries, or apples are ripening. Whatever class or species of animal you seek, its presence or absence always hinges, directly or indirectly, on an area's plant life.

Type of habitat also dictates what species live within a given region. Deer are a timber wolf's natural prey, yet while whitetail populations have exploded across the country in recent years, wolf populations have not, because deer are willing to live in close proximity to humans and wolves aren't. Lynx are now confined to the wilder northernmost regions of the country for the same reason; their primary prey, the snowshoe hare, is thus abundant in locations where lynx no longer exist. The inability of many predators to coexist with people has created a safe haven for their prey, which perhaps regard humans as the lesser of two evils. A gruesome yet fairly accurate way to determine how many predators are in an area is to note the number and type of prey animals killed by cars on nearby roads. A section of forest where roads are dotted with road-killed porcupines is a good indication that the fisher, a large weasel and the porky's most serious natural predator, is absent from the area.

✣ SCAT

Once you've found an environment and habitat suited to the animals you're looking for, the next step is to look for sign, the most prominent being *scat,* or feces. With the exception of beavers, even amphibious mammals don't normally defecate in water. This may stem from some instinct against polluting their own drinking water, but scat deposited on land also serves as a territorial marker, warning other members of the same species not to trespass. Territorial instincts are a natural safeguard against overpopulation, especially among predators, and the most effective means an animal has of broadcasting its claim to a territory is through scat, urine, and musk scents. Coyotes and bobcats patrol regular routes while hunting, and these will be dotted with scat deposits that are periodically freshened. The amphibious muskrat marks its territory by leaving its scat on a prominent log, and river otters declare their presence with scat deposited along streambanks. Interestingly, prey animals such as deer and rabbits may deposit scat anywhere within their chosen territories, apparently unconcerned about using it to establish a defined territorial boundary. This random distribution of scat may be a natural defense intended to flood an area with so much scent that predators will be confused about a prey's exact location.

Predators also tend to defecate directly on the remains of prey after everything edible has been consumed. I've noted this behavior in coyotes, bobcats, lynx, and black bears, and the practice is apparently common. Cached, partially consumed kills are never tainted with scat, only carcasses that have been picked clean; the act seems to be both a territorial marker and a boast of prowess.

Scat deposits can tell you a great deal if you overcome your natural aversion to handling poop and examine it closely. Feces does sometimes carry parasites dangerous to humans, so never handle scat with bare hands. Having said that, I'll admit that I have picked up fresh-looking deer and rabbit droppings to check for residual body heat. Close examination of an animal's droppings can reveal what it has been feeding on, which in turn helps you identify areas where it's most likely to be found.

The physical characteristics of a scat deposit often link it positively to a single family or species. Deer, rabbit, and porcupine droppings each have unique features that make identification fairly certain. Coyotes, bobcats, and gray foxes also have distinctive feces, although their similar diets can make identification by scat alone very difficult. More detailed information about scat identification and other characteristics of individual species is given in later chapters.

It can also help to know the age of a scat deposit. Just as we do, wild animals tend to fall into daily routines, and droppings left at 4 P.M. one day will likely be freshened at about the same time the following day. Aging scat means estimating how long a deposit has been there based on how its texture has changed from evaporation and exposure to the elements. Temperature and humidity are key factors in how quickly moisture is lost from any type of scat, but here are a few rules of thumb: If it feels warm to the back of your hand, it's less than 1 hour old. If it's cold but still wet looking, it was left within the last 5 hours. If the outside is dry and hard but the inside is still moist, it's somewhere between 6 and 24 hours old. Scat that has dried throughout but still retains a dark color is from one to three days old. Deposits that have turned white and crumble when touched are at least four days old. You can see that aging scat becomes less precise the longer it has been exposed to the elements, and if it's raining or snowing hard you can probably toss these rules out the window. Still, they're fairly accurate for most scat types under most conditions.

☙ SCENTPOSTS

Scentposts are another way some species mark their territories against intruders. A scentpost can be as simple as wolf urine on a tree trunk or as complex as the beaver's scent mound—a cone of mud, sticks, and grasses that may stand 1 foot tall with a 3-foot-diameter base. Muskrat scentposts resemble those of the beaver but are about half the size. Cats, especially males, label their territory with a spray of strong-smelling urine on a prominent landmark. Scentposts are refreshed periodically, usually every day or so, and because they're potent enough to warn off animal intruders from a distance, even our relatively useless human nose can often detect one nearby. If you suddenly smell a musky odor on the trail, take a few moments to use both your nose and your eyes to determine its source. Once found, a scentpost is a good place to wait quietly for its owner to return.

TERRITORIAL MARKS

Scentposts and scat are just a first line of defense against rival intruders, and many species complement these warnings with visual sign as well. The scent scrapes left by rutting (mating) males of the deer family serve not just to attract females but also as an obvious warning to rivals that these normally peaceful animals are prepared to fight for breeding rights. Bears leave long claw marks as high as they can reach on tree trunks to impress intruders with their size, and man-made structures such as wooden bridges, power-line poles, or even cabins frequently show the claw marks of a territorial bruin. The grizzly bear's "playful" shoving over of dead trees may actually be meant to advertise its claim to a territory.

Some territorial marks are a bit less conspicuous. Claw marks left on a tree trunk that a bobcat used for a scratching post are easy for us to miss since we have only our eyes to search with, but rivals spot them by scent. The feisty red squirrel, or chickaree, marks its territory with regular feeding stations littered with pinecone debris and droppings. Beavers sometimes mark trees at the outside of their working area by gnawing off a small section of bark, possibly to mark the tree for future cutting but certainly as a warning to other beavers not to trespass. Details about the territorial sign of individual species are given in part two of this book.

♣ TRAILS

When you find an animal trail, you know two things for certain: At least one animal uses it periodically, and doubtless it will use that trail again. Four-footed creatures that travel routinely establish regular trails for the same reason we use hiking trails: They beat fighting your way through the bushes. But open trails are more than a mere convenience for wild animals; they make possible high-speed escapes through dense cover and a chaos of confusing scents from other animals. Snowshoe hares create well-packed runways in deep snow to save energy traveling to and from feeding spots and to give them an edge in speed when running from predators too large to use such a trail themselves.

One problem with animal trails is that it isn't always easy—or even possible—to follow them. Four-legged critters are more able (and willing) to scoot under half-downed trees, jump over logs, and wriggle through deep brush than humans are. A raccoon's highway may be an impenetrable jungle to us, so it sometimes becomes necessary to skirt a difficult area and try to cut the trail on another side. Chapter 1 explained the need for a good map and compass to keep from getting lost as your tracking skills lead you deeper and deeper into the wilderness. But a good compass and topographical map can also help you locate animals; the "topo" contains geographical details that help you identify likely feeding or bedding areas, while a quality prismatic or lensatic compass provides you with the navigational tools to plot a precise course to those places.

♣ BEDDING AREAS

All animals need to sleep, and in most instances their sleeping and denning places are conspicuous. A large, oval-shaped depression in a field of tall grass tells us that a whitetail lay there to chew its cud and nap. Smaller depressions in that same field could belong to fawns, depending on the season and their proximity to larger beds, or they might have been made by coyotes lying in wait for the squeak of a rodent. In winter, a packed trail of cottontail rabbit tracks leading under a snow-covered brushpile or a fallen tree certainly points to a seasonal den. Bathtub-size depressions pressed heavily into the leafy floor of a deciduous forest, usually near a field or meadow, are the beds of elk. A birdbath-size mass of twigs and leaves packed into a hardwood tree crotch is a squirrel nest or "loafing platform."

Sleeping can be a dangerous proposition for wild animals, especially prey animals, which must rest with all their senses alert for the first hint of predators. For this reason, bedding areas are always selected to give an animal its best odds for escape or defense. The porcupine naps on a high tree branch, usually with its tail facing the trunk, because few predators can get to it there and fewer still can negotiate the narrow branch without being slapped by the porky's spiny, clublike tail. Deer make their daytime beds in heavy cover, where their keen noses and sharp ears can detect enemies long before they come into view. Squirrels, which have a sense of smell rivaling the whitetail's, are secure in their leafy nests, because few predators can reach them undetected and none can match squirrels' tree-hopping agility. At the other end of the spectrum, bears sleep pretty much anywhere they choose (which is almost always near a food source). More about bedding areas and dens for individual species is given in part two.

TRACKING TOOLS
3

WHILE IT'S SOMETIMES TOUGH to say anything good about a technology that has made sunblock a necessity, depleted entire oceans of fish, and enslaved us to conveniences of our own design, a few modern advances do benefit outdoorsmen. Many of the products developed for war or sport hunting also lend themselves to wildlife photography and animal observation. Light-amplifying "Starlight" night-vision devices allow nocturnal animals to be observed naturally on all but the darkest nights; handheld heat detectors can signal an unseen animal's location from its body heat; hunting calls can precisely mimic the sounds most likely to entice an animal into view; manufactured scent products can mask human odor or eliminate it entirely, while others broadcast an illusion of food or sex. Had any of these modern hunting aids existed when our forefathers settled the New World, the number of species they hunted and trapped to extinction would doubtless be greater than it is.

❦ COVER SCENTS

Artificial scents have come a long way since early trappers scented beaver traps with castoreum from the animals' own musk glands and Native Americans burned fleabane to attract deer. Perhaps the most important breakthrough of recent years is a nontoxic liquid spray that manufacturers claim will break down odors of all kinds at the molecular level. My own tests of these scent neutralizers have included using them to remove pet odors from furniture, plus a number of field trials that pitted them against the noses of several species of wild animals and one good tracking dog. I'm naturally skeptical of any product that claims to do something I can't perceive, let alone measure, but I have to admit that these sprays do seem to eliminate most odors, even strong ones. My favorite among the best scent neutralizers I've tried is N-O-Dor, from Atsko/Sno-Seal, a two-part mixture that has been at least partly responsible for my getting to within a few feet of deer, elk, and bobcats, undetected.

Cover scents designed to mask human odors (including tobacco, aftershave, and underarm deodorant) work by veiling those odors with a strong musk. The most popular cover scent is fox urine, usually applied to boot soles to disguise the hunter's scent trail, and sometimes used on the ground around a blind or treestand. Raccoon urine is a cover scent that can be used either on the ground or in a treestand without being out of place. These and the rest of the scents covered in this section are available in pocket-size plastic squirt bottles or pump aerosols.

Cover scents do work, but remember that your own odors are still mingled with the stronger odor of the scent, and it's difficult to say at what range animals will unscramble the puzzling mix of odors. Another problem is that older, more experienced members of any species got that way by being cautious, and the sudden odor of a strange fox or raccoon moving through an area may by itself attract attention. Also bear in mind that both raccoons and foxes are predatory species whose odor will send many small mammals into hiding or, even worse, cause them to give an audible alarm. One of the most effective all-around cover combinations is a thorough misting of scent neutralizer, followed by a dozen drops of white-tailed deer musk.

❧ SEX SCENTS

At this writing, the majority of sex scents being produced are for the white-tailed deer, but Buck Stop, Inc., the industry's leading scent innovator, recently expanded its line of products to include mink, bear, elk, and moose scents. With such a broad range of animal scents available in different concentrations and combinations, even first-timers can strategically plan a successful sighting. For specific information about the habits of an individual species and how it uses scents in mating season, refer to the pertinent section in part two.

❧ FOOD SCENTS

Manufactured food scents are designed to attract specific animals, but many will attract other species as well. Apple and acorn scents appeal to hungry deer, but acorn scent can also prove intriguing to fox and gray squirrels, while apple scent can attract a variety of animals, from black bears to elk and porcupines.

A time-proven alternative to manufactured food scents is the use of a transportable form of an actual food. Many animals, including carnivores, are drawn to the odor of ripened fruit; even meat eaters appreciate a little sugar in their diets (did you ever see a dog that didn't like sweets?). An old hunters' trick is to dump a can of apple juice concentrate over a rotting stump or log; several species may then take part in the job of literally eating the wood down to the ground. Most species are also very fond of maple syrup, honey, and, especially, molasses; pouring any of these sweets over a decaying stump will likely result in repeated visits from a variety of critters.

Some food scents can be found in your kitchen cupboard. Concentrated walnut and almond flavorings are attractive to squirrels, and many species are likely to track down the odor of maple flavoring. A few old-timers swear that vanilla extract is just the thing for luring in both deer and bears (it will do in a pinch). Bacon grease, once known as "Indian butter," is sometimes used by backcountry chefs to perk up modest cabin cuisine, and it definitely suits the palates of black bears and raccoons. On a less tasteful note, blood collected from slaughtered animals (you can probably get it free) is likely to attract a host of carnivores. I've also found that in some states, Department of Natural Resources officials are willing to provide photographers with road-killed carcasses as carnivore bait. Note, however, that some states prohibit baiting of any kind. Check with your state officials.

☙ SALT AND MINERAL LICKS

Salt is a necessary nutrient, and, like sugar, it's not widely available in the wild. Many a farmer has seen his cattle's salt block devoured by wild animals, and salt licks have proven so irresistible to wildlife that some states restrict their use by sport hunters. Deer, bears, elk, and moose are among the most exciting visitors to salt blocks, but almost any mammal in an area may come by for a few quick licks sometime during the day or night.

Mineral blocks are a refined version of the salt block that provide not only salt but also other necessary nutrients. To enhance their attraction to wildlife, some mineral blocks are treated with food scents (usually apple). The downside is that toting a mineral block far into the wilderness can be exhausting, and in some places porcupines alone can devour a 25-pound block in days—then proceed to eat the salt-soaked twigs and leaves beneath it.

☙ CALLS

Game calls have been used by hunters for a very long time, but never before have so many brands and types been available. Your success at calling wildlife depends not just on your skill but also on your ingenuity. Varmint hunters know that the squeal of a wounded rabbit will interest most carnivores, but mule deer also respond to it, although no one is quite sure why. The soft calls of a nesting Canada goose or mallard emanating from a vulnerable location could be regarded as a dinner invitation by winter-lean coyotes and bobcats. Likewise, the repeated squeaking of a squirrel call may bring around all sorts of predators to look for the injured squirrel. Bears hanging around deer trails in June and July to get a dinner of newborn venison may come to the low bleat of a fawn, as may cats and coyotes. And the repeated bleatings of an immature doe from the same place will sometimes bring in predators looking for a sickly deer. Actual animal calls recorded on cassette have also proven effective at luring different types of wildlife within gun, bow, or camera range, but their use is sometimes restricted by local laws, so check out the situation before using them.

☙ OPTICS

John Wootters, the world's most famous whitetail hunter, once said that the average hunter will walk by 10 deer for every 1 he sees; doubtless this applies to many other wild species as well. Keen long-range vision is of little value in a dense forest; our sole sensory advantage over our wild brethren is of limited use except at great distances in open country. Fortunately, today's optics are finer than ever before, allowing us to detect and observe animals close up without actually getting near enough to risk detection ourselves.

The terminology of optical devices can be confusing at first, but knowing a few key definitions can help you become better informed about what kind of equipment you'll need. The front lens of a binocular or telescope is called the *objective lens;* it faces the objective being viewed. The lens you look through is called the *ocular lens,* or viewing lens. The numerical description of an optical device gives both the power, or the number of times an objective is magnified, and the diameter of the objective lens in millimeters. For example, 7×35 means sevenfold magnification and an objective-lens diameter of 35 millimeters.

A great deal has been made of light-gathering ability in recent years, particularly where riflescopes are concerned. This in turn has started a trend toward ever larger objective lenses, the theory being that a larger lens will take in more light, thus providing a brighter sight picture in low light. While this is true, the much advertised "Twilight Factor" has less importance in the real world. It takes more than just a large objective lens to get the most out of a spotting scope, riflescope, or binocular. Of primary importance are the metallic lens coatings that allow light to pass into the device's hollow body through the objective lens, but not back out, except at the ocular lens, where you can see it. Optical coatings are often the one feature that makes a particular scope or binocular better than another, so you should always look for them when buying an optical device, including a camera lens. A well-coated and polished lens should exhibit a deep but hazy purplish (sometimes yellow-gold) cast when viewed at an angle to the light. Lens coatings are delicate, not to mention expensive, so always care for coated lenses according to the manufacturer's instructions, and always protect them from exposure to abrasive sand and grit.

The first optical device to go into a tracker's kit should be a good mini-binocular. A rubber-armored Tasco 8×21 mini-binoc is an essential part of my wilderness kit. It folds into a pocket-size package that's carried almost unnoticed by its neck lanyard, and its optical quality is among the best I've seen. Better yet, it retails for around $80, which is about average for a good mini-binoc.

More expensive, more sophisticated, but far more versatile is Pentax's state of the art 8–20×24 UCF Zoom binocular, a compact, professional-quality unit whose mere 17-ounce weight belies its outstanding optical performance. This rugged, compact binoc is larger than my Tasco, but it still wears easily under my jacket and can be tripod-mounted for long-term, stationary observations. Best of all, its crystal-clear coated optics and 20× zoom capability allow it to function as either a binocular or a spotting scope under daylight conditions, doing away with the need to carry both. Suggested retail is $334—expensive, but worth every dime if your budget allows.

The downside to any mini-binocular is its small-diameter objective lenses, which are poor gatherers of existing light. Precision-ground lenses and quality optical coatings help maximize the amount of light reaching your eye, but only so much can be done with such small lenses, so mini-binoculars are best suited to daylight observation.

For most stationary observation or just cruising old logging trails in a 4×4, the magnification and light-gathering characteristics of a quality 10×50 binocular are tough to beat, although the standard 7×35 binoc will also serve you well for less money. For long-range observations—out to 1,000 yards or so—nothing beats a tripod-mounted spotting scope for getting a close look at wary local fauna. Too powerful to be held steady in the hands (20× is average), spotting scopes are designed to sit atop a tripod and remain fixed on a single location. Scanning an area for movement is best done with a binocular; looking through a spotting scope for more than a few minutes will probably give you a headache. When you spot something that merits a closer look, mark its position and zero in with your spotting scope.

There really aren't any bad spotting scopes, but some are better or more versatile than others. If you appreciate multifunctional equipment, as I do, consider the midpriced Bausch & Lomb Discoverer, a powerful 15×-to-60× variable telescope that can be tripod-mounted for use as a spotting scope or converted to a monster 35mm camera lens with the addition of an inexpensive two-piece adapter, available in most types of lens mounts. Its only real drawback is that, because increased magnification requires increased light, the Discoverer becomes almost useless as a camera lens past 30× in full daylight. Even so, that's the equivalent of a 2000mm lens. The Discoverer retails for about $368; add another $43 for the two-piece camera adapter kit.

❧ TRAIL TIMERS

Where there are a lot of animals there will of course be a lot of animal trails, and if you plan to wait near one for a sighting it pays to have some idea which one is most likely to be used. Animals sometimes change regular routes to follow seasonal foods, because part of a trail is blocked, to dodge a predator in the area, or maybe for the same reason folks occasionally drive a different way home after work. And remember, no matter how you might feel about them, wild animals regard you as a dangerous predator; touch nothing unnecessarily when examining a trail to avoid leaving your scent, and disturb as little as possible.

An old trick for checking traffic on animal trails is to string a length of thread or light fishing line across a likely avenue, then come back later to see if it has been knocked down. Tie off one end of the tripline to a tree on one side of the trail, and wedge the other as tentatively as possible under a piece of bark or in a split twig on the other side. By setting a dozen or so triplines on different trails, checking them twice a day and resetting as needed, you can gather enough information to predict an animal's comings and goings with fair precision after just two days.

A modern version of the old thread-across-the-trail trick is a digital clock unit, made by the Trail Timer company of St. Paul, Minnesota. Like the thread timer, the Trail Timer uses a tripline, but it stores the date and time that it was tripped as well as the direction. Units are mounted in their own weatherproof plastic cases and retail for about $15 each.

More elaborate—and expensive—trail-timing devices include the Trail Timer Plus multiple event monitor ($70) and the TrailMaster 500 ($175). Both units use an infrared beam to detect movement, and both can be adapted to actually shoot a 35mm photo of whatever tripped them if you attach an optional camera kit. Among other sophisticated features, the TrailMaster unit claims to discriminate between small animals, such as birds or squirrels, and large ones such as deer.

🐾 HEAT DETECTORS

Handheld infrared heat detectors are a recent innovation that have earned themselves a place in the 21st-century animal watcher's field kit. Personal field tests with the Game Finder II, from Game Finder, Inc., of Huntsville, Alabama, have convinced me that the unit works well for detecting almost any heat source, even through trees. It can operate for 12 hours on a nine-volt battery (less if the weather is cold), and can detect differences in temperature as small as 1°F to several hundred yards, depending on terrain.

The Game Finder was designed to help hunters retrieve downed game, but it also lends itself well to the observer's or photographer's task of finding concealed live animals. Bedded deer or other animals (including large birds) hidden by foliage can be located by their body heat, and this position can then be zeroed-in with a spotting scope or binocular. Game Finder units retail for about $180, with the more advanced Game Finder II selling for around $280. Both include an instructional manual and a nicely produced videotape that not only takes the guesswork out of operating the unit but also offers plenty of tracking advice.

STALKING

4

THE ABILITY TO STALK prey is instinctive in animals designed to eat meat. A house cat taken from its mother as a tiny kitten will nonetheless develop the stealth, speed, and agility that make house cats perhaps the most efficient hunters on earth. Black bears, which seldom hunt because their powerful physique isn't designed for a hard chase, can demonstrate considerable sneakiness when attempting to catch young fawns in spring. Even human toddlers, with no outside instructions, quickly learn to sneak up on grasshoppers, butterflies, and frogs. Nevertheless, most predator mothers—and sometimes fathers—augment their offspring's basic hunting instincts with lessons drawn from their own life experiences.

Except for humans. On the whole, our species hasn't had to hunt for its survival in a very long time, and as a species we're not very good at it. Some anthropologists believe that *Homo sapiens* never possessed the heightened senses of lesser cousins, and that it was only through cunning and ingenuity that we rose to the top of the food chain. Few animals have anything to fear from our physical strength or speed, but they have everything to fear from our abilities to devise tools and to manipulate a situation to our own advantage. This intellect can, with practice, make the Naked Ape as efficient a stalker as any in the world.

♣ CAMOUFLAGE

While it's true that most mammals are to some degree color-blind, it's also true that proper camouflage is necessary when stalking them. The more closely any hunter blends with his surrounding terrain, the less chance he has of being seen. Remember, birds can see colors, typically have better eyesight than we do, and may broadcast alarm calls that put every animal within earshot on the alert for a dangerous intruder. Just as bad are the chattering cry of a surprised red squirrel and the alarm whistle, or "blow," of a deer. Sneaking into the visual range of a specific animal may be the easy part, because first you have to slip past many sentries. Since we walk upright, humans are probably perceived as being larger than we actually are, and the outline of a human shape seems to be the most frightening thing a wild critter could ever see. After all, every other animal in the wilderness is camouflaged to some extent, and it behooves us to follow nature's example.

The trick to an effective camouflage lies in the ability of its pattern and texture to make you look like many small parts of your surrounding environment. Random spatters of color whose shape and hue might be mistaken for leaves, branches, or other terrain features are best for breaking up the distinctive human silhouette. Loose-fitting clothing, such as six-pocket military BDUs (Battle Dress Uniform), printed with such a pattern add a three-dimensional effect with their rumpled, wrinkled appearance.

With so many different styles, patterns, and manufacturers of camouflage clothing around, discussing the pros and cons of each is beyond the scope of this book, and I think it would be a waste of time in any case. Getting right to it, I agree with veteran army sniper Major John Plaster that woodland-pattern camouflage clothing is the best all-around camo an outdoorsman can get. Some types of camo do work better in specific environments, but none has yet matched the woodland pattern's ability to blend acceptably with most types of terrain.

The distinctive roundness of a human head is also out of place in nature, so a good hat is a necessary part of any camouflage outfit. Our military's cloth bush hat is probably the best warm-weather design to come along yet. Its full crown keeps horseflies and deerflies from biting your head, the floppy brim keeps rain off your glasses and camera viewfinders, and the rumpled, misshapen look blends well into virtually all types of terrain. Most bush-type hats also have a series of camouflage loops sewn around the crown to hold bits of foliage, which further breaks up your outline. The washable-fabric bush hat is also one of the best places I've found to wear certain scents.

Nor should you overlook your face and hands, because even a quick flash of light-colored skin may attract attention from every quarter. Painting exposed skin with camouflage creams is the best-known way to disguise uncovered extremities, but there are simpler, less messy alternatives. The Spando-Flage company makes camouflage pullover stretch face masks that are fast, are effective, and retail for around $10. Mosquito headnets are also effective camouflage—as well as sometimes being necessary protection against hordes of bloodsucking insects. Mosquito headnets retail for about $4 each. Hands can be covered with camouflage cream or, if the weather is cool enough, with a light pair of camo-pattern or dark-colored cloth gloves. My own preference (temperature permitting) is a pair of uninsulated leather gloves that have been weatherproofed with petroleum jelly. Petroleum jelly imparts almost no odor and darkens leather; a few drops of scent in the palm of either glove works well for leaving scent trails on tree trunks and branches.

In snow country, German or American military snow oversuits are nearly ideal camouflage, but a pair of white painter's coveralls will suffice. In snow-covered forests it isn't necessary to be outfitted completely in white; white trousers and a camouflage overcoat will do fine. Avoid wearing a white overcoat over camouflage trousers, because this presents an image opposite to that of the surrounding area, where the ground is white with darker colors elevated above it. In a pinch, you can make do with a white linen bedsheet draped around your shoulders like a cape—a quick-and-dirty winter camouflage that I've used to good effect many times.

But for virtually disappearing in most types of wooded or grassy terrain, nothing matches the ghillie suit. Named for the Scottish bond servants, or "ghillies," who once patrolled their masters' lands as game wardens, the tattered, indistinct look of ghillie camo can make its wearer virtually invisible from a distance of only a few feet.

Manufactured ghillie camouflage is available in suit and cape forms, but these are a bit pricey, and the commercial camouflage netting used to make them is less effective than homemade ghillie material. Probably the best ghillie suit is one made from a nylon mesh hammock to which dark brown and green burlap strips have been tied (not sewn). The strips can be cut from burlap bags that have been dyed to the proper colors, or you can buy predyed burlap ghillie stripping in roll form at army-navy outlets. Avoid the military's practice of using spray paint to blend together the strips of burlap. This may work if you're tracking humans, but the powerful odor of ketones and enamel is guaranteed to announce your presence to any animal downwind of your position. The burlap stripping is pretty effective camouflage as is, but if you'd like your ghillie suit to blend a bit better, RIT clothing dyes work well without leaving a noticeable odor.

A word of caution: The frayed, ragged look that makes ghillie camo merge so well with natural backgrounds can also make it quite flammable. Never wear it around an open fire of any kind, and never smoke while wearing it. Spray-on fire retardants are available, but they may impart an odor to the material that frightens animals. For this and similar reasons, it pays to de-scent ghillie camo with N-O-Dor or Buck Stop's Scent Blaster pump sprays prior to every trip afield.

Making a quick, field-expedient type of ghillie suit is one of the projects in my book *Made for the Outdoors* (Lyons & Burford, 1995). There, I describe how to intertwine vegetation from the surrounding area into the netting of a mesh hammock until the finished product matches the terrain to near perfection. In some types of vegetation (bracken ferns, for instance), the hammock ghillie suit can make its wearer disappear from as little as 5 feet away. And when you move on, the hammock can be cleaned of vegetation in a couple minutes, ready for use in different terrain and vegetation or just for stringing up and swinging in the breeze. Ghillie camo made from natural vegetation is also airier than a manufactured ghillie suit, which makes it cooler to wear during those long hours you might have to spend motionless behind a camera viewfinder.

☙ FOOTWEAR

Stalking, by definition, means being on your feet for long periods of time (although some of this is inevitably done on hands and knees), so good footwear isn't a luxury but a necessity. This is not to say that you need to spend a small fortune for a decent pair of boots—although you certainly could—but rather that there are certain criteria any outdoors boot must meet to be considered stalking footwear. And while I always buy as much quality as my wallet will bear, lots of inexpensive boots meet my requirements while some higher-priced name brands don't.

In warm weather, the boot should be light and well ventilated. No boot is truly waterproof, especially in knee-deep water, so waterproofness shouldn't even be considered as a factor. Of far more importance is the boot's ability to go from saturated to reasonably dry in as little time as possible. The GI jungle boot worn in the Vietnam War was ideal for walking alternately through water and on dry land, as are several current civilian models, but military jungle boots are hard (literally) on the bottoms of your feet. Cushioned insoles help, but make certain they're of a type that won't absorb water or you'll be defeating your purpose.

Manufacturers commonly hybridize their outdoors boots by fitting them with hard soles that stand up to walking on concrete, because they realize their products are likely to see as many miles on abrasive paved surfaces as on forest humus. But in the woods, hard soles don't give with terrain changes, and twigs that might have been pressed quietly into the ground by a softer sole tend to snap sharply. This problem is exacerbated by lug soles—which I nonetheless believe are the smartest choice for boondocking—because each lug applies pressure over a small area, again increasing the probability that twigs will snap underfoot. A nice compromise is the new bob sole, with a row of lugs around its periphery for increased traction and lateral stability.

Hard-soled boots also detract from a stalker's sensitivity to the ground, which is vital when you're stalking an animal with your eyes glued to it, ready to freeze instantly and feeling for potentially noisy forest debris with your feet. A good pair of stalking boots should have soles and heels soft enough to compress with a squeeze of your hand. You can get a functional pair of stalking boots from Kmart for around $30, but as your interest in observing wildlife grows, you'll probably demand more durable, more expensive footwear. Bear in mind that stalking requires a lot of time on your feet; a good pair of boots shouldn't feel good when you try them on, they should feel *great*.

Winter stalking in snow country demands a pair of warm pac-boots. Period. Insulated leather "hunting" boots just don't cut it when you're hunkered down in snow for hours watching coyotes at a deer carcass— and a few woodsmen have the missing toes to prove it. The trade-off is that added warmth means added weight and bulk, making pac-boots clumsier and more tiring to wear than warm-weather stalking boots. On the plus side, snow-pacs are today better designed, warmer, and more economical than they've ever been. Again, you can spend in excess of $200 for a pair of winter stalking boots, but a good pair of lightweight mukluks rated to –40° F can be had for around $50. Factory temperature ratings presume the wearer will be walking at a steady pace—not realistic for our purposes—and too warm a boot is always better than one not warm enough.

I recommend avoiding full lug soles in winter, because snow can pack around the lugs and leave you quite literally walking on snowballs. Members of the survival class stranded in the Smoky Mountains during the "Blizzard of '92" were forced to abandon their hiking boots because walking through snow in them proved impossible. Conventional tractor-tread soles and the new bob soles both offer good traction and self-cleaning treads, but most folks find the bob soles more comfortable for long hikes. Two very good choices for a winter stalking boot are the Expedition from La Crosse and Sorel's Maverick, both of which are priced above $200. Military "Mickey Mouse" boots, so called because they make your feet look bulbous and cartoonlike, are a good choice at about $70, but they weigh a leg-tiring 3 pounds a piece.

♣ STALKING TECHNIQUES

After you've gathered the tools of a stalker, your next step is learning to use them in the field. The first thing to remember is that no one can stalk all the time, because stalking demands an ability to freeze in any position and hold that position through several minutes of intense scrutiny. Maintaining such an elevated state of mental and physical control is exhausting, so you should slip into stalking mode only when you're certain your objective is very close. Beaver dams, remote shorelines, and known denning or feeding grounds are good candidates for a stalk, but at a normal stalking pace of about 100 yards per hour, you wouldn't want to stalk everywhere you went even if you could.

It's possible to walk quietly through different types of terrain and still move at a near-normal pace, however. Probably most of my own sightings and photo opportunities occur when I'm walking quietly through the woods. The trick to walking quietly lies in learning to "walk Indian," which means abandoning the off-balance heel-toe walk of a person accustomed to walking on smooth surfaces and adopting the flexible, duck-footed bearing of a hunter. With this technique, your body weight is supported on the ball of your rear foot while your forward foot is brought down with toes pointing outward at about 30 degrees. The first part of your forward foot to hit the ground is the outside of your heel, and your body weight is then transferred smoothly to the forward foot as your rear foot is brought forward, also with toes out at roughly 30 degrees, to land on the outside of its heel. The idea is to press twigs into the ground gently by rolling your supporting foot over them from outside heel to inner (big) toe, distributing your body weight over as wide an area as possible. Each time you bring your rear foot forward, make a conscious effort to raise it higher than normal to clear sticks and other noise-making obstacles. Keep your knees flexible to act as shock absorbers in unpredictable terrain. This will give you the springy step characteristic of folks who seldom turn their ankles in the woods. Learning to walk duck-footed may take a bit of practice, but before long you'll be griping to your companions about how noisily they walk.

Stalking is another matter, and probably the hardest thing about it is learning to slow down. Wild animals don't have schedules to keep, and most of their waking time is spent meandering in search of food. The steady two-legged pace of a human is unique, and few animals stick around for more than a confirming glance when they hear it. The trick, therefore, is not to sound like a human being (your ultimate objective is absolute silence), and this means slowing down to about two steps per minute. Every step is taken slowly, and good balance—which develops with practice—is a must. The forward foot is always brought down against the ground as gently as possible, and always in the place where it's least likely to make a sound. In places where silence is simply unachievable—a mature oak forest in fall, for example—bear in mind that slow, quiet noises are less alarming than quick, sharp ones. The low crunch of leaves as you bring your weight down on them may well go unnoticed, but the snap of a twig underfoot is good reason to freeze for a full minute or two.

Quick, jerky movements are also sure to alarm your prey (remember the birds, squirrels, and other tattletales), so every motion of your body needs to be executed as smoothly as possible. One reason is to minimize noise; the zipping sound of a branch sliding quickly across the fabric of a field jacket is guaranteed to attract more attention than the lower-volume sound of it scraping across very slowly. The other reason is to avoid being seen. The human eye sees at a rate of 60 images per second—a figure that's more or less accurate for wild animals as well—so very slow movements are less likely to attract attention than quick ones. This is also a good argument for long pants and mosquito headnets in bug country.

One element a stalker should be constantly aware of is the wind and its changes, which might reveal your presence via odor. Always begin any stalk into the wind; if its direction shifts, compensate to keep the breeze in your face. In some places, most notably lowland swamps, air currents swirl like stream eddies and winds might blow from all possible directions in the space of a few minutes. While this might seem disadvantageous to a stalker, it's just as confusing for an animal, which will get only a whiff of your spoor before the breeze changes direction again. Under such conditions the best defense is a liberal dose of odor neutralizer, perhaps mixed with a few drops of deer musk as cover.

Windy days are also especially good for stalking because rustling foliage and creaking trees create a confusion of noise, and no animal upwind of you will detect your scent. With animals' two most powerful senses rendered largely ineffective, humans for once will have a physical advantage with our superior eyesight. Other sounds you can use to cover movements include passing airplanes, distant traffic, rain, or those made by animal activity. Resist the temptation to use cover sounds to move quickly; sudden movement is almost certain to attract attention.

Stalking open country, with the animals in sight, requires good matching camouflage, steady concentration, and frequently a belly crawl to get within range. An old Native American trick for sneaking up on a lone grazing deer is to move while the animal has its head down in tall grass, blind to the world above it. Someone once determined that a deer keeps its head down to take a mouthful for roughly five seconds, and my own experiences support this. Advance in a crouch while the deer has its head down, freezing after three or four smooth steps, before the animal raises its head to look about. It may stare intently at you for three or four long minutes, as if aware that something has changed, but will almost invariably put its head down again for another bite eventually, allowing you to gain a few more yards. By keeping the breeze in your face and moving quietly only when the animal has its head down, you may be able to stalk to within 50 yards before it sees you clearly enough to become alarmed.

This trick works because deer, like most forest animals, are nearsighted and have poor distance perception. In other words, they can't tell if an object outside their range of visual acuity is getting closer, farther away, or even moving unless they actually see motion. A motionless "stump" may be scrutinized, but if it doesn't move, make noise, or smell like danger, it will probably be dismissed.

OBSERVING WILDLIFE
5

WHILE STALKING IS A TERRIFIC exercise that helps you become attuned to the environment—and frequently nets you a great photo or two—it's sometimes possible or even necessary to get an animal to come to you. This can often be accomplished with bait, with scents, or just by staking out a well-used trail. Shooting from a blind, or "sitting," is the preferred method of most hunters and photographers, however, because ambushing an animal is simpler than stalking it.

The first step, of course, is to find a place the animals you're looking for are likely to visit, which is done by knowing a species' habits and then scouting for tracks and sign. Once you've established an animal's route and destination (a den or feeding area), it's fairly simple to lie in wait for its return. One thing to remember, however, is that animals living in close proximity to humans frequently become nocturnal, sleeping the day away in secluded bedding areas or dens—this is where stalking comes in—and venturing into the open only under cover of night. If you can see a silhouette, you can capture an animal passing within range of a camera flash on film, but you may only get one shot per night.

Blind hunters need to be especially aware of how much better animals see in the dark than we do. At twilight, when the world is balanced on the edge of day and night and features are getting fuzzy, most animals can see close-up images (because most species are nearsighted) as well as we do at noon. Never think that just because you can't see your hand in front of your face, an animal can't see you move it there.

The big difference between our own eyes and those of lower animals is that we see well into the infrared spectrum of visible light, while they generally perceive more of the ultraviolet end of the spectrum. And since ultraviolet light is most prevalent in what we consider darkness, animals have much better night vision than we do. In daylight, we can discriminate between subtle colors to the point of nonsense; they, on the other hand, can run full speed through darkness that would have us walking into trees.

If animals do move about during daylight, it's nearly always within a secluded bedding or denning area where human activity is infrequent, typically in terrain we find difficult to negotiate. Here's where the hunter who captures his prey on film has an advantage over hunters who kill their game and then must, if they're worthy of the title, haul the carcass out of the woods. Bedding and denning areas are great places to set up a camouflaged tripod, and wildlife photography is a great way for gun and bow hunters to keep their skills sharp during the off-season.

The terms *blind* or *hide* describe a (sometimes) camouflaged cover, usually constructed or erected where you can move about as necessary without being seen from outside. A blind can be as simple as the ghillie suit worn by a hunter lying at the side of a trail, or as complex as the heated plywood shacks (some even have TVs) used by "sport" hunters who seem undecided about taking the part. Most are made from natural foliage taken from the surrounding area (please don't cut live trees—it isn't necessary), but portable pop-up types are great for setting up a hidden camera tripod. These range in style from a simple wraparound camo net to waterproof, tentlike structures with enough height to stand up in.

My own favorite portable blind for traveling far into the wilderness and staying put for prolonged periods in all types of weather is the bivy shelter, a squat, freestanding "minimalist" tent that sets up anywhere in minutes, has a low, unobtrusive profile, and weighs little enough to qualify as a long-range backpacking item. Best among these, in my opinion, is the recently introduced Predator from Slumberjack. It weighs less than 7 pounds and it has enough headroom for you to sit upright behind a tripod, along with a bugproof mesh door with near-silent zippers on either side, a ventilation window, an inside loft for keeping equipment handy, and enough room to absorb a large frame pack and its owner in comfort. Perhaps best of all, its waterproof cover fly is printed with Bill Jordan's Advantage camouflage, a very elaborate and highly effective leaf pattern that makes additional natural camouflage almost unnecessary in most forests. The Predator retails for $140, and when you couple it with a warm sleeping bag you'll be ready to stay on station in cold, miserable weather until the granola bars run out.

When putting up a blind, always remember that the animals living there know their territories as well or better than you know the neighborhood around your home. They'll notice foliage cleared away to form a shooting lane, and they're sure to avoid any new structure for at least a month, until they're satisfied it's harmless. Temporary and pop-up blinds should always be located at least 100 feet from the area being observed or photographed, and you should use natural camouflage as needed to make them as inconspicuous as possible. Permanent blinds have the advantage of eventually becoming an ignored part of the landscape, but they should be built at least 30 days in advance of use.

Once again, scents should be an important part of your setup. Portable blinds should always be kept isolated from chemicals or any product with an odor that might be absorbed into the material. And they should always be thoroughly deodorized with scent neutralizer after setup. A blind will help to contain your own body odors, but your clothing should also be deodorized, and scented products such as aftershave and underarm deodorants are definitely to be avoided.

Other products designed to help keep you hidden include Sport Wash from Atsko/Sno-Seal, a liquid laundry detergent that removes odors from clothing and suppresses the tendency of some dyes to fluoresce in the ultraviolet light of evening, and UV-killer cream, which does the same for equipment. Fabric and other items that reflect UV light stand out in the darkness when viewed through animal eyes, in much the same way that fluorescent colors show up to us in daylight.

Ironically, most of the need for UV killers is self-inflicted. Laundry detergents advertised as "brightening" the wash do so by adding a chemical that reflects ultraviolet rays—not actually brightening the color, just making it appear brighter to the eye. Unfortunately, these brighteners also make clothing abnormally visible to animals on cloudy days or after sunset, regardless of material or camouflage pattern. Laundry soaps used for outdoor clothing and gear should be free of scents, brighteners, bleaches, and softeners.

Blind hunting frequently means staying quiet in one place for half a day or more, so make yourself comfortable. I frequently backpack to blind locations, taking a frame pack loaded with camera equipment, munchies, a canteen, and a few other necessities. Mosquito netting is a must for most summer locations, but insect repellent sprays or lotions have odors that are best avoided if possible. Sitting on an upturned 5-gallon bucket with an earphone carrying a favorite radio station to one ear (headphones are taboo because they cover both ears) actually keeps the mind awake, I believe. Keep back from the blind windows, use plenty of N-O-Dor or Scent Blaster, and try not to make any noise. Aside from this, just relax and enjoy being there.

A situation that's sure to come up for photographers, who may shoot undetected for several hours after their prey makes an appearance, is what to do when nature calls. Urine and excrement are powerful sign of human presence, and either is sure to repel all sorts of wildlife. The best way to dispose of urine with a minimum release of scent is into a resealable bottle. This has always been fairly simple for men, and now there are form-fitting devices for women, too. Barring this, urinating into a hole at least 4 inches deep then covering it over with dirt will hold scent to a minimum. A few drops of red fox scent on top of the filled hole helps confuse any residual odor.

Excrement, especially feces, should be deposited at least 100 yards from the blind in a direction perpendicular to, or at least downwind of, the one you expect animals to come from. Feces should be buried as deeply as the terrain and tools permit, and the location well scented with Buck Stop's earth, pine, or red fox cover scent. Always remember that human waste is extremely toxic; never defecate within 100 feet of any body of water, and make sure that all traces have been completely buried. Nature will do the rest.

PART
2

TRACKING MAMMALS

DEER
(CERVIDAE)
6

NO FAMILY OF ANIMALS holds more fascination for outdoorsmen of every discipline than the deer family, whose members include white-tailed and mule deer, elk, caribou, and the stately moose. A lot of the impetus and money for research into deer behavior comes from commercial interests in the sport-hunting industry, and probably most of what has been written about the animals is for this audience. The population growth enjoyed of late by some species has been largely due, for better or worse, to sport hunters and those who cater to their buying power.

Members of the deer family are distinguished from other hoofed mammals by the fact that adult males grow tined antlers prior to the autumn mating season, then shed them about midwinter. With caribou, cows normally sprout a sometimes massive set of antlers, and about 1 of every 15 whitetails also grows antlers. Shed antlers are prized by porcupines, squirrels, and rodents, which eat them for the calcium and other nutrients they contain.

Human beings also prize deer antlers. Hunting publications promote the idea that bigger antlers equals a craftier prey and therefore a greater prize, when in fact the size of any deer's antlers after adulthood is determined mainly by nutrition. Rarely will a whitetail buck living in a wholly natural environment develop more than 12 tines on his antlers, although overfed bucks living in an artificial environment created by intensive agriculture often grow 20-plus points. The irony is that such large-antlered deer are often so accustomed to humans and so dependent on the food we provide that they become easy prey. Frequently the toughest and smartest bull or buck in the woods is an animal that trophy hunters would disdain.

Seasonal color changes are common to all deer, with a lighter red or brown coat being the norm in summer and a heavier dark gray to almost black coat during the winter months. The summer coat blends fairly well with dead standing grasses in the open areas where deer feed, while the dark winter coat makes the animals tough to see among the leafless trunks and branches of a snow-covered forest.

With the exception of the gigantic moose, deer are well adapted to the role of prey. All are fast runners, all are equipped with noses that would put a bloodhound to shame, and all have an acute sense of hearing made directional by the animals' large, swiveling ears. But deer have evolved to survive amid many natural enemies; even a carnivore as small as a mink will kill a fawn given the opportunity. Because so many predators consider them food, most deer species are prolific, with females giving birth to twins or even triplets if food is abundant. Females outnumber males by about four to one, and this, if combined with a lack of natural predators, can create localized population explosions in which deer/car accidents and agricultural damage are serious problems.

❧ WHITE-TAILED DEER (*ODOCOILEUS VIRGINIANUS*)

HABITAT AND RANGE

The whitetail, also known as the "flagtail" and "Virginia deer," is the most common deer species in the lower 48 states. Nearly extinct over much of its range by the 1940s because of unrestricted hunting, whitetails have made a phenomenal comeback. Whether this is due to good management or, equally likely, to the resilience and adaptability of the species, whitetails can be found in some part of all of the lower 48 states except California, Nevada, and Utah. The species' range to the north covers at

Len Rue, Jr.

1. White-Tailed Deer

least the lower portions of Canada's southern provinces; to the south, it extends well into Mexico. There are no whitetails in Alaska.

The name *whitetail* comes from the animals' practice of raising their large tails to show the white underside when fleeing danger. The highly visible raised white tail warns other deer and gives fawns a mark to follow when running after their mothers.

Like many species, whitetails are typically larger the farther north they live. Maine boasts bucks of weights topping 300 pounds, while the minuscule key deer (*Odocoileus virginianus clavium*) of Florida weighs in at 50 pounds or less. Another subspecies, the Coues deer (*Odocoileus virginianus covesi*) of Arizona, averages less than 100 pounds for adult bucks. One theory is that size and strength are dictated by the harshness of an environment. In Canada, whitetails must cope with a host of predators and winters that show no mercy to the weak, while key deer want for little in their tropical home and have fewer natural enemies.

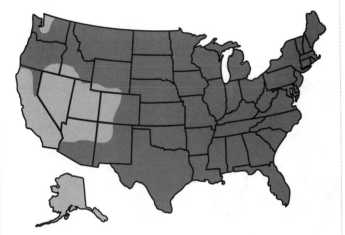

*Distribution of white-tailed deer (*Odocoileus virginianus*).*

Sport hunters play an important role in controlling whitetail populations now that their most important predators, the cougar and the wolf, have been exterminated over most of their original ranges. Unfortunately, human hunters lack the efficiency of natural predators—despite modern weapons—while the whitetail's reproductive capabilities remain geared toward losing a full third of the population every year, whether to predation or starvation.

Although there have been numerous cases of disoriented animals running amok through city streets, whitetails are essentially creatures of the forest. Their natural routine is to bed down during daylight hours in a swamp, an overgrown clear-cut, or another secluded place that offers enough cover for a few secure winks. At midday—about 11 A.M. to 1 P.M.—they habitually rise and move about but rarely venture out of the security of the bedding area unless hungry. By late afternoon, from about an hour before sunset on—depending on how far they have to travel—deer begin their nightly migration to feeding areas.

As a general rule, whitetails inhabit approximately 1 square mile of land throughout their eight-year life span. This range varies more or less, depending on how far seasonal foods and watering places are from the bedding area, but you can be that the animals are intimately familiar with every rock, tree, and stump within it. Noticeable changes as small as a candy wrapper left on a trail virtually guarantee a change in the animals' routines.

Generally considered an eastern deer, the whitetail's range overlaps nearly all the mule deer's territory west of the Rocky Mountains, and, as both species are steadily increasing in number, either may be encountered in western states. Whitetail bucks are smaller than mule deer bucks, weighing from 200 to 300 pounds at maturity, but whitetail does are usually larger than mule deer does, with an adult weight of 150–250 pounds. Tracks, scat, and most sign are virtually identical for the two species, but whitetail antlers consist of two main beams with single tines branching from them, while mule deer antlers have Y-shaped tines.

One noteworthy whitetail behavior is the way it stamps a forefoot and moves its head from side to side when studying something suspicious (such as the click of a camera shutter), occasionally extending its nose to test the air. If you're well camouflaged, odorless, and silent, such encounters may occur with mere feet between you and the animal. Good as it is, the whitetail is not infallible; if you remain motionless through it all, chances are the animal will lose interest and go about its business. Staying absolutely still is critical, because, although deer see poorly, they key instantly on movement. Stamping a forefoot is believed to be meant to prod concealed animals into showing themselves, and possibly to serve as a warning to other deer nearby.

FOODS

Like all the most successful species, whitetails have a broad diet that includes a wide variety of food options. Summer is the season of plenty, with clover, alfalfa, and grasses drawing deer into open fields to feed, usually under cover of darkness. They may also be seen foraging for aquatic plants in the shallows of ponds and lakes. Lacking upper teeth, all deer must pin foods between their hard upper palates and their bottom teeth to tear it free, leaving ragged-looking browse unlike the scissorslike cuttings of rabbits, marmots, and porcupines. The strictly vegetarian whitetail owes much of its survivability to an efficient digestive system that can convert almost any type of vegetable matter into energy.

When the frosty nights of autumn kill off many food plants, apples and acorns are consumed ravenously for their proteins and fats, needed to put on weight against the coming winter. By mid-October, the month-long mating season, or rut, begins, and breeding does in particular require a layer of fat to sustain them and the fawns they'll carry until spring.

Winter is tough for whitetails in snow country. When ground forage becomes inaccessible, they move as a group to the protection of cedar swamps and other thick cover, where trees block the cold wind and provide meager winter forage. Throughout the winter months they subsist on a woody diet of tree buds, cedar foliage, and thick dead grasses along the banks of waterways. Deer yards in cedar swamp are easy to identify, because foliage will be stripped from the lower branches to a height of about 7 feet—as high as an adult can reach from its hind legs. A hard winter may kill a full third of a population through starvation and injury (broken legs are not uncommon), and those that suffer the most are the young and the old. Whitetails inhabiting northern lumbering regions have even learned to associate the sound of a chain saw with food (buds and twigs from felled trees), and some are actually drawn to engine noise.

When spring returns, it finds survivors of the whitetail yard with an irresistible craving for green plants. From March until May, deer may literally overrun drainage ditches and low-lying fields to get the first succulent vegetation of the year. During this period they might be seen feeding at any hour of the day or night, and their proximity to roads can make driving on rural highways downright hazardous.

MATING HABITS

Whitetail mating habits have been studied extensively by the sport-hunting industry, and much is known about this aspect of their lives. The mating season, or rut, generally extends from mid-October to mid-November, but in different regions—even within the same state—its timing may vary by a week or so. Adult bucks appear ready to mate year-round, but breeding is initiated by the scent of does coming into heat. Eligible males respond with a release of hormones that causes them to swell physically, makes them bolder, and carries their own unique sexual signature.

Breeding males react to the scent of receptive females by creating *scrapes*, or pawed-up patches of strongly scented earth laid within and around the perimeter of each buck's chosen territory. Scrapes are usually sited along well-used trails that does travel regularly, and there may be a dozen strung out through the woods. Individual scrapes vary from a few cursory hoof marks to 3-foot patches torn up by hooves and antlers; size is probably indicative of a scrape's importance to its creator. Being the more cautious sex, bucks prefer to site scrapes behind cover, but you may also find scrapes around the edges of open feeding areas, where does congregate to feed in preparation for seven months of pregnancy.

Scrapes are the whitetails' version of a human playboy's answering machine. After creating one, a buck urinates on it, leaving a strong, musky odor that can be detected by a human nose at several yards. The buck then leaves to create another in a string of scrapes that will eventually ring his territory, fighting off rivals with his polished antlers as he travels from one site to the next. A receptive doe, drawn by the odor of male pheromones, will deposit her own urine on the scrape to indicate interest then leave, dribbling urine down the insides of both hind legs and over the tarsal (scent) glands on the insides of each knee. A buck returning to check his scrape—usually every six hours or so—will set out in pursuit right away. He has no time to waste, because does remain in heat for just 24 hours and competition is fierce. Unmated does are likely to come into heat again before a rut ends, but a buck has to move quickly or lose his chance.

Although more polygamous than other New World deer, whitetails have no interest in the opposite sex beyond the act of procreating. Does don't care what male impregnates them—this will be determined by physical contests between the bucks themselves; they simply want to be pregnant. Bucks go their own ways after the rut and take no part in the rearing of young.

SEASONAL HABITS

Fawns are born from early May to June, seven months after breeding, and any runts or late arrivals might not make it through their first winter. Does typically bear a single fawn in their first pregnancy, with twins being the norm thereafter—triplets if food is abundant. Young fawns instinctively know to lie motionless, relying on the camouflage of their spotted coats to conceal them. Mothers eat their fawns' urine and feces—a common trait among animal mothers—for the first two weeks or so to help keep them as scent free as possible. Does rarely defend their offspring, and never to the point of being injured themselves, preferring instead to sacrifice one fawn to save the other. In just a few weeks fawns will have become miniatures of the mother, too inexperienced to avoid many dangers but otherwise equipped with the speed, agility, and senses of a whitetail.

Fawns nurse from their mothers throughout their first year, but can subsist on wild plants after their first month. They stay with their mothers for two years, with young bucks being driven away in their second summer to prevent inbreeding. Does, which outnumber bucks by an average of four to one, are ready to breed after two years, while bucks don't usually become serious contenders for mating until four years of age. The normal life span is about eight years; adults of both sexes reach peak maturity at four years.

TRACKS

Like most hoofed mammals and all members of the deer family, whitetails have cloven hooves that are in reality two modified toenails. In a normal track, the two roughly teardrop-shaped halves print side by side to form a split heart. When an animal is walking on slippery surfaces such as mud or snow, its hooves are likely to be spread into a V, which helps keep the whitetail from sliding forward.

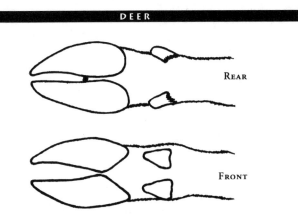

Front and rear feet of white-tailed deer. Note size and position of dewclaws. These same physical characteristics apply to most other deer species, and even nonrelated hoofed animals.

A question repeatedly debated among deer hunters is whether or not a whitetail's sex can be determined by its tracks. One famous outdoorsman claims that does, being built for childbearing, carry most of their body weight on the hind quarters, thus causing their back hooves to be especially wide. The opposite is supposedly true of bucks, which carry more weight in their shoulders and chest. But animals, like people, have widely varying physical characteristics that make this theory unreliable. A more reliable indication of gender is the fact that adult bucks tend to drag their toes lazily when walking on flat surfaces, while does normally step higher and more lightly. The toe dragging is more pronounced during the rut, when mature bucks run themselves ragged trying to get a year's worth of sex in one month and frequently fight hard for the privilege. Tired does may also drag their toes when pressed hard by hunters, but the trait is

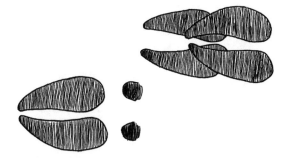

Tracks of the whitetail. Track at bottom is a front print with dewclaws showing, as they might on soft ground. Paired tracks above are as they might appear with a walking gait on firm ground, hind track superimposed on front track.

most common in males. When there are several inches of snow on the ground, however, all deer tend to drag their toes.

When a whitetail is moving at a normal walk on flat ground, its track pattern will show the hind prints registering in and slightly to the rear of the front tracks. Bear in mind that all deer lean slightly forward as they step, so only the toes may register on sod or hard ground. The stride length is about 1 foot, while the straddle is normally about 6 inches.

The track pattern of a normal walk changes in several inches of snow, when the animals have to lift their hooves from a hole with each step. The stride length will likely increase to about 20 inches (the longer strides compensate for the more difficult walking), and hooves will print separately in a regular, staggered formation.

At a gallop, the track pattern also shows individual prints, but in this case the stride increases to 6 feet or more. The straddle also increases, but only by a couple inches. Hoofprints are deep and well defined, angling downward at the toes, and some loose soil may be sprayed backward from the print.

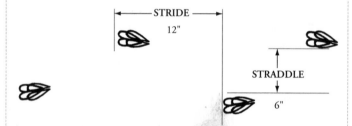

Walking pattern of the white-tailed deer, which is typical for many other species as well. Hind feet register on top of footprints.

At a dead run the whitetail adopts the "rocking horse" gait common among most running mammals—an exception being the mule deer, which bounds with all four feet together. In this gait the forelegs act as a fulcrum: Both front hooves are planted together, while the hind feet are brought forward to land ahead and to either side of them. Prints are especially deep, and front toes may actually plow under the sod. All tracks will probably contain a spray of loose soil. The stride increases to approximately 20 feet and the straddle distance between hind prints may measure 2 feet.

Track pattern of a leaping whitetail. Note how all four feet print together. Changes in direction are indicated by the direction in which hooves point.

SCAT

Whitetail scat is very similar to that of other hoofed mammals with similar diets, and in areas where the whitetail's range overlaps that of the closely related mule deer, positive identification from scat alone may be impossible. When the animals' diets are regular, droppings take the form of pellets in capsule or, less commonly, acorn shapes. Pellets are usually deposited in groups of 20 or so, and the same spot may be used repeatedly, apparently as a scentpost. Most droppings are found on well-traveled trails, but deer tend to unload wherever the urge comes upon them.

Whitetail scat in pellet form. Dark brown in color, becoming lighter and more fibrous with age. Scat shown is common to all members of the deer family (Cervidae), *with a few differences in size and shape.*

Scat pellets are normally dark brown in color, firm, and contain visible traces of plant fibers. Dimensions don't always indicate the size of the animal depositing them, but pellets may range in length from ½ inch for fawns to more than 1 inch for large adults. The diameter generally runs about one-third of the length. In winter, when yarded deer are forced into a dry and woody diet, scat pellets are lighter in color and more fibrous.

As is the case with humans, a sudden change in diet has temporary adverse effects on the whitetail's digestive system. When the woody diet of winter changes to one of succulent green plants in spring, droppings become more liquid and massed, looking much like miniature cowpies but with an average diameter of about 2 inches. The same is often true in autumn, when the animals gorge themselves on ripening apples, acorns, and farm produce.

SIGN

Whitetail sign is varied and usually abundant. Among the most obvious are "buck rubs," ragged patches of bark stripped away from the trunks of small trees by antlers. One reason that deer create them is to scrape off the "velvet" covering that nourishes antlers during growth; another is to leave a visual warning to potential rivals that a territory has been claimed. Small saplings are used most often, but a large-antlered buck will some-times rub trees barely small enough to fit between his antlers as a demonstration of his size. Fresh rubs still wet with sap are likely to be encountered from August through November, usually in the vicinity of rubs from years past.

Antlered males also spar with shrubs and small trees to get in a bit of practice for the real thing. Dogwood, willow, birch, or almost any other shrub bearing some resemblance to a set of antlers is a likely candidate, and one used for sparring will show obvious signs of abuse: stripped bark, broken branches, scattered foliage. Antlered whitetails of all sizes and ages exhibit this behavior in late summer, and it's likely that abused shrubs also serve as territorial marks for breeding bucks.

Like elk, whitetail bucks occasionally wallow in mud during the mating season. This isn't a common practice, but messed-up muddy spots containing gray and white hairs, and usually smelling strongly of musk, are definite signs that a rutting buck has been there. Understandably, wal-lows are most likely to be found in swampy areas or near water. The size of a wallow apparently is determined only by the amount of available mud, but elk wallows will contain lighter-colored hairs—and of course there will always be identifiable tracks in the mud. The purpose of wal-lowing in urine-scented mud is to spread as much of the buck's sexual odor over as large an area as possible, increasing the range at which a receptive female or potential intruder can detect his presence.

Mushrooms and toadstools with bites taken from them are another sign of whitetail presence. Little is known about why deer and other ani-mals eat portions of sometimes toxic fungi, but the practice is common. Since so little of them is ingested, toadstools are almost certainly not eaten as food. Perhaps they're eaten for the same reason cats eat catnip.

VOCALIZATIONS

The best-known whitetail vocalization is its alarm whistle, or "blow," a sharp exhalation emitted when an animal has been actively frightened by the sight or scent of a predator. The sound, made by blowing forcefully through the nostrils, resembles a sudden release of high-pressure air, and is usually followed by the sight of disappearing hindquarters.

Other sounds emitted by whitetails of either sex include a low mooing sound, reminiscent of a cow but quieter. The pitch of these calls varies with the size and age of an individual. Fawns have the highest-pitched and quietest calls, usually prolonged but muted bleats that can scarcely be heard at more than a few years. Does have a lower voice, although not quite so low as a young buck. Fully mature bucks (four years and up) have the lowest voice of all, very much like the quiet lowing of a cow.

One virtually unmistakable whitetail vocalization is the piglike grunting of a rutting buck. This sound is a product of the mating season and is heard only in October and November, when competing males announce their readiness loudly to both rival bucks and receptive does. The sound, sometimes described as a "buck snort," frequently is accompanied by hoof stomping and the rattling of brush. To a photographer or hunter, the grunting of a sexually aroused buck also means a subject whose attention is likely focused more on mating than on potential predators.

MULE DEER (*ODOCOILEUS HEMIONUS*)

HABITAT AND RANGE

The mule deer, so called because of its large, perpetually moving ears, is mainly a western deer, although—as with the whitetail—its range and numbers are growing. The black-tailed deer, a subspecies found along the Pacific Coast, is identical except that its upper tail is black to dark brown above, while the mule deer has a white tail tipped with black. This minor difference may be due to nothing more than a dominant gene, as is eye color in humans, and the animals are otherwise indistinguishable.

Len Rue, Jr.

Mule Deer

*Distribution of mule deer (*Odocoileus hemionus) *and black-tailed deer.*

Unlike the whitetail, the mule deer is not a creature of the deep forest but prefers more open, usually mountainous country. Its range covers most of western North America, from British Columbia east to Saskatchewan, down through western North Dakota to northwestern Mexico, and west to the Pacific Coast. Isolated populations are also found in Minnesota, Wisconsin, and northern Iowa, and have also been reported in the extreme southwestern corner of Alaska. In most places where mule deer live, you'll also find whitetails; the exceptions are prairies, deserts, and other wide-open places where "mulies" are comfortable but where whitetails feel too exposed.

An interesting disparity exists between the sizes of bucks and does of the two species. Mule deer bucks weigh from 110 to 475 pounds and are often much larger than whitetail bucks, which have an adult weight of 200–300 pounds. Yet mature mule deer does may weigh between 70 and 160 pounds, while whitetail does are nearly twice as large at 150–250 pounds.

Another major difference between mulies and whitetails is that the former migrate with the seasons. Whitetails typically spend their entire eight-year life span roaming a square mile of real estate—which doubtless accounts for at least some of their reputation for clever escapes. Mule deer prefer to summer at higher elevations, where the air is cooler and breezes keep biting insects at a tolerable level. When snow makes food inaccessible in the mountains, mulies head for warmer, more open plains and valleys to feed until spring.

Thanks to good management, more or less, and a scarcity of natural predators, mule deer populations are on the rise—and in a few places their numbers have increased to the point that they've become pests. Their major natural enemies as adults are cougars, wolves, and humans, while coyotes, bobcats, and bears prey upon the young and weak. Many are killed by motorists, who are often killed themselves, and well-intentioned humans sometimes contribute to these tragedies. Jackson Hole, Wyoming, has long been noted for residents who feed mule deer, elk, moose, and bison through the winter, creating an unnatural environment in which herds overpopulate, potentially dangerous wildlife loses its fear of humans, and few animals have ever had to forage naturally in winter.

FOODS

The mulie's diet pretty much parallels that of other deer, although the open country, even desert, that it prefers provides different browse than that available to its forest-dwelling cousins. In summer it grazes chiefly on herbaceous plants such as clover and alfalfa, but also eats such shrubs as blackberry, thimbleberry, and huckleberry. All things being equal, there's little variation in the diets of mule deer, whitetails, elk, and moose, and in the northern Rocky Mountain region where all four still exist, any or all may browse the same areas.

Winter is tough on mule deer in their northern range, and, like white-tails, they may yard up as a herd in places where the terrain offers both shelter from cold winds and woody winter browse. As with all deer, their food options are broad—aspen, willow, dogwood, sagebrush, rabbit brush, cedar, juniper, and fir—depending on climate and availability. Acorns and apples are eaten until snow makes these favorites inaccessible. The animals also paw through the snow along streambanks to get at thick dead grasses from the previous summer, and a few suffer broken legs—a mortal injury in winter—from the treacherous footing there.

While mulies seem generally less tolerant of humans than whitetails, they have also learned to associate farming with food, and the crop damage they cause is sometimes extensive. Apples, corn, beans, and rye are perennial favorites.

MATING HABITS

The mule deer rut generally coincides with that of other deer, running from October through November, with some variations throughout its range. Mating is initiated by the scent of does coming into heat, which prompts adult bucks to secrete hormones that cause them to swell phys-ically and carry their own distinctive sexual aroma. Antlers that have been developing since April are now polished against trees to make them appear more impressive to rivals, but it seems unlikely that the polishing is an intentional effort to sharpen the tines. Probably the reason behind it is to lighten the antlers' color and make them more visible against most backgrounds.

Mule deer antlers can be distinguished from those of whitetail by their unique tines (there's little chance of mistaking either species' antlers for those of the much larger elk or moose). Both deer have a pair of normally identical antlers with main beams that start from the skull on each side, above the eyes and between the ears. A single brow tine projects upward near the base of each antler to protect the animal's eyes while it spars with other bucks. A mule deer's main beams end in a forked Y, however, as do the tines branching from them, while whitetail antlers have single, unbranched main beams and tines.

Combat between mulie bucks competing for does is a bit less vicious than some whitetail matches. Young bucks of two or three years may spar with one another, or occasionally even an adult, but when adults of four years or more in age meet as competitors for breeding rights, contests are taken seriously. If posturing and grunting fail to discourage a hopeful rival, a competing male lowers his head and locks his antlers with the rival's, entering into what essentially becomes a pushing match to see which animal is the stronger. It may be only a few seconds before the weaker animal acknowledges defeat and withdraws, or the feud may last several rounds, with both fighters resting periodically. There appears to be little genuine animosity among rutting males in any deer species, but testosterone levels are high, and one or both bucks are frequently stabbed by antler tines. If mule deer suffer fewer severe injuries during rutting contests than whitetails, it may be due to their different antler structure. In unusual instances, antlers can become inextricably wedged together, resulting in the eventual demise of both bucks, but such tragedies are rare.

Like all deer, mule deer bucks communicate their availability through pawed-up sections of earth, called scrapes, scented with strong-smelling urine and musk. Scrapes vary in size from a few hoof marks to several feet of plowed-up earth; many of the smaller scrapes are made by immature males. Breeding bucks create strings of scrapes around their chosen territories, which may be some distance from their home range, and patrol them constantly. Does in estrus urinate on active scrapes to indicate interest, but then leave, dribbling urine over the scent-producing tarsal glands on the insides of their hind legs. When the buck returns and finds his invitation has been accepted, he sets out in immediate pursuit. Females have little interest in what buck impregnates them, and will breed with any male strong enough to get past the competition.

Mule deer bucks are thought to be more polygamous than whitetail, gathering a harem of several does by midrut. But whether a buck of either species has one mate or a dozen probably has as much to do with his own social standing and the availability of does as it does with any specieswide instinctive traits.

SEASONAL HABITS

After the rut, bucks and does lose interest in one another. Does of more than two years of age are likely to be pregnant and, with winter approaching, their attention shifts to gathering nourishment. Gestation lasts about seven months, with fawns born in May and June. Young females giving birth for the first time typically have a single fawn; twins are the norm thereafter, or triplets if food is abundant. A doe with fawns may not participate in the first rut following their birth, but will breed again when her young are 18 months old, driving them off just before the next generation is born.

Bucks may be gregarious, especially before and immediately after the rut, while does with fawns are usually solitary. In fact, mule deer does are quite territorial and often fight upon meeting, an instinctive reaction designed to ensure that each family group has sufficient food. A truce is called during winter in the north when, like whitetails, mule deer of all ages and both sexes yard up until spring.

TRACKS

To quote the legendary tracker Olas J. Murie, "I must confess that I have found no way to distinguish the footprints or droppings of our three kinds of deer (whitetail, blacktail, and mulie)." This statement is as true today as when he penned it in 1954; all things being equal, whitetail and mule deer tracks are identical.

But all things are not equal if you look closely enough, and Mr. Murie knew this as well as anyone. Any deer track (not counting elk and moose) found east of Minnesota will always be a whitetail print. In places where the two species coexist—Montana, for example—it helps to know that mulies prefer open areas (I suspect mule deer have sharper eyesight than whitetails). In mountainous country, this means they spend a lot of time walking on abrasive rock, while the more reclusive whitetail avoids such exposed places. For this reason, mule deer hooves are likely to have rounded, well-abraded edges and blunt tips whose prints contrast with the sharp features of whitetail prints. Some mulies spend most of their time around the edges of a forest if food is abundant there, of course, and solitary whitetail bucks frequently travel along rocky ridgelines, but a fresh track that lacks sharp definition found in a place where both species live was most likely made by a mule deer.

Mule deer tracks; 2 to 3 inches long. Paired tracks at top show walking gait typical of the deer family, hind prints registering in foreprints.

While there may be considerable differences between the sizes of adult whitetail and mule deer bucks, the differences in hoof size are not as pronounced as you might think. An adult whitetail leaves prints a hair under 3 inches in length, while a large mule deer track is no more than ¼ inch longer. Track size is no help in determining whether its maker was a whitetail, a mule deer, or even a young moose.

But careful study of track patterns can be a help. Like some African antelope and unlike any other American deer, mulies run with a distinctive bounding gait known as "stotting," in which all four hooves leave then make contact with the earth simultaneously. This curious pogo-stick running gait has also been called "rubberballing," which is as descriptive a term as any.

Mule deer track patterns. Note how all four feet land together, a running gait unique in North America.

At a full run, mule deer hit the ground with all four hooves coming down close together, the forefeet ahead of the hind feet, and all four printing individually in a slightly staggered pattern. The straddle across the forefeet is about 5 inches; the hind feet register a bit farther apart. The distance between the front and hind prints averages about 1 foot, while the distance between sets of prints may run 9 to 12 feet. Each track will likely have a spray of loose soil to its rear.

At a relaxed walk, mule deer track patterns resemble those of other deer, with the hind prints registering in and slightly behind the front prints. The stride is the most important factor in making a positive identification in this case: Adult mulies have an average walking stride of 22–24 inches, compared to 12–14 inches for whitetails and 30–60 inches for elk.

SCAT

As Olas Murie stated earlier, there's no reliable way to differentiate between the droppings of mule deer and those of whitetails, or even those of mountain goats or small elk. All have similar diets and all leave drop-pings that are pellet or acorn shaped, or massed when they're feeding on a diet of succulents.

Once again, knowing a species' preferred habitat can help. Mountain goats typically stay at higher elevations than mulies, which in turn fre-quent higher elevations than whitetails. That isn't a whole lot to go on, but this is one of those situations where an ability to find and interpret other sign is necessary to fill in the blanks.

SIGN

As with tracks and scat, mule deer sign is very similar to that of the white-tail. Both species create scrapes and rubs, both lack upper front teeth (as do all deer), and males of both species spar with shrubs and bushes. Again, the types of terrain and of vegetation can be important clues for determining a specific species' sign.

But there are a few differences that can help you with identification. One is the tendency for mule deer to urinate immediately upon rising from their beds, which are usually located under cover in tall grass or around forest edges. Mulie bucks habitually urinate directly onto the bed, probably as a proprietary claim to that spot, while does typically step a few feet to one side before relieving themselves.

Buck rubs may also be noticeably different from those left by other deer species, because of the mulie's unique Y-shaped antler structure. The twin points at the end of each antler branch tend to leave dual parallel scrape marks, while the single points of whitetail or elk antlers leave indi-vidual marks. The distance between these parallel gouges varies with antler size and individual characteristics, but several pairs spaced 2 to 4 inches apart on a tree trunk can be taken as proof of a mule deer buck.

VOCALIZATIONS

Although not as vocal as elk, mule deer have more calls and use them more frequently than do whitetails. There are the muted bleatings between a mother and her young common to all deer, and rutting bucks make much the same grunting noises as whitetails, but mulies also appear to have a rudimentary language. Reports of mule deer "talking" among themselves while feeding on a winter night (remember, snow forces deer to be gre-garious) are common. Their vocalizations include a wide range of grunts, growls, snorts, and bleats, but it's likely that at least some of those heard on quiet winter nights are simply declarations of personal space.

AMERICAN ELK OR WAPITI (*CERVUS CANADENSIS*)

HABITAT AND RANGE

"Elk" is said to have been originally a British name for the animal we know as the moose. Somehow it became mistakenly applied to the wapiti (a Shawnee name meaning "pale deer"). Incorrect or not, the name stuck,

Len Rue, Jr.

American Elk or Wapiti

and now when anyone speaks of elk, we think of the majestic wapiti, North America's second-largest deer.

Today, elk are creatures of open forests, plains, and meadows, but before the 1800s they were almost strictly grazers, as were bison. Elk were once common throughout much of North America, before over-hunting, logging, and human encroachment drove survivors into northern wilderness areas. Elk populations are found these days along the Pacific Coast from northern California through British Columbia, and in the northern Rockies from Alberta to Colorado. Attempts to reestablish elk herds in areas where they were once native have resulted in sometimes sizable populations in Arizona, Minnesota, and several other states. Like those of whitetails and mule deer, the elk's northern range stops well south of Alaska.

Based on my own experiences with these large deer, it isn't hard for me to understand how our forefathers, for whom hunting skill was a matter

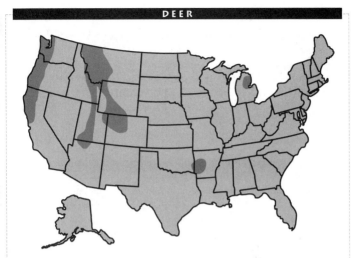

*Distribution of elk (*Cervus canadensis*).*

of survival, could have hunted them out of existence over so much of their original range. For one thing, elk are big targets, standing up to 5 feet tall at the shoulder and with a body length of 7 to nearly 10 feet. Females (cows) weigh from 450 to 650 pounds at maturity, and adult bulls average 600–1,100 pounds——enough meat to get a family through the winter. Size may have also worked against the elk in that few predators are willing or able to tackle such gigantic prey, which probably accounts for their marked tendency to be more curious than afraid when approached by a relatively puny human. Any frontiersman armed with a rifle would have found them easy prey.

Elk do have natural enemies besides humans, most notably the puma, grizzly, and black bear, but a healthy adult of either sex really has little to fear from any carnivore on the continent. With a superb nose, excellent hearing, and a top running speed of 35 mph, the elk is well equipped to avoid the few predators that do have the strength to bring it down. Fearing injury to themselves, large predators—grizzlies, for example— typically charge an elk herd just to make its members run, concentrating their real efforts on animals too weak or injured to keep up with the rest. Instances of smaller carnivores such as coyotes taking elk are limited to calves or half-dead adults. A mother elk or harem bull may rush to defend a young calf, but if a coyote or a bobcat can inflict a lethal would before being driven off, the herd has no choice but to abandon the carcass.

Other names such as "ghost of the forest" have been attached to elk, because of their light-colored body hair and because of a surprising ability to move quickly and quietly through open woods. Some outdoor writers have remarked upon the wapiti's stealth, contrasting it with the crashing made by a startled whitetail as it dives into cover. The inference

that a half-ton elk is somehow quieter than a 200-pound whitetail is erroneous, however, because it overlooks the fact that a whitetail's first
instinct is to get out of sight immediately, running through places where
an elk wouldn't fit. In the open woods and meadows preferred by elk, a
whitetail travels at least as quietly as its much larger cousin, and as hunting legend John Wootters once pointed out, most folks actually see only
10 percent of the whitetails they encounter.

FOODS

Once again, the diet of an elk closely resembles that of other deer: clovers,
grasses, and succulents during the growing season; willow, aspen, raspberry, and other woody browse after snow makes grazing more work than
reward. Elk are more likely to feed on lichens, such as reindeer moss
(*Cladina rangiferina*), than any other deer—except reindeer, of course—
and their fancy for aquatic plants is surpassed only by the moose's. Pond
lily, water shield, and lotus are among favored aquatic foods, while elkslip
(*Caltha leptosepala*) is eaten by wapiti to the west of the Rockies, and
marsh marigold (*Caltha palustris*) by those to the east. Moose also eat
both species of elkslip, although both are toxic to most other animals,
including humans.

Like all deer, elk are fond of apples, corn, and other farm crops; only
their lower numbers and normally remote habitat have kept them from
becoming agricultural pests, as have mulies and whitetails. Or maybe
they avoid farmlands because ignorant cattlemen of the 19th century
slaughtered them by the thousands to keep range pastures free for business use.

MATING HABITS

The mating habits of wapiti are similar to those of other deer, featuring
scrapes (mud wallows in this case), antler rubs, and ritual combat using
their huge antlers. But there are a few striking differences: Bull elk are
perhaps the most polygamous deer in the world, gathering harems of up
to 60 cows if conditions and competition from rival males allow. As with
other deer species, the ratio of cows to bulls is weighted heavily in favor
of the females, which outnumber males by roughly five to one, so the
strongest bulls have ample opportunity to spread their genes around.
Even though a herd may appear to be led by a powerful bull, however, its
members actually follow the wisest and most experienced cow.

In March, bull elk begin growing new antlers to replace those lost in
December. By late May, adult bulls are sporting large antlers covered with
a nourishing layer of "velvet." During these spring months, adult bulls of
all ages may run together, although I've seen large males traveling with
small harems even this early. I've also watched groups of velvet-antlered
bulls grazing peacefully with cows in early spring, although it's interesting to note that when these herds are startled, cows and bulls generally go
their separate ways as a group.

Elk antlers are nothing if not impressive, with main beams of up to 5 feet in length and with a treelike structure that appears unbearably heavy. By his fourth year, a mature, well-fed bull will have developed three tines on each beam (not counting brow tines), although an abundance of nutritious food may stimulate growth of additional tines, usually in pairs. By August, when bulls begin gathering their harems in earnest, saplings, shrubs, and small trees stripped of bark by heavy antler rubbings will be in evidence, usually with bits of dislodged velvet around their bases.

The availability of food has a lot to do with how a mating season unfolds. If food is scarce, or if a herd is too large for the land to support, some cows may not come into estrus, and those that do may not become pregnant. It also appears that scarcity of food can delay the puberty of young bulls, but a simple lack of nutrition probably has as much to do with this as do any natural genetic safeguards.

Like other deer, elk communicate their sexual availability through scents, but with elk the buck scrape takes the form of a mud wallow scented with copious amounts of urine and feces. Bulls roll in wallows to cover their bodies with scent, creating bathtub-size depressions with low walls of displaced mud ringing their perimeters. A receptive cow drawn by the odor will herself roll and urinate in the wallow to indicate acceptance of the bull's invitation to mate, but then she'll probably leave, forcing him to chase her. Mating wallows are musky smelling and have light-colored hairs lining their bottoms as well as fresh hoofprints all around. Abandoned wallows from previous years are likely to be filled with water and have grasses growing around them.

By October, bulls have gathered complete harems and stand ready to defend ownership with polished antlers. Immature bulls that submit to the harem master's authority may be allowed to stay, but competitors that attempt to steal all or some of a bull's females will be met with force. Injuries and death are only infrequently the results of mating battles; the real objective is to force an opponent's head to the ground, at which point the vanquished bull generally withdraws. Breeding and fighting continue through November, when the cows themselves end them by going out of estrus.

Calves are born after a gestation period of about nine and a half months, the longest of any American deer, with most arriving in late July and August. Cows ready to deliver withdraw from the herd to give birth to one or—if food is abundant—two calves, weighing from 25 to 40 pounds. Young are born with brown-and-white-spotted fur, like whitetail fawns but much larger. After a week or so, when the calf is strong enough to travel, its mother will rejoin the herd. Calves are entirely dependent on their mothers' milk for the first month—the most dangerous time of their lives in terms of predation—but may suckle for nearly a year.

SEASONAL HABITS

Like all deer and most wild animals, elk are primarily nocturnal, moving to open grazing areas in early evening and returning to secluded bedding areas before full daylight. One exception may be the first month or so of a spring following a hard winter, when all deer are more hungry than afraid and may be seen feeding on patches of bare ground at any time of day. Elk also yard up when snow covers grazing areas, but their yards are generally in more open areas than are whitetail yards, because of the animals' larger size and ability to reach higher for browse. Elk are also known to eat quantities of aspen, poplar, and other tree bark, especially in winter; this is a food source exploited by moose, but rarely by whitetails or mule deer.

From the time a rut ends in late November until the next begins the following August, mature bulls tend to run together, and old foes seem to forget their differences, at least until the next rut. When spring rains wash the snow from fields and meadows, permitting hungry deer to feed on last year's grasses until new growth appears, it isn't unusual to see a dozen or more large-antlered bulls in velvet feeding peacefully shoulder to shoulder. An occasional mock battle may occur, and there does appear to be a social hierarchy, but there's seldom any real animosity.

Cows and bulls often graze together in early spring, when food is in short supply and most feeding areas are still snowbound, but the two sexes generally go their separate ways after feeding. Juvenile bulls follow their mothers for the first two years, gradually spending less and less time with the cow-dominated herd as puberty draws closer. It appears that bull calves are actively encouraged to leave the cow herd in their second year, probably to curb inbreeding.

Cows run together in groups year-round. The leader of the herd is always an older, dominant cow, even when the whole group has been gathered into a harem. Alpha cows are territorial, but since they normally lack antlers they have to settle for scraping patches of bark from live saplings with their lower incisors to establish domain. Such territorial gnawings are easy to identify, because all the bark will have been scraped upward or sideways only, never downward.

TRACKS

While some tracking books warn that elk prints might be confused with those of moose and smaller deer, most are distinctly different from the hoof marks left by other species. Like all deer (as well as cows, pigs, goats, and sheep), wapiti have cloven hooves that normally print in a split-heart shape on soft earth; elk tracks are more clearly rounded, however, almost like the caribou's. The most obvious feature of an elk print is the way its rounded outer edges print more heavily than its inner surfaces, outlining tracks on sod and humus deeply, although sometimes nothing but a vaguely cherry-shaped hoof outline is left on hard-packed dirt roads. The dewclaws on all four feet may register in several inches of mud or snow, and hoofprints may be splayed wide on slippery surfaces. I've also noted that elk appear to walk nearly flat footed, while moose, whitetails, and

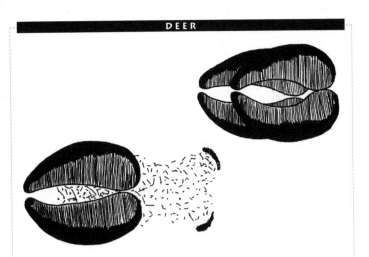

Elk tracks; 3 to 5 inches long. Darkly shaded areas show portions pressed hardest against the earth. Paired top track indicates a walking gait, with hind hoof printing over foreprint. Bottom track, with dewclaws printing to its rear, is characteristic of those made in snow or mud.

mule deer lean heavily onto their toes while walking. More than a quick glance may be required to positively identify a set of tracks.

As you might expect, wapiti are much easier to track than most wild animals, including whitetails and mule deer. A hoofed animal with that much weight is bound to leave some sort of mark in or on almost anything it walks over. Add to this the animals' tendency to travel in groups of one type or another throughout the year and you have a species whose comings and goings are obvious to practically anyone.

It should be noted that some elk habitats may be located in rocky or mountainous regions, while others are confined to lowland forests and meadows. Elk that spend much of their time walking over abrasive rock will leave tracks with more rounded edges on soft ground, often showing chips, gouges, and other evidence of damage. The sharper the features of an elk track (bearing in mind that features deteriorate with age), the less time that animal spends on rocky terrain; this can help you pinpoint its bedding and feeding areas.

Surprisingly, the straddle of an elk measures about 5 inches, or about the same as that of a mule deer and whitetails, so don't expect to find the foot-wide path of domestic cattle. The stride of a walking adult elk averages 30–40 inches, occasionally longer, with the hind prints registering in and just behind the foreprints, in typical deer fashion. In difficult walking conditions—mud, sand, or snow—walking tracks print individually, and the stride may increase to 60 inches.

At a gallop, the stride may increase to as much as 8 feet—less than that of smaller, more nimble deer, but sufficient to carry the big animals through the woods at speeds of up to 35 mph. Like most hoofed animals

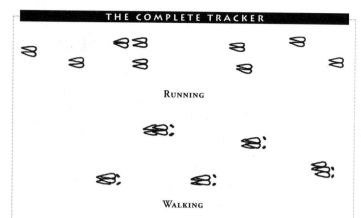

RUNNING

WALKING

Track patterns of elk.

(except mule deer), wapiti run with a "rocking horse" gait, in which the rear hooves land ahead and to either side of the front feet at the end of each stride. All running prints are especially deep, and a spray of loose soil or snow should be visible behind each track, thrown there when the animal pushed off.

SCAT

Here again, there are few differences between elk scat and the droppings of its cousins. Given a steady, consistent diet, pellets deposited by mule deer, whitetails, elk, and sometimes even moose may all be of the same general size, shape, and texture. Elk pellets have been described as being more like compressed sawdust because their diet is normally more woody than that of other species, but this is seldom enough on which to base a decision, especially in winter, when all deer have a woody diet.

A distinct difference between wapiti scat and the droppings of smaller species, however, is the amount deposited at one time. Whereas an adult whitetail may leave 20–40 pellets at a time, elk deposits are generally two to four times larger. This difference in volume becomes especially apparent when a rich diet causes the animals' scat to become a soft mass, similar to a domestic cowpie but smaller. "Elkpies" average 4–6 inches in diameter, while those of whitetails and mule deer run about 2 inches across. Massed moose droppings are similar to those of elk but generally more solid, with a diameter of roughly 2 inches, although I've seen moose that feed from deer hunters' bait piles leave 8- to 10-inch chips very similar to those of domestic cattle.

SIGN

Probably the most easily identified elk sign is its wallow, described earlier as part of the wapiti rutting ritual. But wallows are used throughout the summer months as well, and you might see a fresh one as early as April or May. Rolling in mud serves to loosen the dead winter coat and helps dislodge annoying parasites. A coating of mud also provides some degree of protection against the bloodsucking insects that begin hatching even before the snow has melted. Wallows are, of course, sited in areas where the ground is wet and muddy, usually near a body of water and nearly always in a secluded area where animals feel relaxed enough to drop their guard a bit. Mule deer bucks are also known to wallow, particularly while rutting, and moose make a habit of it around streams and lakes where they feed, so don't arbitrarily assign a wallow to a wapiti until you've first checked for other sign.

Gnawed trees, especially aspen and poplar, are common in both elk and moose country during winter, and the one-way, bottom-teeth-only scrape marks of the two animals are virtually identical. Bark from these and other trees is also a mainstay of the beaver's diet. Wintering elk or moose gnawings may be found on felled trees, however, where they're unlikely to be confused with the chisel-like cuttings of the beaver. Differentiating between elk and moose gnawings can best be accomplished by reading other sign, knowing the usual winter range of either species in a given area, and, of course, observing the animals themselves. Moose gnawings are not necessarily found higher up on a trunk than elk, because moose have shorter necks, but gnawings within inches of the ground can be attributed to elk for this same reason. Wintering forests are easy to identify at any time of year: Older trees will have developed a thick, rough layer of black bark over some or all of their lower trunks— scars left by previous generations of wintering elk or moose.

An elk sign that is especially prevalent in late summer, when bulls are at their most handsome and are anxious to use their new antlers, is a scattering of uprooted plants in open meadows. When bulls begin gathering their harems, they habitually urinate on the plants and toss them onto their backs, using their antlers as pitchforks. This practice will continue throughout the rut (weather permitting), and apparently helps a bull spread his scent over a greater area, perhaps making him seem larger to potential rivals.

VOCALIZATIONS

Elk are the most vocal deer in North America, and probably no one old enough to read these words has gone through life without hearing at least a recording of the bull elk's mating call. To me it sounds somewhat like a loon's call with a certain squealing quality, ending with two or three guttural grunts, also with a squealing tone. The call is far more pleasing than my feeble attempt at describing it implies.

Bull elk mating calls are naturally heard more often during the wapiti mating season, from August through November, and most often at dawn and dusk. In most cases, the calls sound from an open meadow where a contentious bull, with or without a harem in tow, is announcing his dominance to would-be rivals.

Cows use a squeal—perhaps better described as a high-pitched whistle—to communicate with calves and with one another. Calves emit a similar sound with a slightly higher pitch, although the calling between a mother and her young calf is frequently too soft to be heard at more than 50 yards. One (I think) funny wapiti characteristic is the way a herd of cows with calves babble among themselves with low mooing sounds and grunts when joining up again after being startled into flight. Like other deer (except moose), elk have light-colored rump patches, highlighted by darker fur around the hindquarters; this helps youngsters keep Mother in sight while fleeing, but in a herd setting there's bound to be some confusion when the animals settle down again.

MOOSE (ALCES ALCES)

HABITAT AND RANGE

Moose were originally known as "elk" to New World explorers, before that British label was mistakenly applied to the wapiti, where it has stuck fast ever since. Moose are the largest deer in the world, with bulls weigh-

Len Rue, Jr.

Moose

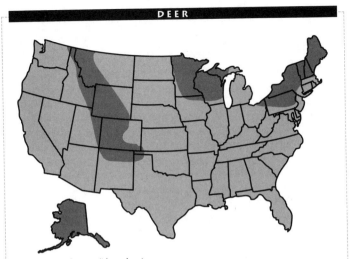

Distribution of moose (Alces alces).

ing in at a whopping 900–1,400 pounds, and cows at 700–1,100. The shoulder height at maturity ranges between 6½ and 7½ feet, and body length may reach 9 feet.

Moose are solitary creatures of the North Woods normally found in remote forests, where lakes and streams provide aquatic foods in summer and shrubby browse in winter. Their range covers nearly all of northern North America, from Alaska to Newfoundland and south through the Rocky Mountain range to Colorado. Moose are also found through the northeastern United States in a line extending from Minnesota through Pennsylvania and back up to Maine. They're noted for migrating up and down mountain slopes with the seasons, but these horse-size deer are equally at home in the swamps of northern Michigan and the Massachusetts hardwoods. In their preferred four-season habitat, the factor that most determines their range is the presence of humans.

Moose are normally shy, slipping quietly away through the woods at speeds of up to 35 mph when approached by humans. But photographers in particular need to be constantly aware of the gigantic deer's unpredictable nature. Mothers with calves of any age are almost guaranteed to be fiercely protective and quick to anger, while rutting bulls have been known to charge anything they perceive as an intruder into their territories, including livestock, automobiles, and even trains. Whatever the circumstance or season, it pays to accord a moose the same respect you'd give a grizzly bear. Even grizzlies rarely consider tackling an adult moose.

In keeping with their station as the world's largest deer, moose lack the light-colored rump patch and flag tail evolved by other deer to provide a visual alarm to others and to give young a beacon to follow when fleeing danger. Their horselike coats range from dark brown to dark gray in winter, and offer surprisingly good camouflage to such a massive animal.

A long dewlap hangs under the moose's chin, but its purpose, if there is one, is unknown.

FOODS

From spring through fall, moose subsist largely on aquatic plants such as pondweed, water shield, pond lily, lotus, and marsh marigolds (elkslip). Other deer may eat water plants occasionally, but only moose make them a staple, an adaptation that allows these giant vegetarians to coexist peacefully with other plant eaters. The shorelines of lakes and beaver ponds within the species' range are good places to look for moose, especially in the early morning and early evening. Moose will feed along shorelines, sometimes with their heads completely under water, until winter snow and ice makes such foraging impossible. They're very good swimmers and have been known to swim 12 miles at speeds of up to 6 mph.

Because all moose live in snow country, where the vegetation and trees are similar (if not the terrain), their winter feeding habits are fairly predictable. Winter browse consists of a variety of trees and shrubs, most of which grow near water. Willow is a staple, but twigs and buds of aspen, birch, dogwood, pine, cedar, and maple are eaten, as is the bark of some trees, particularly aspen and poplar. Smaller trees broken and bent over to afford the animals access to their tender tops are a sure sign of moose.

If snow becomes too deep, moose may congregate in what might loosely be called a yard, just as several may feed from the same banks of a lake in summer. They will tolerate one another for the common need, but they can't be called gregarious at any time of year.

MATING HABITS

The moose rut begins in mid-September and continues through October. During this time, bulls are at their peak size and strength, and even grizzlies give them a wide berth. The unique, flattened antlers that have been developing since April are now polished from rubbing against trees and may span nearly 7 feet, although 4 to 5 is average.

Like elk, bull moose use mud wallows instead of scrapes to advertise their availability to females. Such wallows are, of course, sited on muddy ground and generally measure about 4 feet square, with low walls of displaced mud surrounding the perimeter. Rutting wallows smell strongly of urine and musk; bulls roll in them to increase the distribution of their mating scents, and cows roll in them to indicate their interest in the bulls' offers.

When two bulls meet as rivals, threat displays are usually sufficient to cause one to withdraw, but an occasional battle does occur. The objective, in typical deer fashion, is to lock antlers with an opponent and force his head to the ground, whereupon the subdued bull submits to the other and quits. Occasional injuries are to be expected from such a clash of titans, but almost no moose die unless their antlers become inextricably wedged together, a rare and sometimes fatal dilemma for both animals.

Like other American deer, moose shed their antlers in late December, but collectors need to move quickly because porcupines, squirrels, and other rodents eat them for the calcium and other nutrients they contain.

Like whitetails, moose are fairly polygamous, with bulls claiming just one breeding cow for several days then another, until females are no longer in heat. At rut's end, the two sexes will have nothing more to do with each other until the following year. The gestation period is eight months, with one to two calves born in late May or June. Calves are lighter colored than their parents, but are not spotted. Baby moose (something of a contradiction in terms) are dependent on their mothers' milk for their first month, but mature quickly. At two to three weeks they can swim well and begin eating plants. At six months calves are weaned, and at one year, just before mothers give birth again, they're driven off to fend for themselves. Females may breed at 18 months, but young bulls will probably not become serious contenders until age three or four.

SEASONAL HABITS

Depending on terrain and vegetation, moose may or may not migrate with the seasons. From spring through fall they can normally be found foraging for aquatic plants along the shorelines of remote lakes, where they also swim and roll in mud to escape biting insects.

In mountainous country, where suitable ponds and lakes are found at higher elevations, moose may prefer to summer far above sea level. Stronger and steadier winds occur here, making hot days more tolerable and offering added protection against biting flies.

In Maine, summer movements of moose are determined by the size of the biting insect crop. In bad years moose become semiaquatic and head for the coast, where they're frequent sights in urban areas rife with humans but more or less devoid of blackflies, horse and moose flies, and mosquitoes.

When winter snows and frozen shorelines make foraging for water plants impossible, moose are forced into yards, as are elk and whitetails. More than a dozen normally solitary moose may winter together, and while there doesn't appear to be a ruling hierarchy, they seem to get along fine by respecting one another's space.

TRACKS

Moose tracks are much like whitetail and mule deer prints, but the hoof-prints of an adult moose measure 5 to 6 inches in length while mulie and whitetail prints never exceed 3½ inches. Elk tracks may be nearly the same length, at just under 5 inches, but are generally more widely rounded; moose hooves are typically pointed, perhaps even more so than whitetails. Moose tend to lean forward onto their toes when walking, and on solid ground only the toes may be obvious, making prints easy to mistake for those of a smaller species. Elk tend to step more flat-footedly, and the outsides of their hooves usually print more deeply than the insides.

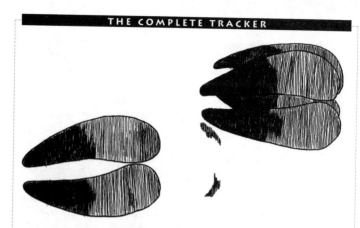

Moose tracks; 5 to 7 inches long. Bottom track shows dewclaws printing faintly behind. Paired set at top indicates a walking gait, with hind foot printing into front track.

However, there are individual characteristics among animals—just as with us—and occasionally an "intermediate" print turns up that looks like either or neither of these species.

At a normal walk, the moose straddle approximates that of other deer, at 4 to 6 inches, despite differences in size, while the stride ranges between 3½ and 5½ feet. Track patterns appear to vary more than those of other deer, sometimes with rear hooves registering inside front prints, but frequently with all four hooves registering individually. On slippery surfaces, hooves tend to be splayed in typical deer fashion as a protection against sliding.

Moose gaits.

At a gallop, the moose stride may increase to 8 feet or more, and again, all four hooves register individually. Although moose can run at up to 35 mph, they seldom need to, so the "rocking horse" gait, in which hooves land as pairs, front feet ahead of and inside rear prints, is rare.

SCAT

When I think of moose scat, the word "plentiful" comes to mind, and the image is fairly accurate: An average scat deposit will fill a 1-quart jar, with some deposits being half that size and others containing twice as much. During the summer, when moose feed extensively on aquatic vegetation, droppings are normally massed or even liquid, and some closely resemble domestic cow chips. Others may be smaller masses, 2 to 3 inches in diameter and formless.

Various common forms of moose scat. Pellets (1 to 1¾ inches long) indicate a dry, fibrous diet, common in winter. Massed deposits (1 to 2½ inches long or larger) indicate a more succulent diet.

One form of dropping that can be identified as exclusively moose is a soft scat that looks something like a toadstool, with a roughly spherical shape at one end and a narrow stem joining it to the generally mushroom-shaped opposite end. Once seen, such deposits are easily recognizable as belonging to moose, but the reason behind their unique shape is open to conjecture.

In winter, when the animals are forced into a diet of willow twigs, shrubs, and tree bark, moose scat takes the form of pellets that resemble compressed sawdust. Pellet sizes are extremely variable, averaging from 1 to nearly 2 inches in length, with a diameter of ½ to 1 inch. Some have concave depressions in one end that are distinctly moose, but others are virtually indistinguishable from other deer species' scat and some even resemble porcupine scat. Once again, it pays to consider all available sign.

SIGN

Even discounting their deep tracks and copious scat deposits, moose are obvious creatures. Willow and dogwood shrubs bent over at a height of about 7 feet (depending on an animal's size) are a sure sign that moose winter in the area. Gnawed patches of tree bark showing one-way scrapes are another sign of winter feeding, but bear in mind that moose gnaw-ings are often identical to those of elk.

Like all deer, bull moose thrash shrubs and saplings with their antlers prior to and during the rut, and such disturbances will reflect the size and power of their creator. These territorial marks are typically larger and more violent than are the thrashings of smaller deer; sometimes entire shrubs are pulled up by their roots. After August, antler rubs on young trees and saplings will be in evidence, often with bits of torn velvet around their bases. Moose rubs are understandably larger and deeper than those of whitetails or mule deer, but they can again be confused with those of elk where both species coexist.

Moose of both sexes and all ages wallow in mud. Because moose feed mainly on aquatic plants during the summer months, they're exposed to the worst concentrations of blackflies and mosquitoes. Rolling in mud applies a temporary bugproof coating that offers some relief. The wallows are large, typically measuring about 4 feet square and 3 to 4 inches deep, with low walls of displaced mud around the perimeters. The bottoms are usually lined with dark brown or gray hairs, as opposed to the blond or tan hairs found in elk wallows. After August, when bulls are in their prime, wallows are usually scented strongly with musky urine, a territor-ial scentpost and an advertisement of availability to breeding cows. Since mud wallows must, of course, be in mud, lakeshores and riverbanks are the best places to find them.

VOCALIZATIONS

Many attempts have been made to describe moose calls in print, but it's probably easiest to remember that the animals sound very much like domestic cattle. Females communicate with calves using a low mooing sound, and calves respond with higher-pitched bleats, neither of which can be heard at any distance. During the rut, females advertise their will-ingness to breed with a loud, cattlelike bawling that can be heard from several hundred yards. The late Olas Murie described this sound as "Uh-o-ow-wa," which is probably as close as a written description gets.

Bulls are generally silent for most of the year, but when the rut gets into full swing they can become quite vocal. Bulls have a mighty bellow, similar to that of their domestic counterparts, that serves as a challenge and an invitation to breed. They also have a low, huffing grunt during the rut, heard especially around scented wallows (*never* approach a rutting bull at his wallow) and when a bull is on the trail of a receptive cow. Bulls, too, have a low mooing call, used mainly to communicate with cows, but this noise is too quiet to be heard beyond 50 yards or so.

SWINE
(SUIDAE)
7

AMERICAN WILD BOAR
(INCLUDING FERAL HOG) (SUS SCROFA)

Although a distant cousin of the much smaller native peccary, or javelina, North America's only species of wild boar is descended from shaggy-haired European and Russian wild swine brought to the New World more than a century ago as game animals. In 1893, 50 were imported from Germany's Black Forest to a hunting preserve in New Hampshire's Blue Mountains. In 1910–12, Russian wild boar were released on a game preserve in North Carolina near the Tennessee border, and again in 1925 near Monterey, California. Some were also released on California's Santa

Feral Hogs

Cruz Island. In the century since their introduction, these tough survivors have escaped captivity to become firmly established, mainly in southeastern and western coastal states. In many places wild boar have interbred with domestic feral hogs escaped from farms to produce rather strange offspring with the physical characteristics of both species. They aren't well suited to snow country, and, with the exception of a few artificially maintained populations on game preserves, none are found in any northern states except Oregon and southern Washington.

Like deer, swine belong to the order Artiodactyla, meaning they have hooves with an even number of toes on each foot—in this case, four (dewclaws are actually toes). The similarity ends there; swine are aggressive omnivores that essentially eat anything with nutritional value, plant or animal. Adult males weigh 165–440 pounds, females 75–330, but, unlike their domestic counterparts, these pigs are fast, agile, and often fearless. With powerful, bisonlike bodies, oversize heads, and hooklike tusks (actually modified upper canines) that curl around to point upward from either side of the mouth, wild boars are formidable fighters. They can sprint at up to 30 mph for short distances, and they've been known to attack humans, especially rutting boars or sows with young. In some states, wild boar and feral hogs have become so numerous that they threaten to starve out species such as deer and black bears, and can be legally killed at any time of year. In Tennessee, there have been reports of black bears—whose omnivorous diet puts them in direct competition—killing wild boar, but also reports of wild boar killing bears. Mountain lions, bobcats, and coyotes prey on young piglets; their usual tactic is to rush in and inflict a lethal bite to a piglet's throat before its fiercely protective mother can come to the rescue. Wild boar are also capable of driving most predators away from a fresh kill to claim it as their own.

HABITAT AND RANGE

As you might expect from animals with such diverse diets, wild boar and feral hogs are at home in most wooded areas that offer concealment as well as a variety of plants, roots, nuts, and small animals that they can catch as food. Pure-blooded wild boar are found only in Tennessee, North Carolina, and parts of California, but feral and hybrid wild hogs can be found along the Atlantic Coast from North Carolina to Texas and north to Arkansas and Oklahoma. Populations are also found in western Texas, Arizona, California, and Oregon, with scattered game preserve populations in New Hampshire, Vermont, Pennsylvania, Michigan, and a few other tourist-oriented states. The factor that most limits the expansion of wild boar and feral hog ranges is climate; their stocky, short-legged bodies put them at a serious disadvantage in deep snow, and even shaggy-haired, pure-blooded wild boar are poorly equipped to survive moderately cold weather. Their home range is generally limited to about 10 square miles, but when food is in short supply, animals may roam 50 miles or more.

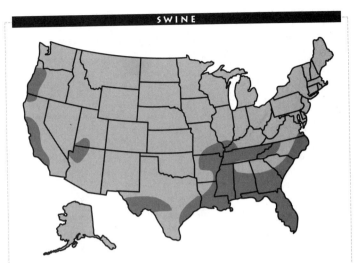

*Distribution of wild boar (*Sus scrofa*) and feral hog.*

FOODS

With wild boar, feral hogs, or—for that matter—farm-bred domestic pigs, it would be simpler to list what they *won't* eat. Grasses, sedges, plantains, and clovers are just a few of the plants they eat regularly. The tough, cartilaginous snouts and tusks of wild boar (feral hogs lack tusks) are effective rooting tools that allow them to reach taproots and tubers that other plant eaters find inaccessible. Beech, hickory, and pecan nuts, as well as acorns, are favorites, but competition for these rich treats from squirrels, deer, and other animals is fierce. It's said that American wild boar don't attain the 500-pound weight of European wild boar, even though they're the same species, simply because the New World contains so many competitors for food.

But wild pigs have an edge because their diet also includes meat. Carrion is preferred since it requires no effort—except possibly that of stealing it from rival predators, most of which will withdraw without a fight. Snakes are stomped to death with the boar's sharp hooves, and all pigs seem relatively immune to rattlesnake venom. Rodents, squirrels, and any other animals unfortunate enough to be caught are also eaten, and even prey as large as a newborn fawn is killed if it can be chased down.

Although the European wild boar is faster and more agile than feral hogs, owing to its more lithe body and longer legs, no swine species can be called a good hunter. They have superb noses, good hearing, and adequate eyesight but lack the speed, endurance, and claws common to animals whose primary food is meat. Instead, wild pigs are opportunistic, as are black bears, and sometimes fights between these two powerful rivals are to the death.

MATING HABITS

Breeding begins in late November and generally peaks in December. Boar are either solitary or run together in small, exclusively male bands most of the year, but breeding males (one and a half years and up in age) go their separate ways during mating season. Sows travel in family groups, and sometimes herds contain up to 50 females and young. Females outnumber males by about four to one. Mating is initiated by females coming into heat, and apparently nothing more than a sow's sexual odor is needed to bring the two sexes together. There are no elaborate scentposts or scrapes, and mud wallows probably serve as nothing more than just that.

Boars are polygamous, but they don't collect harems, although it might appear that way. A rutting boar running with a herd of females is simply one lucky enough to have found a large family group, and will likely impregnate every one of its receptive females over 18 months old. After mating, boars and sows go their separate ways.

Young are born in secluded, grass-lined nests about 16 weeks after impregnation; most arrive in April. Gregarious sows separate from the other females just prior to delivering 3 to 14 piglets (5 is average). Piglets are born 6 to 8 inches long, with a dark brown coat and 9 or 10 lighter longitudinal stripes that help them blend into grass and brush. Within a week, piglets are able to travel with their mother, and within a month they're eating solid foods, although they won't be weaned until they're three months old. Young boar are ejected from the family unit at one year to prevent inbreeding, but sows may stay with their mother. Both sexes become sexually mature at 18 months and are full grown at six years. Their average life span is 20 years.

SEASONAL HABITS

Wild boar are especially active around dawn and dusk, possibly because these are the times when other animals that might be considered prey are stirring. They appear to be primarily nocturnal, but may also be seen at midday. Beds are usually well hidden in brushy thickets, and may range from sausage-shaped depressions pressed into the undergrowth to piles of brush and grass accumulated by the pig, which then crawls underneath to sleep in solitude.

Wild boar don't yard up like deer, largely because their range is limited mostly to regions that stay green year-round. Like bears, they do follow seasonal foods. In spring and summer they root along forest edges for underground treats such as burdock root and cow parsnip, and also feed on sedges and grasses in meadows, where an unlucky ground squirrel or vole might add an extra bit of protein to their diets. Autumn will find them harvesting whatever fruits and nuts are available, again with an eye out for unwary squirrels, and winter is likely to bring them into swamps, where some food plants and edible fungi are available year-round. Mushrooms and toadstools are light on the nutritional side, and few animals actually regard them as food, but wild swine, like the truffle pigs of Europe, appear to eat them with relish.

TRACKS

Whitetails overlap the wild boar's entire range, and in some instances a close look may be needed to distinguish between their tracks, particularly since pigs are likely to follow established deer trails. In northwestern Texas, where wild pigs share their territory with a variety of other cloven-hoofed animals—pronghorns, javelina, mule deer, and maybe an occasional bighorn sheep—tracking may require of you a sharp eye for detail.

FRONT   HIND

Wild boar and feral hog tracks, 2 to 4 inches long. Shaded areas indicate portions of hoof pressed hardest into the earth.

The most striking difference between wild boar prints and those of fellow hoofed animals is their distinctive U shape. The inside hooves of other animals form a fairly sharp, straight-sided V when the hoof is spread, and when the two halves print closely together there's typically only a small gap between them. In contrast, a wild boar cannot bring the two halves of its hoof flush together because of their concave inner profile. The outsides of a swine's wide hooves are also well rounded, generally more so than those of other species within its range.

Another notable difference between swine and other hoofed animals is the location of their dewclaws, which are positioned low on the leg and generally print on all but the most hard-packed soil. Front dewclaws are most prominent, printing as elongated dashes at an outward angle behind and on either side of the hoofprint. Dewclaws on the rear feet also print most of the time, but register as dots just behind the hoofprint. In loose soil or wet sand, where most hoofed animals leave dewclaw marks along with their hoofprints, pigs are again distinctive because their entire foot registers, from hoof tips to dewclaws.

Wild boar seldom walk or run but instead trot from one place to the next. They leave a very narrow trail—almost a single line—with a straddle of 2 inches or less and (for adults) a stride of 18 inches. Rear hooves print in and slightly behind front prints, and the hoofprint itself, minus dewclaws, generally measures 2 to 2½ inches in length.

Trotting track pattern of wild boar. Note straightness of pattern, with hind prints registering in the slightly larger front tracks.

Feral pig tracks are usually distinguishable from those of wild boar, but remember that the two interbreed readily and offspring may exhibit the physical characteristics of either or both. In general, feral hog tracks are rounder and less sharply defined than those of wild boar, but the inside surface, where the two hoof halves meet, is straighter, resulting in prints that are less splayed. The straddle is a bit wider for the stockier feral hog, averaging about 4 inches, and all tracks tend to print individually, the front feet registering 1 to 2 inches ahead of the rear prints. The dewclaws may register on soft ground, but not as prominently as those of the wild boar. Note also that feral hogs take shorter steps than do wild boar, with a stride that measures between 10 and 11 inches.

SCAT

As you might expect of an animal with so many food options, swine scat can vary considerably, depending on what its creator has been eating. Most common is a cashew-shaped pellet, deposited individually when the animal has been dining on fibrous plants such as grasses and sedges, but often deposited in a mass of compressed pellets when it has been eating fruits and other succulent foods.

Wild boar scat. Pellet or sausage-shaped droppings about 2 to 3 inches long, sometimes massed. Considerable variation in scat size reflects a large diversity in adult weights.

Another scat form is nearly round; this occurs mostly when the animal's diet has been especially coarse and dry. These spherical or semi-pellet-shaped droppings generally exhibit a kind of sprue, where the pig's sphincter muscle clipped them free of the anus.

There are two things to remember when you're trying to determine whether or not a scat deposit was left by swine: The first is that elk and moose, whose droppings can be quite similar to the wild pig's, don't exist within the wild boar's range. The second is that swine are true omnivores and will eat meat perhaps even more readily than plants, providing they can get it. Bits of undigested hair and bone in what might otherwise resemble deer scat is a sure sign of wild pigs.

SIGN

The sign most commonly left by wild boar and feral hogs is disturbed soil and overturned sod resulting from their "rooting" for tender grass and plant roots. All pigs, domestic and wild, have tough, cartilaginous snouts designed for plowing under sod and plant roots to tear them free. Wild boar have the added advantage of tusks, which they use as hooks. Excavations may be 6 inches deep, with loose soil scattered all around, and range in size from several square inches to several square yards, depending on the number of animals involved and the prevalence of edible roots.

Mud wallows are a common sign, more so with pigs than with any other animal, which doubtless explains pigs' preference for swampy terrain. Wallows may be several inches deep and are likely to be more expansive than those of other hoofed animals, reflecting the proverbial joy a pig apparently feels rolling in mud. Close examination will reveal dislodged hairs at the bottom, which will be straight and coarser than those left by other wallowing animals.

Wild swine also seem to get genuine pleasure from scratching themselves against trees, particularly rough-barked varieties such as oak, maple, and some evergreens. Rubbings may be more than 3 feet high and will always exhibit rough hairs caught in the bark, sometimes with mud clinging to them. Feral swine lack tusks (although some with mixed blood have them), but wild boar frequently mark scratching trees by gouging the bark with their tusks.

Another clue to the type of pig you're trailing is the tendency of true wild boar to ford streams by crossing on downed logs or gravel bars, where the water is shallow. All swine are good swimmers, but wild boar avoid deep water, while feral hogs typically plow right across to the opposite bank.

VOCALIZATIONS

The calls of wild swine are not much different from the grunts, snorts, and squeals of domestic pigs. Boar grunts are deeper toned than sow grunts, and grunting seems to be the most common form of communication for both sexes. High-pitched squeals indicate fear or anger; the pitch of such squeals is highest in piglets, lower in sows, and lowest of all in mature boar. To a tracker, such squeals are always cause for caution.

NEW WORLD PIGS (TAYASSUIDAE)

8

COLLARED PECCARY OR JAVELINA (DICOTYLES TAJACU)

The collared peccary or javelina belongs to the family Tayassuidae and is North America's only native pig. The other member of this family, the white-lipped peccary (*Tayassu pecari*) ranges from southern Mexico to Paraguay. Javelina differ from wild boar and hogs in several ways, but most notably in size. Wild boar may weigh in excess of 400 pounds, while adult peccaries range from 30 to 65 pounds, with females typically being smaller than males. Unlike swine, deer, and other hoofed animals belonging to the order Artiodactyla—a group in which members have an even number of toes (including dewclaws)—the peccary has only a single dewclaw behind its cloven rear hooves (two dewclaws on the forefeet), placing it in the order Perissodactyla.

Len Rue, Jr.

Collard Peccary

The collared peccary gets its name from a narrow, irregular band of white to yellowish fur that runs from beneath each side of its lower jaw and across its shoulders, contrasting with the grizzled gray-black fur covering the rest of its body. Peccaries have only a vestigial tail, as opposed to the coiled pig tail of feral hogs and the long, straight tail of wild boar. Another difference is the upper canines, or tusks: Feral hogs lack them altogether, wild boar have tusks that curl around to point upward from either side of the mouth, and peccaries have straight tusks that grow downward like elongated fangs. These straight, spearlike tusks are responsible for the animal's common name, "javelina," which is derived from the Spanish word *jabalina* or "spear."

Peccaries have the same tough snout, large head, powerful body, and aggressive, even vicious, nature common among all pigs, but some scientists believe the species is in transition toward becoming a cud-chewing ruminant such as the deer, goat, and cow. Whereas swine have one stomach, peccaries have two. Peccaries also have fewer teeth than swine, and they alone have a skunky-smelling musk gland in the middle of their back, just forward of the hindquarters.

HABITAT AND RANGE

While it can be said that peccaries are fairly common within their range, it's also true that in the United States peccaries are found only in Arizona, in Texas, and in the extreme southern corners of New Mexico. South of the border, javelina range well into the Mexican states of Sonora, Chihuahua (a small portion), Coahuila, and Tamaulipas. Like wild swine, they're unsuited to cold weather, but tough little javelina are right at home in the badlands of scrub brush, cactus, searing midday temperatures, and sparse water. The animal once ranged as far north as Arkansas,

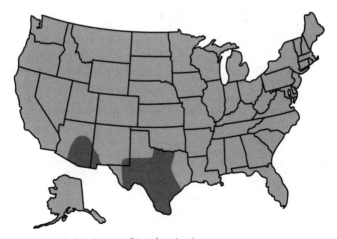

*Distribution of collared peccary (*Dicotyles tajacu*).*

where it was known as the "razorback" because of the thick line of erectible fur along its spine, but early settlers hunted it to extinction over much of its original range, eating its flesh (which is very tasty) and using its tough hide for leather goods.

FOODS

The peccary is best known as the little wild pig that eats cacti, a diet some say is largely responsible for its ornery disposition. In fact, peccaries are particularly fond of prickly pear cactus, eating not only the fruits but also the leaves, spines and all. Their tough mouths and digestive systems are apparently equal to the task of digesting cacti, and the flesh provides an important source of water as well as nutrition.

But peccaries have a lot more dietary options than just cacti. They may wander to elevations as high as 6,000 feet in search of scrub oak acorns, they eat mesquite and lechuguilla, and they root for burdock and other edible roots. More gregarious than swine, peccaries normally travel in groups of up to 30 animals, and signs of their rooting are obvious.

Peccaries are also fond of meat when they can get it. With a top speed of 25 mph (slightly faster than most humans), no claws, and the stealth of a bulldozer, the little pigs are poor hunters, so most of the meat they get is carrion. Mice, lizards, and other slow-moving animals are eaten as opportunities present themselves, and all snakes are fair game. Like other pigs, peccaries are largely immune to rattlesnake venom and waste no time stomping the life out of such delicacies with their sharp hooves.

MATING HABITS

Peccaries have no fixed breeding season, and mating may occur at any time of year. Biologists theorize that this individual rather than collective mating behavior occurs largely because food is abundant year-round in the peccary's preferred range, and gestation doesn't have to revolve around the onset and passing of cold weather.

Unlike swine, peccaries have a scent gland on their backs, just ahead of the hindquarters, that exudes a skunklike odor under normal conditions and becomes much stronger when the animal is alarmed or agitated. It's believed that this scent gland acts as a bonding mechanism that allows individuals within a group to recognize one another, thus helping keep the herd together. The scent gland probably also plays a role in sexual communication, much as do a deer's tarsal glands, but a lot remains to be discovered about javelina mating rituals.

The gestation period for a pregnant javelina sow is four months, and piglets may be born in any month of the year. Twins are the norm, because, although peccary sows have four nipples, only the rear two produce milk. But litter sizes may reach as high as six when food is abundant, with piglets suckling in pairs. Piglets are born with a yellow or reddish coat that turns darker as they mature. They gain strength quickly and are able to travel with their mother within a week, but are probably wholly dependent on her for sustenance for at least a month. Peccaries are noted for the way piglet pairs nurse from behind their standing mother rather from the side, as do most other four-legged mammals. It's likely that the fiercely protective peccary mothers adopt this stance because it allows them to meet a potential threat head on, which seems in keeping with the species' literally pig-headed nature.

The life span of the peccary has been estimated at 15 to 20 years and, although the animal occupies only a small portion of the United States, its population growth merits a hunting season in those states—mainly Arizona and Texas—where it does occur. Mountain lions and jaguars are its main natural enemies, but few predators are willing to risk certain, possibly serious injury by tackling an adult javelina if there's easier prey about.

SEASONAL HABITS

Like most wild animals, peccaries are most active at dawn and dusk, trotting as a group from one feeding or bedding place to the next and stopping to eat any foods they encounter along the way. Being pigs, they like to wallow in mud, and they're good swimmers if an opportunity presents itself. But since peccaries typically inhabit regions where water is scarce, most settle for dustbaths.

Peccaries sensibly bed down during the day, sleeping away the hottest hours in a hole rooted into the earth or a cave if available. Dens are private; only one adult or mother with piglets occupies each, even though herd members are sure to stay in close proximity to one another. In wooded country, dens may be found inside hollow logs, in excavated coyote burrows, or under the roots of standing trees.

TRACKS

Like those of swine and most other hoofed animals, peccary tracks are cloven. But unlike the case of most hoofed animals, especially swine, the twin dewclaws on a peccary's forelegs and the single dewclaw on its hind

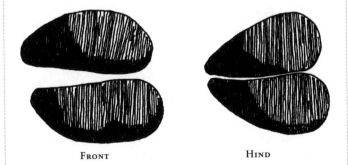

FRONT   HIND

Peccary tracks; 1 to 1½ inches long. Single dewclaw doesn't print. Shaded areas show portions pressed hardest into the earth.

Trotting peccary track pattern, with rear hooves registering in front tracks.

legs rarely print. Its tracks resemble those of a small white-tailed deer but are generally more rounded; the width is about the same as the length. The front tracks are noticeably larger, with an average length of 1½ inches versus about 1¼ inches for the hind tracks.

Peccaries seldom walk anywhere but prefer to trot from place to place. Track patterns are irregular, with the front and hind prints sometimes registering in pairs, sometimes individually, and sometimes the rear hoof registering behind the front, sometimes beside it. For this reason, the average stride is widely variable, ranging from 6 to 10 inches. The straddle is surprisingly wide for a wild pig, measuring 4 to 5 inches on average.

At a full run, the javelina's gait seems almost a faster-moving trot. Running stride, straddle, and track patterns could be confused with those of a trotting pig, except that the running tracks will have been made with noticeably more violence, and with a spray of loose soil and stones in the rear.

SCAT

Because the javelina diet excludes almost nothing even vaguely edible, from cacti to grasses to rodents and insects, its droppings are understandably variable. Most common, when the diet is largely dry, is a roughly pellet-shaped mass of individual droppings that range from round to oblong to crescent in shape, and ½ inch to 3 inches long. Such deposits resemble miniature piles of horse dung, although breaking droppings apart will likely reveal undigested insect parts, hair, and bits of bone.

When peccaries are feeding heavily on succulent foods such as cacti or fresh carrion, their scat deposits will be liquid and nearly round, and again will often contain some clue as to what the animal has been eating. The diameters of liquid scat deposits vary considerably, from about 1 inch to more than 3.

Like all animals, peccaries tend to stay put in areas where food is plentiful. Dens or denning caves in these areas are likely to be used by peccaries to sleep away the daytime heat; these can be identified by the numerous scat deposits around their entrances. Like most animals, the little pigs leave their dens to defecate, but they generally don't make too much work of it. A den with scat deposits of various ages around the entrance is a likely place to wait for javelina, but always approach dens with caution and common sense: A cornered peccary can be ferocious.

Peccary scat; overall length 2 to 3 inches.

SIGN

Aside from the obvious trails made by a traveling band of javelina, the most noticeable sign of the animals' presence is rooted-up soil. Overturned sod, uprooted plants, and undermined shrubs are all indications that peccaries have been feeding. Chewed cacti, especially prickly pear, is a sure sign of the little pigs' presence.

Wallows similar to those of larger swine are also common, and such wallowing areas are likely to be used by an entire herd. If water is available, wallows will likely be located along a muddy bank, where tracks and disturbed earth are evident along with traces of coarse, dark hairs. Wallow dimensions may or may not conform to the body shape of their makers, but the typical depression will be an oblong shape 35–40 inches long and 3 to 4 inches deep.

In more arid regions, wallowing takes the form of dustbathing, and shallow depressions in loose sand and gravel denote where animals have rolled around to scratch themselves. Dislodged hairs will be present and tracks will be in evidence, although a close look may be required to find and identify either.

Peccaries also like to scratch themselves against standing trees and shrubs, leaving scuffed bark to a height of 22 inches. Bits of dislodged bark and hairs can be found around the bases of these scratching posts, and hairs will usually be caught in the bark remaining on the trunk.

VOCALIZATIONS

The peccary's normal call consists of low, piglike grunts, with which it apparently communicates with others of its kind. Piglets emit the same sounds but at a higher pitch. These pigs can also squeal, but such sounds are heard only when an animal is in imminent danger or ready to fight.

NEW WORLD ANTELOPE
(ANTILOCAPRIDAE)
9

PRONGHORN ANTELOPE
(ANTILOCAPRA AMERICANA)

This family has only one member, the pronghorn, or American antelope, but it has an interesting story. The family name, Antilocapridae, translates to "antelope goat" (Captains Lewis and Clark reported it to be a wild goat), but in reality the pronghorn is related to neither of these animals. Scientists have determined that it's the last and apparently best-adapted survivor of a family of hoofed animals that inhabited North America some 20 million years ago. The name "pronghorn" derives from its unique horn structure, which features one short forward-pointing tine branching from each curved main beam, giving the horns a pronglike shape.

The pronghorn is the fastest runner in North America, a trait that appears to have left it without serious natural enemies—except humans. Coyote packs will occasionally maneuver animals into a cul-de-sac, exploiting the pronghorn's inability to jump over obstacles that deer could clear easily, and puma take a few, but predation is usually limited to the weak, injured, or very young. With a top running speed of 70 mph and the strength to maintain that speed for 4 to 5 miles, the pronghorn can easily outrun any animal on the planet. The cheetah is slightly faster, but only for a short distance, and attempts by frustrated "sport" hunters of the 1800s to bring down pronghorns with trained cats were predictably futile. If an animal is somehow cornered, it can fight effectively with its sharp hooves, but its horns seem to be reserved strictly for mating contests.

At an easy cruising speed of 30–45 mph, a pronghorn can cover up to 15 miles without stopping, its mouth open wide to suck in the oxygen needed for such herculean muscle activity. Accordingly, pronghorns are creatures of the open prairie, where good grazing areas might be miles apart. Their slender legs are actually stronger than those of a domestic cow, despite the fact that pronghorn antelope are small, with bucks weighing 90–140 pounds and does averaging 70–105.

The most obvious difference between pronghorn bucks and does is that bucks grow horns while does are normally bare headed. Another difference between the sexes is that bucks have a black stripe running along the top of their muzzles from eyebrows to nose and a dark patch directly

Pronghorn Antelope

under the jaw on each side. Does lack these dark patterns; they have an unadorned brown muzzle and no dark patches under the jaw.

The American antelope is also endowed with keen eyesight, although the commonly held belief that its eyeballs are equal to an 8× binocular appears an exaggeration. We do know that its large, protruding eyeballs provide a nearly 360-degree field of vision, and that it can detect the movement of a walking man up to 4 miles away, especially if he's silhouetted against open sky. With acute vision, an almost unbelievable running speed, and the protection of living in herds, with at least one or two pairs of bulging eyeballs peeled for danger at all times, pronghorns seem nearly predatorproof.

Well, almost. As cattlemen began to fence in the prairies in the 1800s, antelope, which cannot jump over tall obstacles, found their range shrinking behind walls of barbed wire. Even worse, pronghorns are grazing animals, and any animal that competed with cattle in the last century was arbitrarily exterminated. Pronghorn herds that once numbered with those of bison shrank almost as rapidly, and by the mid-1920s there were only an estimated 20,000 left on the planet.

HABITAT AND RANGE

Today, thanks to good management and hunting dollars, pronghorns number about a half million, and herds are found from southern California and Nevada across to western Texas, and from southern Saskatchewan to eastern Mexico. Their thick fur allows them to inhabit fairly cold regions, although they cannot exist in places where deep winter snows make running impossible. Seasonal migration habits vary depending on region, latitude, and availability of food, but pronghorns living in the North, or at high altitudes during the summer months, will migrate to warmer areas when snow falls. Like deer, they can scratch through shallow snow to get at the vegetation beneath, but unlike deer they're virtually crippled by as little as a foot of snow because they have almost no jumping ability. And since running, their main defense against predators, is practically impossible in deep snow, pronghorns take advantage of their speed and mobility by traveling to more favorable country.

No one really knows how far the pronghorn would migrate in a wholly natural environment, because its nomadic wanderings have long been restricted by expressway fences, fenced cattle ranges, and a growing human population that consumes more of its natural habitat each year. Movements within that narrowing range are dictated by the presence of preferred foods such as sagebrush, ground plants, and grasses, and by whether or not a site offers a clear running field. Over most of the animals' range, pronghorn grazing areas overlap those of mule deer and sometimes elk, the result being a sometimes confusing array of similar tracks and droppings. One difference among these species is that prong-

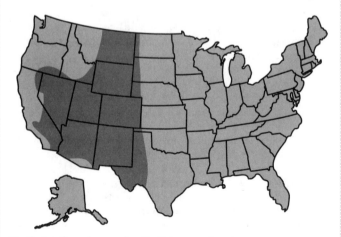

*Distribution of pronghorn antelope (*Antilocapra americana*).*

horns tend to avoid water—although they can swim well—and they seem to dislike walking in mud.

FOODS

One reason the American antelope seldom visits watering places is because, like a camel's, its body can extract the moisture needed to survive from green plants. Succulents such as the omnipresent common plantain (*Plantago major*) are rich in moisture as well as nutrition, while sagebrush, rabbit brush, and a wide variety of grasses and forbs offer plenty of food options. Some cacti are also eaten in the more arid part of their range, as much for water as for nutrition. Probably reindeer moss and other lichens are eaten, too, particularly after these spongelike growths have absorbed water from rain or melting snow.

MATING HABITS

The pronghorn rut begins as early as late July or August in the animal's southern range, and from September to October in the northern. Breeding is initiated by the scent of does coming into heat and will continue for roughly a month. Mature bucks, about four years old, stake out territories and begin gathering harems of up to 20 does, with which they'll travel until rut's end.

Ritual combat between rival males is usually limited to staring contests that are—to me at least—more comical than menacing. If a good staredown doesn't discourage an intruder, bucks may engage in a shoving contest with the horns they've been growing since March or April. The contest ends when the stronger animal forces his opponent's head to the ground. Few injuries result from these contests, and horns never become inextricably tangled the way tined deer antlers can.

When the rut ends, males and females go their separate ways. Dominant bucks are often strictly solitary except when mating, but immature bucks normally run together, in what are known as "bachelor herds," until individual members grow strong enough to leave and try their luck at the mating game. Does also tend to hang together, and at the end of breeding season any females 18 months of age or older are likely to be pregnant.

Like black bear sows, pronghorn does experience a phenomenon known as "delayed implantation," in which the fertilized egg is carried for about 30 days before it attaches itself to the uterine wall. The purpose behind delayed implantation is first to schedule the birth of young to match the onset of warm weather, but second—and more important—to allow time for the egg to be spontaneously aborted if food proves scarce.

After a gestation period of seven months, brown, unspotted fawns are born in May or June. The average weight of a newborn pronghorn is 8 pounds, but birth weights can vary considerably, from less than 3 pounds to more than 12. First-time mothers give birth to single fawns, with twins and occasionally triplets (if food is abundant) being the norm thereafter.

In a matter of hours, fawns are able to stand; after two days they can outrun an Olympic gold medalist, and after a week few predators can touch them in a footrace. Mothers will attempt to defend their young with flailing hooves, but not to the point of risking serious injury to themselves; they prefer instead to sacrifice one fawn and escape with its sibling. A large white patch of fur on the animals' rumps gives fleeing fawns a mark to follow as they chase after their mothers in the dark. Young does may stay with the "mother herd" for several years, but males are banished to bachelor herds at 18 months to guard against inbreeding. The life span is judged to be 7 to 10 years.

SEASONAL HABITS

Pronghorns migrate with the seasons, particularly in their northern range, following the availability of food plants. Today, natural migration habits are hampered or even prohibited by impassable man-made obstacles, but wanderings may encompass more than 100 square miles where terrain and humans permit. Pronghorns are designed for open country, although in a few places, such as the Bull Mountains of central Montana and the Wind River Mountains of Wyoming, there are "timber goats" that frequent forest edges at the bases of mountains. Interestingly, these antelope don't run for deeper cover when alarmed but instead break into the open, where their speed can be used to advantage.

Likewise, antelope never bed down in cover, apparently feeling uneasy about sleeping in places that restrict their keen eyesight and good depth perception. Unlike that of other ungulates (hoofed mammals), pronghorn sleeping is essentially restricted to catnaps, short periods of sleep interspersed with other activities such as feeding, breeding, or just running really fast for the heck of it. As a result, pronghorns may be seen moving about at any time of day or night.

TRACKS

Pronghorn tracks print in the cloven heart-shaped pattern common to most hoofed mammals, although, like those of deer, the animals' hooves tend to be splayed wide when they walk on slippery surfaces, as a guard against sliding. Their tracks are generally narrower and more pointed than those of whitetails or mule deer, and the inside surface of each hoof half is more concave, which prevents the halves from coming flush together.

One reliable identifying feature of pronghorn tracks is that front hooves, which may be 2 to 3 inches in length, are longer and wider than rear hooves. You should also note that, although antelope belong to the order Artiodactyla, hoofed animals with an even number of toes, they lack dewclaws altogether. This makes the legs more streamlined for high-speed running. Cloven tracks in an inch or more of snow that don't show dewclaws were made by pronghorns.

Pronghorns seldom walk anywhere, traveling to and fro at a trot or sometimes a full run. When they do walk, their hind feet don't register in

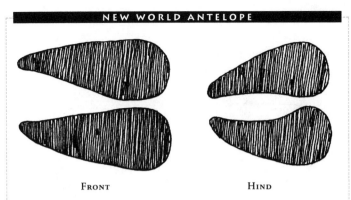

FRONT   HIND

Pronghorn track; 1½ to 3 inches long, front hooves larger than hind, no dewclaws.

the front tracks and all tracks register individually, with the front feet printing slightly behind and to the inside of rear feet in pairs. The straddle is 4 to 5 inches, and the walking stride is about 12 inches.

At a trot or a full run, the stride and straddle remain about the same, but the distance between sets of four prints (two pairs) may increase to up to 20 feet, depending on the animal's pace. The amount of loose soil thrown to the back of each hoofprint is indicative of speed.

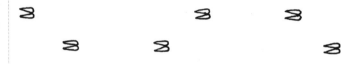

Track pattern of pronghorn running slowly.

SCAT

Because the animals' diets and digestive systems are similar, pronghorn scat is easily confused with that of whitetails and mule deer. Pellets left as the result of feeding on dry (winter) vegetation are usually elongated or acorn shaped, measure less than 1 inch in length, and have a pronounced nipple shape on one end where the sphincter muscle clipped them free. Deer pellets may also exhibit this nipple shape, but not as routinely as those of pronghorns.

When antelope are feeding on succulent vegetation, their scat becomes softer, again paralleling deer, and deposits may be segmented or massed in roughly cylindrical shapes that measure 2–3½ inches in length. Still others may resemble miniature piles of horse dung. Liquid, cowpielike droppings don't occur because of the animals' low fluid intake; remember, most of the water they take in is derived from the plants they eat.

Pronghorn scat. Pellets about 3 inches long, massed deposits up to 3½ inches.

SIGN

The most noticeable sign of pronghorn presence are their beds. These are normally found in groups, although bear in mind that, outside rutting season, large bucks are often solitary. Beds are always in the open, with an unrestricted field of view all around, and appear as pressed-down, roughly oval-shaped areas of grass that measure 4 to 5 feet in length. Mule deer and whitetail beds (actually cud-chewing stations) may also be in the area, because the feeding areas of all three species sometimes overlap, but deer beds seldom number more than three—a doe and two fawns—while beds left by antelope herds may number more than 20.

VOCALIZATIONS

The most commonly heard antelope vocalization is the alarm call, a fairly high-pitched blowing sound similar to the whitetail's but a bit more prolonged. This call most often precedes thundering hooves, but if the animal is unsure about what spooked it, it will sometimes just stare intently and stamp a foot, trying to get whatever it is to reveal itself.

During the rut, bucks can be heard snorting loudly, especially in the presence of a potential rival. Snorting appears to be limited to mating and isn't heard at other times.

Like deer, antelope have a soft bleating call used to communicate with one another at close quarters. This sound can't be heard at any great range, especially not the call between a mother and her fawns. Mothers also use a sharp, doglike bark to warn fawns of danger.

BEARS
(URSIDAE)
10

NATIVE AMERICAN LEGEND HAS it that the beaver taught man to build houses, the blue heron taught him to spear fish, and "God's Dog," the coyote, taught him to hunt. But before Brother Bear could teach man the greatest secret of survival, how to sleep through the winter, a foolish hunter killed one of them, and man was forever condemned to struggle for food as best he could from autumn till spring.

Bears are the largest carnivores in North America, and the brown bear—also known by the names grizzly and Kodiak, depending on where it lives—is the largest land carnivore in the world. The polar bear (*Ursus maritimus*) is the only one of our three native bears to subsist almost exclusively on meat, and it's also the best hunter; these traits result from life in an environment where predation is the only source of food. Black and brown bears are omnivorous creatures of a more benign environment, though, eating practically anything they can find.

Native Americans felt a special kinship with bears because of their humanlike qualities. Most four-legged animals walk on their toes, with knees bet rearward and body weight thrust slightly forward, a habit that literally keeps them on their toes and ready to flee instantly. Bears, raccoons, porcupines, and humans are all flat footed, however, with knees pointing forward and heels printing as deeply as toes. Since this design typically denotes a slow runner with a powerful body, it's probably no coincidence that flat-footed animals are among those with the least to fear from predation.

Traits common to all bears include powerful bodies, relatively weak eyesight and hearing, and an excellent sense of smell. All are superbly adapted to their natural environments, but only the comparatively mild-mannered black bear has shown an ability to coexist with humans. With no natural predators, bears have little need for keen hearing, which is mainly a defensive capability, and the thickets they prefer make keen eyesight less valuable than a sharp sense of smell.

Most folks probably know that bears aren't true hibernators, the Arctic-dwelling polar bear least so of all. Brown and black bears enter into an energy-conserving state of lethargy through the winter months, but body temperature remains only slightly below normal, 96 degrees, and they can be awakened at any time—usually in an ornery mood. Unseasonably warm temperatures may also bring them out of the den at any time during the winter. Denning periods vary by region, but it isn't unusual to see fresh bear tracks in several inches of snow. Black and brown bears have access to sugar-bearing fruits and fat-rich fish that enable them to layer on huge amounts of fat, storing energy to burn as a survival ration when food is scarce.

Cubs are born during the winter denning period, blind and weighing from ½ pound (black bear) to 1 pound (brown bear). Mating takes place in late spring to early summer, but fertilized eggs are carried inside the sow's body for 6 to 7 months before implantation on her uterine wall. If food has been scarce, the eggs are aborted. Cubs, usually twins, nurse for about two and a half months in the den, growing rapidly, and are ready to begin eating solid food when they emerge from the den with their mother. They stay with her for 18 months, learning the mechanics of survival, and spend their first winter denning together. Grown cubs are run off in their second spring, just before the mother mates again. Bears' life span in the wild may be as long as 35 years, although 25 years is average.

Bears offer potentially dangerous situations that every tracker should be familiar with: All mothers will defend their cubs (although I've found myself between a black bear and her cubs on two occasions, and simply backing off slowly worked). All bears will defend a carcass they've claimed, whether they killed it or not, and until the bones are stripped clean the owner won't be far away. And all bears, especially brown bears, can be very dangerous when surprised. Never forget that bears have poor hearing and eyesight; if you approach one from downwind it may not detect your presence until you're face to face. Confronted at close quarters, an adult bear's first instinct is often to charge. *Never* run from a bear (or any other wild predator); this can excite its predatory instincts, causing it to give chase. With a top running speed of 30–35 mph, the bear *will* catch you, and then. . . . Most bear charges are feints, used to size up a potential adversary, and if you stand your ground—as I've had to do on several occasions—there's a good chance the animal will turn away.

BLACK BEAR (*URSUS AMERICANUS*)

This is the most common bear in North America. Despite its name, the black bear's fur may range from black in its eastern range, to brown or cinnamon in its western, and even to white on Alaska's Gribble Island. It can be distinguished from the brown bear by the facts that the brown is much larger, with a more concave muzzle, flatter forehead, and distinctive muscular hump behind the shoulders. Unlike the brown bear, the black has demonstrated a remarkable ability to coexist with humans, and while few people ever see one of these reclusive animals in the wild, the species is far from endangered. Sows weigh 200–300 pounds and boars 350–600, depending on age, availability of food, and time of year.

Len Rue, Jr.

Black Bear

HABITAT AND RANGE

Although humans have taken over much of its original habitat, the black bear's current range covers most of Alaska, most of Canada (except Saskatchewan) northern California to Washington, Montana down to New Mexico, and the northern parts of Minnesota, Wisconsin, and Michigan. It exists along the eastern coastline from Alabama up to Maine, throughout the Appalachians, and in a few other pockets scattered around the country.

The black bear's preferred habitat is always around dense cover—cedar swamps, thickets, brush, and clear-cuts populated with saplings—places where animals can sleep in peace or lie in wait for any prey that might come along. It will range into low mountains to eat berries and acorns, but seldom climbs above 7,000 feet.

Like all bears, black bears are solitary except when mating, with males and especially females with cubs avoiding contact with one another throughout a territory, the size of which is determined by the availability of food. Several may share the same territory if food is plentiful, but the dominant male will defend his territory fiercely against any that challenge his authority. Females with cubs go far out of the way to avoid males, because a mature boar will sometimes kill cubs to bring the mother into estrus.

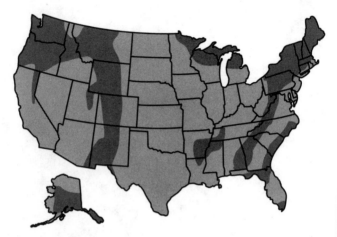

*Distribution of black bear (*Ursus americanus*).*

FOODS

One reason black bears are such good survivors is their ability to eat just about anything of nutritional value. Rotting logs and stumps are turned over and frequently torn apart to get at fat-rich grubs, worms, and spiders. A bear will also knock the top off an anthill, insert a paw until the angry insects cover the impenetrable, dense fur, then lick the sugar-filled ants off with its raspy tongue.

And of course black bears also eat honey, although it's a relatively new food for them, because our "native" honeybees are actually immigrants from Europe. Black bears need no protective clothing or smokes for hive raiding. Their thick fur is beeproof (although their noses aren't), and it didn't take long for calorie-craving bruins to figure out that honey was worth the odd sting.

Vegetation makes up a large part of the black bear's diet, sometimes most of it. Grasses, sedges, tender young plants, and roots of many kinds are eaten, and flowers are nipped off for the sugars they contain. Bears emerging from their dens when little plant life is available frequently will rip through the outer layer of bark on aspen, poplar, and some pine trees to get at the sweet and tender cambium layer beneath. Rose hips, apples, and acorns and other nuts are also favorites.

No food source is overlooked. An average black bear needs roughly 50 pounds of fat to get it through the winter denning period, so feeding is constant throughout summer and fall. Berries, fruits, and fish are followed as they become available, sometimes over great distances. Squirrels provide an important source of food by gathering caches of pine and other nuts, which the bears locate with their keen noses then casually eat.

MATING HABITS

Black bears mate in June and early July, and this is the only time they'll tolerate each other's presence without fighting. Females are ready to mate at 3 to 4 years of age, males at 4 to 5 years. Boars are drawn to the scent of a breeding female a week or so before she actually comes into heat, which gives the pair time to get used to each other. When the sow is ready, she allows the male to mount her; couplings, which are frequent for a week or more, may last an hour at a time. Once a female is pregnant, she loses interest and chases the boar off, whereupon he may seek out another mate. Sows normally mate every other year of their lives (sooner if cubs are killed), and a typical female produces 20–30 cubs in her lifetime.

But although the sow's eggs are fertilized, they're carried unchanged inside her fallopian tubes for five months before implanting themselves on the uterine wall. If a female is sickly or unable to put on the fat needed for denning, the pregnancy is spontaneously aborted. Embryonic growth takes only two months, with two to five blind, hairless, 8-ounce cubs born in January. First-time mothers generally have just one cub, with twins being the norm thereafter. Mother may sleep through delivery, but the relatively helpless newborns instinctively make their way to a milk-rich nipple to suckle. They grow rapidly until emerging with their mother in May. Cubs begin eating solid foods about two weeks after emerging, but continue to suckle until the following autumn.

By ten months, cubs may weigh in excess of 50 pounds, but they can be easy prey without their mother, who will protect them fiercely, even to her death. Humans, brown bears, and male black bears are the most dangerous enemies, but rather than fight, a mother's first reaction is to send her cubs up the nearest tree, then follow them. Cubs are extraordinary climbers by just five months. Their sharply curved claws—in contrast with the straighter claws of a brown bear—are well designed for climbing, and a cub's lighter weight allows it to climb out of reach of most predators. I've sometimes wondered how often many hikers, myself included, have walked right by a treed mother and cubs without seeing them.

Black bear mothers are among the best in the animal world, lavishing constant attention on their young and even holding them on the lap in a humanlike sitting position. But even with all this care, cub mortality is about 33 percent for the first five years of life. Cubs den with the mother their first two winters, but are chased off to prevent inbreeding the following spring, just before the sow is ready to breed again. The first year of life for a banished cub is the most perilous, but the dangers steadily decrease as it gains size, strength, and experience. At five years of age, a typical cub weighs 200 pounds, and can easily kill—if not catch—a deer of equal weight.

SEASONAL HABITS

The black bear's most notable seasonal habit is denning, sometimes still incorrectly called hibernation. Dens may be in hollow logs, stumps, or sometimes small caves, but the most common is a large excavation under the roots of a standing tree or into the side of a dirt hill, always in a secluded place where the animal can sleep without interruption. Space inside is kept to a minimum to conserve body heat. Sites are prepared a month in advance of the late November–December denning time, and owners stay close to them during this month. Feeding is constant the last several months prior to denning, with animals taking in upward of 20,000 calories a day. They need 50–60 pounds of fat to sustain them through the winter, and stop eating abruptly after reaching almost exactly the required weight, even though they might not den up for another two weeks. The animal's last meal consists of grasses, pine needles, and other fibrous plant materials that form an anal plug in the lower colon.

When the time is right, a black bear enters its den and falls into a deep but not unbreakable slumber. Body temperature remains a near-normal 96 degrees, but the heart rate slows to 10 beats per minute. Unless awakened by unseasonably warm temperatures that fool it into thinking spring has arrived, the bear will sleep almost without moving for the next five months. It will not urinate, defecate, eat, or drink during that time, which explains why Native Americans thought sleeping through the winter an enviable ability.

The metabolism of a denned bear is nothing short of astounding. Water and calories are provided by the 4-inch layer of fat, protein is extracted from the muscles, and the serious problem of osteoporosis that occurs in every other animal when it lies dormant for even a week is prevented by the efficient recycling of absorbed calcium. Even more remarkable is the way a denning bear's liver and kidneys transform nitrogen urea, a very toxic component of urine, into amino acids (proteins) that help sustain the body. And medical researchers have long been fascinated by the bear's complete lack of arterial blockage from fats and cholesterol.

When bears emerge from the den in May, they're groggy, a condition that seems to grow more pronounced and prolonged as a bear ages. Anal plugs formed by the animals' last meals of fibrous vegetation are usually discarded near the den entrance, but the bears won't begin eating until their bodies adjust to being active again, living off stored fat for the first two to three weeks after awakening. Once they do begin eating, however, bears feed almost nonstop until September, sometimes even forgoing sleep in their drive to put on weight. They roam constantly throughout the summer and their ranges may vary from 10 square miles in prime bear country to more than 50 in less bountiful areas. The heat of the day is spent in a hidden, shaded thicket, but animals may move about at any time to wallow in mud, which loosens the old winter coat and dislodges biting parasites, and they sometimes swim to cool off in hot weather.

TRACKS

Black bear tracks are remarkably humanlike. All feet have five digits, and the hind foot bears a striking resemblance to our own. But a bear's toes form a rough semicircle in front of the foot, with the middle toe being the longest and the outermost toes on either side the shortest. Another difference is the location of the big toe, which is outermost on a bear (our own is innermost). This gives them a shuffling gait, with the rear foot coming down on the outside of the heel and rolling toward the big toe, sometimes causing the inside little toe to print lightly or not at all. When they want, bears can walk with a stealth that makes deer sound like they're wearing bongos; I've had black bears pass as close as 6 feet before the sound of their movement alerted me.

Front feet feature a rough resemblance to our own hands, with toes again arranged in a semicircle, like human fingers, that ends abruptly at the base of the "palm." A single dewclaw on the back of the foreleg may print, in snow or mud, as a single dot. All toes have sharply curved claws that are much shorter than the straighter 4-inch claws of an adult brown bear, with the claws of the hind feet printing about 1 inch ahead of the toes; 2 inches ahead for front feet. The hind feet of an adult black bear average about 7 to 9 inches long by 3 to 5 inches wide; the front feet are 4 to 5 inches long by nearly the same width.

The stride of a walking black bear is about 1 foot, with front tracks registering behind rear tracks in pairs on either side, and usually with all feet printing individually; at a fast walk, however, the front feet may print inside the rear tracks. The toes of all four feet, but especially the hind feet, point noticeably inward, a track pattern common to all four-legged, flat-footed animals. The straddle is 8 to 10 inches—much wider than most animals, and the width of a bear trail reflects this.

At a fast lope, both front feet print in staggered pairs behind both hind feet, also in staggered pairs. This is the "rocking horse" running gait common to deer and most four-legged animals, in which the front feet are planted as a fulcrum while the hind feet are brought down ahead of them. At a full run—about 30 mph—the space between the sets of all four tracks may exceed 3 feet.

HIND   FRONT

Tracks of black bear. Front, 4 to 6 inches long; hind, 6 to 9 inches long.

WALK

RUN

Black bear track patterns.

Bear trails are about 1 foot wide, and some ancient paths have been used for centuries by generations of black bears. Well-used paths are packed down or even rutted to a depth of several inches. On the aptly named Bear Mountain, in Michigan's Huron Mountains, I found a time-less trail that had been worn several inches into a low ridge of solid granite. In grassland or forest, regular trails look as if they were made by barefooted humans, except for the telltale claw marks, and are similar to the trails of forest-dwelling cougars.

SCAT

There's a tendency to describe black bear scat as "doglike," but I'll go out on a limb here and say that I think it looks humanlike. When plants, insects, and carrion make up most of a bear's diet, its scat is cylindrical and typically deposited in a coiled form, sometimes in individual seg-ments. Bits of hair, fur, bone, insect parts, and plant fibers distinguish it from human feces, as does the large size of the deposit. Color ranges from dark brown to black.

When fruits and berries are in season, scat deposits assume an almost liquid form, reflecting the richness of these foods. Such deposits are almost black and contain undigested seeds—nature's way of ensuring that a plant species' seeds are not only spread about, but fertilized as well.

Unlike deer and like many predators, black bears generally make an effort to distance themselves from their odorous feces, because the scent frightens off potential prey. Scat is rarely or never left on a regularly used trail, but always several yards to one side of it and usually under cover. Even on remote logging roads the animals tend to go into the woods on either side to defecate. However, bears do use scat deposits to mark their territories, particularly adult boars. Deer carcasses picked clean by bears can often be identified by the large scat deposit left on top, apparently as a territorial mark and a brag. Of course, this is done only after the animal

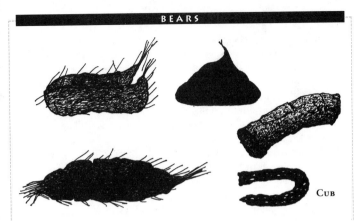

CUB

Bear scat, typical of both brown and black bears. Size varies greatly.

has finished with the carcass, which may take several days. Never approach a partially eaten carcass: Its owner is never far away, and dominant males in particular may rush to defend their caches.

SIGN

Black bears leave plenty of sign if you know what to look for. Most prominent are the territorial claw marks left mainly by adult boars. Trees selected for marking are generally smooth-barked varieties in which claw marks will contrast most visibly—aspen, birch, white pine, and beech—but sometimes dead standing trees are heavily clawed, probably as much to find insects as to mark a domain. It sometimes appears that the animals just plain like to claw into soft wood, perhaps for the same reasons cats do. Claw marks on standing trees are usually diagonal, sometimes vertical, infrequently horizontal, and typically extend as far up the trunk as the animal can reach (6 to 7 feet). Man-made structures may also bear claw marks, among them utility poles, footbridges, and even outbuildings in places where food is plentiful.

Rough-barked trees, such as maple, oak, and large poplar, serve as scratching posts. Scratching is a favorite summer pastime among black and brown bears, relieving the torment of parasites and loosening the thick, matted coat from the previous winter. Good scratching trees may be used repeatedly for several years, and are easily identified by the large amounts of long black or brown fur caught in their abraded bark.

Fruiting trees such as apple, chokecherry, and the richly sweet serviceberry may also exhibit obvious marks from feeding bears. Sometimes bears even rip whole limbs free to reach fruit. Smaller fruiting trees and shrubs such as the pawpaw may be ripped out by their roots. In contrast, berry bushes such as raspberry and blueberry are relatively undisturbed, their fruits plucked neatly from the branches by a bear's lips.

Mud wallows are a bear sign most common in summer, when the itching of biting bugs and last winter's coat become almost unbearable (no pun intended). If an ample supply of food is nearby, black bears often spend most of a summer on streambanks, where they can swim to cool off and roll in mud. Wallows are bathtub-size depressions that contain long hairs at their bottoms, sometimes matted in clumps. They're smaller than moose wallows, they contain darker hair than elk wallows, and the hairs are less coarse than those found in a wild hog wallow. And of course there'll always be tracks in or around a wallow that identify its owner.

Downed logs torn to pieces with bits of rotted wood scattered about are another telltale bear sign. Black bears will work very hard to tear apart even huge logs to get at the insects, grubs, and spiders living inside. Their handiwork can be identified by large claw marks and destruction indicative of brute strength. And since nature is always logical, the black bear's destruction of rotting logs speeds their decay, enriching the soil more quickly and promoting new growth.

VOCALIZATIONS

The solitary black bear has little need for the sometimes complex language of more social animals. A mother will communicate with her cubs using gentle grunts and moans, but if danger threatens, a sharp bark from her will send them up the nearest tree.

When working hard to tear apart a log, scratching against a tree, or wallowing in mud, black bears make considerable noise, grunting with each exertion. Their breathing is loud, especially when they're agitated, making sharp huffing sounds that are uniquely bear. If you hear such a sound nearby, move off at least 100 yards before you stop to observe; the animal might be guarding a kill or cubs. Another bear call that I've had a rather perilous opportunity to hear is a rumbling, doglike growl that means "go away or I may hurt you." This growl was issued at close range and was accompanied by a raised line of fur down the bear's spine, laid-back ears, and a show of teeth.

BROWN BEAR
(URSUS ARCTOS HORRIBILIS)

As its scientific name implies, the "horrible northern bear" (nowadays the *horribilis* is sometimes dropped) was regarded as an enemy by settlers to the New World. Armed with underpowered single-shot muzzleloading rifles, frontiersmen were poorly matched against the huge teeth and claws of this aggressive bear, which can weigh more than 1,500 pounds. In truth, brown bears generally avoid humans, but the presence of easily caught domestic animals has often caused them to invade ranches and farms. Dead livestock was a serious matter to early settlers, who lived off what they produced, but when ranchers and farmers were attacked by bears defending these domestic kills, war was declared, and the brown bear was persecuted mercilessly. As the largest land carnivore on the

Len Clifford/Leonard Rue Enterprises

Brown Bear

planet, with no natural enemies, its instinct is to attack when threatened, and incidents of bear hunters being killed by their intended prey only enhanced its reputation for bloodthirstiness. Although more carnivorous than black bears, much of its reputation as a killer was undeserved because, as naturalist John Muir put it, "To him almost everything is food except granite."

At one time it was believed that the Alaskan Kodiak (*Ursus arctos middendorffi*) was a separate species, because bears, like deer, are typically larger the farther north one travels. Some confusion probably resulted from the brown bear's variation in fur color, which ranges from yellow-brown, to brown with silvery (grizzled) guard hairs, to black. Biologists have now decided that grizzlies, Kodiaks, and brown bears all belong to a single species.

Although black bears may also have brown fur, the two are easily distinguishable. Apart from the brown bear's huge size, its muzzle is uniformly dark colored—in contrast with the brown patches normally present on either side of a black bear's muzzle—and black bears lack the muscular shoulder hump characteristic of brown bears. Also, the black bear's muzzle is shorter and more rounded, while a brown bear's muzzle is comparatively concave.

Another difference is that black bear claws are shorter and curve sharply downward, while those of brown bears are long, nearly straight, and better designed for killing. As a result, adult brown bears are poor tree climbers, although one attack in 1968 proved they can climb large trees by using branches as ladder rungs.

*Distribution of brown bear (*Ursus arctos horribilis*).*

HABITAT AND RANGE

Today the brown bear is cornered into portions of Montana, Wyoming, and Idaho in the lower 48 states, where its population numbers fewer than 1,000 animals. Its northern range covers most of western Canada from Alberta north, all of Alaska (with an estimated population of 50,000 animals), and a large portion of the central Northwest Territories. It's also found in northern Russia, from whence our own are believed to have come, across a land bridge some 50,000 years ago. The brown bear's "normal" habitat is semi-open mountainous country, but at one time it inhabited all of Asia, northern Africa, and much of Europe. When the conquistadors arrived in the New World, the big bear's range covered nearly all of North America.

As with the black bear, a brown bear's personal range is largely determined by the availability of food, and some are said to travel up to 1,000 miles between dennings. In most cases, the range is more in the area of 100 square miles, perhaps with an occasional long trip to fish for spawning salmon. If food is plentiful, the normally solitary animals congregate more or less peacefully, but at other times they can be downright hostile toward one another. Concealed thickets are used to sleep away the heat of the day, and you should exercise real caution to let sleeping bears lie.

FOODS

It's been said that only 20 percent of brown bears' diets consist of meat. That may be true on any given day, but it's tough to assign arbitrary rules to animals that have such a broad range of food options. Their digestive systems can assimilate plant proteins nearly as efficiently as a herbivore's, so grasses, sedges, and many plants and roots are staples of brown bears' diets. Flower tops are eaten for the sugars they contain, and most types of berries and fruits are eaten for the same reason—even foul-tasting soap-berries. In spring, before there's enough new growth to sustain them, bears also gnaw through the outer bark of softwoods, particularly pines, to get at their sugary sap and tender inner bark. Acorns, fungi, lichens, and almost any vegetation with a hint of nutritional value are also eaten.

Brown bears will go to a lot of trouble to get ants, grubs, and insects. Their powerful claws can make short work of a half-ton log and also work well for levering up rocks that hide bugs, worms, snakes, rodents, and lizards, all of which are eaten with relish. The long, nearly straight claws can also excavate a rodent burrow with surprising speed, and a ground squirrel foolish enough to be visible running into its burrow will likely end up as a snack.

Powerful as they are, brown bears are relatively poor hunters. They frequent secluded moose trails in spring, hoping to surprise a newborn calf, but adult moose are too large to prey upon—the objective is to eat, not fight. In the North, the same applies to caribou herds; a hungry bear will sometimes bluff-charge a herd to see if one is weak or injured, but its top running speed of 35 mph is no match for the caribou's own 50-mph sprint. In fact, an adult caribou bull with large antlers can weigh up to 600 pounds—a dangerous adversary the bear would rather not face. A common brown bear tactic is to let wolves do all the work of bringing down weakened caribou and then blithely steal their kill.

Salmon are a vital part of brown bears' diets, and their autumn spawning runs give the bears rich food that helps them put on the weight necessary for denning. Although not as adept at fishing as the black bear, browns are nonetheless capable of taking their fill of spawning salmon, and good fishing spots frequently draw the normally unsociable animals close together. The most aggressive and dominant individuals usually get the best fishing spots, but bloody fights do sometimes erupt when two bears lay claim to the same site. Salmon brains and roe are especially rich in fat, and spawning runs are perhaps the only times when a brown bear can get all it wants to eat. By denning time, a healthy adult brown bear will have put on up to 400 new pounds of fat, or about 25 percent of its body weight.

MATING HABITS

The brown bear mating season is short, running from late June through early July, which seems in keeping with the animals' naturally antisocial behavior. Sows initiate breeding through a sexual scent released perhaps two weeks before they actually come into estrus. This delay seems designed to allow an amorous boar and sow time to become accustomed to one another before becoming intimate, and it may also serve as a culling process to ensure that the strongest males have time to detect the sow and to run off weaker rivals before she mates. Mating lasts for about a week and is constant, with enamored males eating and sleeping little until the sow, who somehow knows when she's pregnant, spurns the boar, who in true romantic style then sets out to find another mate before the rut ends. Females carry the fertilized eggs in their fallopian tubes for roughly five months before these implant themselves on the uterine wall and being developing. Sows that are sickly or underweight at denning time spontaneously abort the embryos.

Cubs are born in the den from January through March. Sows with cubs from the previous year will not become pregnant again until their cubs are two to three years old, although young boars may leave their mothers at two years. Newborn cubs weigh 1 pound at birth—twice the weight of black bear newborns—and litter size ranges from two to four cubs, with twins being the norm. The tiny cubs grow rapidly in the den, nourished by their mother's fat-rich milk. When they emerge from the den in May, cubs weigh about 10 pounds and are ready to begin eating solid foods, although they won't be weaned until they reach 16 months. Brown bear mothers are extremely protective, occasionally defending cubs to the death. Wolves will prey on a cub if they get an opportunity, while males of their own kind sometimes kill and even eat brown bear cubs to bring the female into estrus again. Cubs can climb trees to escape predators but lose this ability at about 12 months. Cub mortality may run as high as 50 percent in the first year.

Female cubs may remain in their mother's home territory until adulthood, but young boars must leave if they hope to find mates. Females have their first litters at five to seven years. Males breed at about the same age, competition from larger boars permitting. The average life span is 25 years, with some individuals living well into their 30s.

SEASONAL HABITS

The brown bear's most notable seasonal habit is denning through the winter. Denning is generally prompted by the disappearance of food plants, usually in November or December, and lasts until the following April or May. Dens are located in the shelter of a small cave or rock crevice, or sometimes excavated into the side of a hill. Den size, of course, varies with the size of an individual, but dens are always kept as small as possible to help conserve body heat and the calories burned to produce it. Dens are lined with moss and grasses to make a comfortable bed, and good dens that are used year after year will be lined with several generations of vegetation.

When denning browns emerge in spring they remain groggy for the first two weeks or so, a condition that takes longer to shake off the older a bear gets. During this adjustment period they won't eat, instead living off leftover stored fat until their sluggish bodies awaken completely. By June their appetites will be nearly insatiable—just in time for them to prowl the thickets for newborn deer and moose.

Since a bear's entire life revolves around eating, its habits, range, and choice of habitat are always dictated by the availability of food. Feeding is constant throughout the summer, and animals travel sometimes ancient paths to follow food sources as they become available. Wandering bears go out of their way to avoid one another, with weaker individuals giving way to larger, stronger bears, and a female with cubs going well out of her way to avoid adult males.

TRACKS

Brown bear tracks are easy to follow, even when they aren't on an established trail. Tracks may not be of plaster-cast quality, but an animal this heavy is bound to leave prints on almost any medium it walks over. Brown bear tracks have the same configuration as black bear tracks—five toes on each foot, pawlike front feet, and hind feet that look remarkably humanlike, except for claws and a big toe positioned opposite our own. One difference is size: Grizzlies in the lower 48 leave hind prints 10–12 inches long by 7 to 8 inches wide, and Alaskan Kodiaks have hind feet that sometimes exceed 16 inches in length and more than 10 inches in width. Another especially notable difference is the claws: Brown bear claws are much longer and straighter than black bear, with those on the forefeet extending as far as 4 inches ahead of the toes. The hind claws are roughly half as long and may not register on hard-packed surfaces. The heel pads ("palms") of the front feet may print lightly or not at all, and the same goes for the inner "little" toes of the hind feet.

HIND   FRONT

Tracks of brown bear; front paw, 4 to 8 inches long; hind paw, 6½ to 12 inches long. Adult weights can vary by as much as a quarter-ton, with sows usually much smaller than boars. Bears in the far north typically are much larger than their southern cousins.

The walking track pattern of a brown bear is again nearly identical to that of the black bear, with the front and hind prints registering in pairs on each side, the front foot behind the rear. At a normal walk, all prints register individually, the front feet about 4 inches behind the rear, and a stride length—the distance between track pairs—of 2 feet or more. A bear in a hurry will take longer strides, increasing the distance between track pairs as well as the distance between the front and hind prints in each pair. Conversely, a slow and deliberate stroll normally results in an abbreviated stride length and track pairs that register directly on top of one another.

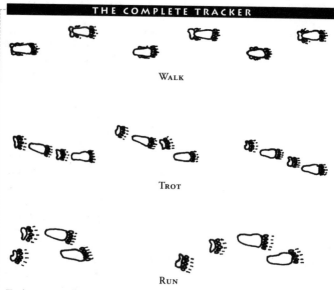

Walk

Trot

Run

Track patterns of brown bear.

At a fast lope, the stride increases to 8 to 9 feet and the track pattern shifts to the familiar "rocking horse" gait, with the front feet printing in pairs behind the hind, which are also paired. Unlike most other animals that use this running gait, though, bears bring both hind feet down close together, one slightly behind the other, instead of spreading the rear feet wide apart, as deer and rabbits do. Maybe this unique track pattern has something to do with the brown bear's comparatively slow 35-mph running speed.

SCAT

Brown bear scat is similar to the black bear's, but deposits are up to twice as large, and the browns' more carnivorous diet is usually evidenced by large amounts of hair and fur, often containing bits of rodent bone. When bear diets consist mainly of insects, plants, and occasionally red meat, scat is generally firm, more than 2 inches in diameter, and deposited in a coil shape that may itself measure 8 to 10 inches across. Large amounts of animal hair causes scat to be more segmented and broken up, while scat resulting from a diet of mostly plants and roots is typically smooth and more uniformly cylindrical, and often contains insect parts.

In late summer and early autumn, when calorie-craving bears are drawn by the sweetness of ripened berries and fruits, scat deposits are typically soft, massed, or even liquid. This condition, also seen in the scat of other species, is actually a mild case of diarrhea caused by the sudden transition to abnormally rich foods. We all know what that's like.

SIGN

Brown bear sign are very similar to the black bear's, but correspondingly larger. Adult males are especially territorial, staking claims to areas that provide a good supply of food as they come to them. "Bear trees" are common territorial landmarks, with deep, ragged claw marks, most of them diagonal, gouged through the outer bark to a height of 12 feet or more (versus 6 to 7 feet for black bears). Claw marks are typically accompanied by toothmarks, where the animal bit into the trunk, at a height of 6 to 7 feet. Both types of marks are left as high up on the trunk as their maker can reach to advertise physical size and strength.

Clawed and bitten trees may also serve as comfortable scratching posts, and favored trunks will show definite signs of hard rubbing. Scratching dislodges parasites and removes last winter's matted coat, and bears often claw into pines to start their sticky sap running, then rub against the adhesive bark as if it were a giant lint remover, sometimes leaving large amount of hair glued to the bark.

Soft inner (cambium) bark from some trees is also eaten, particularly in late spring before the growing season is fully under way. Spring sap is high in sugar and, as syrup makers know, abundant. Pine sap is especially sweet at all times of the year, but this sweetness is combined with a strong taste of turpentine that the bears seem accustomed to. Food trees show evidence of tooth- and claw marks, and are easily distinguished from the one-way, bottom-teeth-only gnawings of moose and elk.

Since insects make up a large part of the brown bear's diet, rotting logs are frequently torn apart using strong front claws to get at the nutritious bugs, grubs, and worms living inside. Standing stumps and dead trunks are routinely pushed over, although not always torn apart. Claw marks will be evident in either case.

Fruiting shrubs and bushes are popular bear browsing places, and tracts of berry bushes may show signs of abuse as foliage is crushed under the bears' huge feet. Hard-to-reach fruits and berries are brought down to eating level by ripping entire shrubs out by their roots; this seemingly destructive practice does no harm, and it actually contributes to the overall health of a berry patch by removing large plants that inhibit the growth of new bushes.

Brown bears are primarily nocturnal, sleeping away the heat of the day in secluded thickets, frequently on beds scraped together from moss and grasses. Approach such bedding areas with caution. When your objective is merely to scout an area, it pays to make a lot of noise to warn hidden bears well in advance of your approach. Brushy thickets may also conceal the partially camouflaged remains of an animal carcass dragged there to be eaten at leisure. *Never* approach such a carcass; its owner will be nearby until everything edible has been consumed and will defend the cache against all comers. Carcasses that have been picked clean are often marked with large scat deposits in their centers, a boast of prowess as well as a territorial claim.

Brown and black bears both use established trails that make walking long distances less tiresome. Some of these may be centuries old. Black bear paths look very much like human hiking trails, but brown bears have a much wider stance and a straddle that may exceed 2 feet. As a result, their trails normally consist of two deep, parallel ruts that make walking tough for any animal except a brown bear. In a few cases, old trails consist of a series of regular depressions where generations of bears have walked precisely in the tracks of their ancestors. Abandoned trails of this type remain obvious for years, because the depressions collect water, making the grasses growing in them taller and healthier than those of the surrounding area.

VOCALIZATIONS

It's an exaggeration to say that brown bears have a language, but they're relatively intelligent and can communicate at the most basic level. A sharp bark from a mother brings her cubs to her when danger threatens, and softer moans or grunts soothe them; an occasional snarl—with a slap that always seems to miss—keeps them informed about who's running the show.

Other vocalizations include a surprising range of moans, whines, and grunts that haven't yet been deciphered. A throaty, prolonged "waaa-aaaah" cry means a bear is ready to fight, while heavy, forceful panting denotes anxiety.

Bears also communicate with body language. White, spittle-flecked lips are a sign of stress, often seen when bears first congregate at a favorite fishing hole. Contrary to the work of a few dramatic taxidermists, bears cannot roll back their lips like a dog to snarl, but a bear walking very slowly with its head held low and wagging is to be avoided.

WOLVES AND FOXES (CANIDAE)

11

THIS FAMILY OF ANIMALS has occupied a place in the human heart and imagination since before recorded history. Our domestic dog, in its many manipulated forms, is a member of this family, although there's disagreement about whether it descended from the wolf or from a unique species that found domestication preferable to the rigors of the wild.

All wild American canids share a number of distinguishing features: Every species has strong but slender legs, with knees that bend opposite our own; all have four toes with nonretractable claws on each foot; and all are characterized by lithe bodies, thick fur, long tails, and directional pointed ears. The three groups—foxes, coyotes, and wolves—are all hunters with extraordinarily keen noses, sharp hearing, and mostly color-blind eyes that see exceptionally well in the dark, but not at long distances in any light.

Native American canids vary considerably in size and coloration, from the 6-pound swift fox to the 130-pound gray or timber wolf. Every species is a fast, highly successful predator that neither hibernates nor needs to put on excess fat to survive a hard winter. Some, such as the red fox, are lone hunters that rely on their own abilities to find food, while coyotes and especially wolves are renowned for the drill-team precision with which pack members (usually family) can bring down animals much larger than themselves. The high level of energy expended in pursuit of prey requires a great deal of protein, so wild canids' most important food is meat, but insects, fruits, and other vegetation are also part of their diets. Carcasses are picked clean, and, if an animal is strong enough, the bones are cracked to get at the fatty marrow inside. Carrion is an important source of food in snow country, which put canids in the enviable situation of having more to eat during a harsh winter than a mild one.

While gray wolves have been extirpated over nearly all their original range, either by prejudicial humans or by their own inability to live alongside us, foxes and especially coyotes have thrived to the point of being declared fur-bearing game animals in many states. None are dangerous to humans, myths and fairy tales aside, and if there has ever been a verifiable case of any wild canid preying on live humans, I can't find it.

Livestock is sometimes preyed upon, but that problem is less frequent than some would have us believe, and always preventable. Also, foxes and coyotes are frequently accused of stealing chickens and other small farm animals that more likely fell prey to raccoons, weasels, or predatory birds.

TIMBER WOLF (*CANIS LUPUS*)

Largest of the North American canids, the gray or timber wolf has been hunted, poisoned, and trapped to extinction over nearly all its original range in the United States. To Native Americans, Brother Wolf was revered as a spiritual creature that prayed to the moon and had much to teach its two-legged relatives about survival and life in general. Then came the invasion of even more superstitious savages from Europe, who saw the wolf as a sinister creature of nightmares. The newcomers carried with them fantasies of werewolves, witches, and vampires, and a dread of all wild carnivores. Reports of livestock predation were (and still are) loudly exaggerated, while early explorers looking to make names for themselves sometimes showed real creativity when relating tales of their adventures in the New World. The wolf paid dearly for their flights of fancy.

Gray wolves are not always gray; some are all white, adolescents are frequently all black, a few are silver grizzled, and many have face and body markings almost identical to Siberian or malamute huskies. One

Leonard Lee Rue III

Gray or Timber Wolf

difference is that huskies, true to their name, are more stoutly built, while wolves are lanky, long legged, and lean. The shoulder height of an adult wolf averages 16 inches, and the body length 40–60 inches. Males are normally larger than females, with adult weights ranging from 60 to more than 130 pounds. Wolves have thick, bushy tails, 14 to 17 inches long, that are never held aloft over the back in the manner of dogs but always held horizontally while traveling. The smaller coyote always trots with its tail fully down.

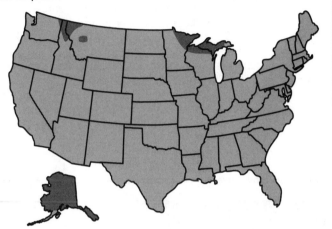

*Distribution of gray or timber wolf (*Canis lupus*).*

HABITAT AND RANGE

Once common to every forest in the United States, timber wolves are now virtually extinct in the lower 48. Populations are found in the north-ernmost regions of Montana, North Dakota, Minnesota, and Wisconsin, in Michigan's upper peninsula, over most of Canada, and throughout Alaska. Reports of wolf sightings in other states are usually traceable to coyotes, wild dogs, or just wishful thinking. Wolves have pronounced fear of man, no doubt amplified by the shoot-on-sight status they held for nearly 300 years, and human presence is probably the key factor limiting their range.

The gray wolf is a creature of the forest, where its keen nose and sharp ears counter those of its main prey, deer, moose, and caribou. These and other prey animals determine its range, as does the number of animals in a pack (more wolves need more food). A large pack may traverse more than 250 square miles.

FOODS

Wolves are particularly well adapted to prey on members of the deer family. Wolf senses of smell and hearing are at least as keen, and their eye-

sight is a bit sharper, day or night. A few young or very old males are solitary, but most run in packs of up to 15 animals, with 5 or 6 being the
average. Packs hunt with surprising intelligence, culling out weak and
injured individuals and frequently setting up elaborate ambushes. Fawns
and moose calves are prime wolf targets in spring, which keeps these prolific species from overpopulating, but healthy adults are seldom preyed
upon unless a pack is starving. A broken jaw or ribs cracked by a flailing
hoof can be lethal to a wild predator, so the nearer to death a prey animal
is, the better a wolf likes it. Unless hindered by deep snow, all members
of the deer family can beat the 30-mph running speed of a timber wolf,
so if an animal isn't caught within a quarter mile, or if it turns and fights
vigorously, a pack will probably move on to easier prey.

Wolves and other canids constantly gaze skyward for sign of crows,
ravens, or vultures circling a dead or dying animal in the distance. The
relationship is symbiotic, because, although carrion-eating birds can find
potential food animals with ease, they need a strong, sharp-toothed
predator to open the carcasses for them. Again, people are never preyed
upon, but starving packs have been known to eat human corpses in hard
times, which only enhances our fear of them.

Even without the strength of a pack, wolves are capable hunters. They
can dig a ground squirrel out of its burrow, snatch a ruffed grouse from
its snow nest, and catch spawning fish from a stream. Rodents are a mainstay, and, as wolf biologist Farley Mowat proved (even to the point of
living on a diet of rodents himself), large carnivores can lead normal lives
on a diet of nothing more than voles and mice, with an occasional meal
of insects and carrion.

Like most carnivores, wolves eat a variety of plants to get vitamins and
minerals. Grass, flower tops, mushrooms, and lichens may all be eaten,
but ripened berries are especially favored for their high sugar content.

MATING HABITS

Gray wolves mate in February and March, but only the leader, or "alpha,"
male and female, which mate for life, will breed. Other pack members,
usually offspring and relatives, don't mate within the parent pack but
instead leave to establish their own families at one to two years of age. All
pack members are submissive and loyal to the alpha pair. When the pregnant alpha female goes off to a prepared den in April through June to
deliver as many as 14 pups (7 is average), the entire pack will support her
while she cares for the newborns. Food is delivered by the alpha male
until pups emerge at one month, but no other pack members are allowed
close to the den.

Once pups become active, pack members take turns baby-sitting while
the alpha female leaves to join in nightly hunts. All pack members are very
protective of her young, even to the point of fending off hungry bears that
might make a meal of the pups. Adults returning from a hunt are mobbed
by pups that lick and bite at their muzzles and throats to stimulate regur-

gitation of partially digested meat, which is then re-eaten. Pups continue to nurse through their first summer, developing their hunting skills on rodents under the watchful eyes of guardian adults. Predation upon wolf pups is light, thanks to the protection provided by adults, but bears, especially the huge brown bears, can and do eat them. Pack members continue to watch over and feed pups until the following spring, when they'll have grown sufficiently to participate in hunts or even strike out on their own. The average life span is thought to be 10–18 years.

SEASONAL HABITS

Timber wolf packs are nomadic, venturing hundreds of miles in search of food, the alpha male leading his followers with keen senses and the experience of past years. Routes, like those of bears, are well established in the range of a veteran pack, and often follow the trails used by yarding deer, elk, and moose, or, in the Far North, the migratory routes of caribou. The only time a pack really settles into one place is for a month or so between April and early July, when an alpha female gives birth and the pups are too weak to follow the adults. Dens, usually unlined excavations in a hillside or (sometimes) in a small cave or crevice, always seem to be sited in an area where the rodent population is high, which makes hunting forays away from the denned female and her helpless young less necessary.

A wolf pack on the attack is one of the most awe-inspiring sights in nature. In the classic example of gray wolf tactics, a quick chase after a group of feeding deer determines which animal is weakest, and that animal is cut out from the rest. Slashing canines rip at tendons in the victim's hind legs, hamstringing it, and when it falls a quick death is administered by crushing its windpipe between powerful jaws anchored by sharp teeth.

Wolves also employ a number of fairly ingenious traps for cornering large prey. In midwinter, a pack may deliberately herd a moose cow and her calf onto a frozen lake or pond, where crusted, windswept snow and ice place hooves at a serious disadvantage. Teamwork keeps the adult moose on the defensive, but the real target is her calf; if it can be fatally wounded, its mother will have no choice but to leave the carcass. Other hunts may use natural terrain features such as rocky cul-de-sacs to drive prey to an ambush point, where other pack members wait to bring down the weak and injured.

Packs are territorial, and, although ranges may overlap where the hunting is good, groups tend to avoid one another; confrontations are rare except under starvation conditions. Wolves in general don't den but rather settle in one place to sleep away the daylight. In winter they curl into balls atop the snow and cover their noses with warm, bushy tails, welcoming the added insulation of a layer of falling snow. Fierce winter storms are weathered in this manner, but normally at least one pack member will be awake and on the lookout for danger (or opportunity) at all times. Solitary wolves select sleeping places that offer effective concealment, but larger packs may use the safety of their numbers to bed in more open terrain.

TRACKS

The first thing a tracker should know about wolf tracks is that they're sometimes indistinguishable from those of certain large dogs, particularly the husky breeds. Both have four toes with nonretractable claws on each foot, and both walk weight-forward on their toes, but the real confusion comes from their both having identically shaped front and hind pads. The front foot of a timber wolf is noticeably wider and longer than its rear foot, with a roughly arrowhead-shaped heel pad and two lobes pointing rearward on either corner. A wolf's rear heel pad is slightly smaller than its front pad, also triangular, and has three prominent lobes at its rear, one at each corner and one in the center. This also describes the feet of a malamute.

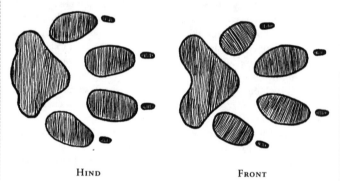

HIND   FRONT

Gray wolf tracks, 4¼ to 4¾ inches long; long front feet larger than hind feet. Note heel pad shapes, which may be identical to some domestic dog breeds.

Generally speaking, adult wolf tracks are longer and wider than those of a similar-size dog, a characteristic that gives them snowshoelike support when pursuing deer in deep snow. Front feet average 4 to 5 inches from claws to heel by about the same width. But there are big dogs and small wolves, and wolves' habit of using trails already broken by dogsleds, snowmobiles, or deer can make tracking them confusing.

The biggest difference between dog and wolf tracks is where they're found. Wolf country is typically far from civilization, while dogs rarely stray far from their domestic habitat. In fact, a dog stranded in the remote territory of a wolf pack is in mortal danger, because hungry wolves have on occasion eaten man's best friend.

At a normal walk, the front and rear feet from opposite sides print together in staggered pairs, with the front feet often registering in and slightly behind the hind prints. The stride is a rather lanky 26–30 inches,

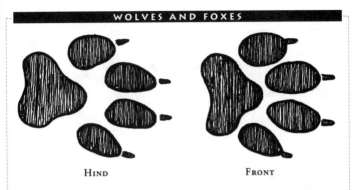

HIND   FRONT

Typical mongrel dog tracks.

with a narrow straddle of 4 to 6 inches that prints tracks almost in a straight line. Since most of the animal's weight is pressed onto its toes, the heel pads may register faintly or not at all on hard ground. Unlike cats, which walk with claws retracted, the claws always print ahead of the toes in any canid species.

At an easy trot, the wolf's track pattern changes only slightly: All four feet now print individually but in staggered pairs, with one rear foot registering behind and to one side of the opposing forefoot. The stride remains 26–30 inches, and the animal achieves a speed of roughly 15 mph at what essentially amounts to a fast walk.

At a fast run—30–35 mph—tracks show the familiar "rocking horse" gait, but with a design that seems unique among wild canids. Three feet, one front and two hind, come down together, with the other forefoot printing 8 to 10 inches behind. Usually the forward trio of tracks will print in a V shape, with the forepaw registering between and just behind the rear paws. Leaps between track sets may be from 6 to more than 8 feet.

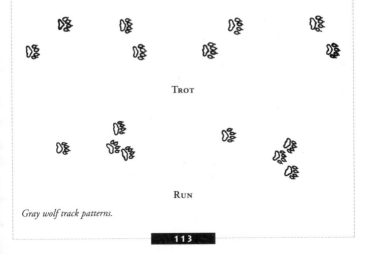

TROT

RUN

Gray wolf track patterns.

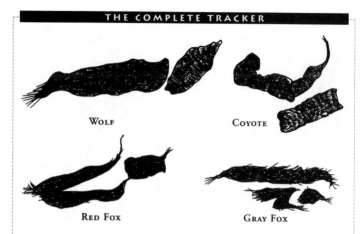

WOLF

COYOTE

RED FOX

GRAY FOX

Typical scat samples of wild canids. Since diets are similar, physical characteristics overlap.

SCAT

The droppings of wolves, coyotes, and foxes are remarkably similar, owing to their shared bloodlines and similar diets. Feasting on the rich meat of a winter-killed deer can result in smooth, doglike scat, cylindrical and deposited in coil form, sometimes segmented or broken. Its diameter averages 1½ to 2 inches. Size can help you identify a scat deposit, but remember that there are small wolves and big coyotes, and bear scat can be identical to wolf scat.

In midsummer, after winter-weakened deer have been culled and fawns are too fast to catch, rodents of all types become a staple of the wolf diet, along with a few plants and ripening berries. Scat takes on irregular segmented or cigar shapes, 5 to 7 inches long by about 1½ inches in diameter, containing large amounts of animal hair and bits of bone. Plant fibers may also be present, and deposits will likely have raspberry seeds and chokecherry pits.

SIGN

Much gray wolf sign is in scent form, invisible to humans but easily detected by "lower" animals. As with all canids, dominant male wolves frequently mark the same trees or other prominent landmarks with urine during their stay in a seasonal territory. We can't smell these scentposts from even a few feet away, but we can see the trail left by a pack that travels this route at least once a day.

Scentposts and scat deposits are also marked by a stiff-legged scraping of front and rear feet, first one side then the other, against the forest floor. This ritual, which most of us have seen dogs perform after they've urinated or defecated, is intended to scrape the feet clean of any trace of waste scent. The action leaves four distinct scrape marks, each about a foot long and always next to a scentpost or scat deposit.

Carrion partially covered with dirt and grass or snow is another wolf sign, but one you should never approach. Bears will also camouflage a partially eaten carcass, sometimes after appropriating it from a wolf pack, and until the bones have been picked clean a bear will always be nearby, ready to defend its cache. A carcass partially camouflaged with snow in midwinter most likely belongs to a wolf pack, which probably won't defend it against a human—but keep your distance anyway.

Wolves and coyotes also tend to chew off part of a deer or moose leg then carry it to a place where it can be gnawed in peace. Coyotes are rarely strong enough to crack large leg bones to get at the fatty marrow inside, but wolves can. Toothmarks left by wolves are normally wider than those made by coyotes, resembling shallow, rounded gouges about ¼ inch across and less than 1 inch in length.

VOCALIZATIONS

Few animals anywhere have a more complex system of audible communications than the gray wolf. Barking seems relatively unimportant—many individuals are incapable of barking—but all gray wolves use a variety of yelps, whines, and growls, frequently accented with body language, to communicate with others in the pack. Submission to a more dominant pack member is displayed through a low crouching or cowering stance accompanied by whining and repeated attempts to lick the stronger wolf's face. A pack member may refuse to yield to the alpha male (usually over food) with a showing of teeth, laid-back ears, a raised line of fur along its spine, and vicious-sounding snarls and growls, but usually in concert with a submissive posture. Despite appearances, members of a pack seldom harm one another, because each member is a vital part of the whole; a military-like hierarchy is needed to maintain discipline, however, and an alpha male must frequently assert his authority with growls, stiff-legged posturing, and perhaps a paw thrown over the submissive's back.

Wolves are best known for their howling, which is a language in itself. The howl of the gray wolf is generally a long monotone and lacks the yapping that usually precedes a coyote howl. The evening begins with a community howling session precipitated by barks and yelps from various pack members. Soon the entire pack is howling, with a drawn out "oooo-oooooh" that to me resembles a strong north wind moaning through leafless winter trees. Even pups, stirred by the deep instinct to hunt, will join in. Communal howling doubtless has a practical purpose, but it looks like a pep rally.

A hunting pack sometimes splits up to cover more ground, and scouts broadcast their positions to one another through the "lone wolf" howl, a low moaning sound that lasts only a few seconds and fades away smoothly. A successful scout—one that finds an unclaimed deer carcass or needs help in bringing down an injured animal—will use an "assembly" howl, a low, throaty monotone sometimes punctuated with barks or yaps.

Len Rue, Jr.

Coyote

COYOTE (*CANIS LATRANS*)

To cowboys, Indians, and all kinds of woodsmen, the coyote has long been a symbol of everything wild and free. Its common name derives from the Nahuatl word *coyotl*. The Kiowa called it "the trickster," a compliment to its cunning, and several tribes knew it as "God's Dog" or "the little wolf." But when the uncharted frontier that the early settlers knew was parceled out to create farms and ranches, the coyote was presented with an irresistible abundance of easily caught chickens, goats, and sheep. Cows are far too big for coyotes to prey upon, but young calves were sometimes taken on open range. Predation was never more than light, considering the coyote's numbers, but stockmen were quick to add the little wolf to their roster of species to be exterminated. Animals were shot, trapped, and poisoned—the last two methods killing a large number of other species as well—and many states paid substantial bounties on their hides. When I was growing up in northern Michigan, the state offered rewards of $25 for dead males and $50 for females; today this has been amended to the more economical shoot-on-sight status.

Despite more than a century of persecution, the coyote has thrived, largely because less adaptable competitors, such as the wolverine, wolf, and mountain lion, have disappeared over much of their original ranges, leaving the more resilient coyote with an abundance of prey. Today, coyotes are easily the most important predators in the United States, providing vital protection against the legendary fertility of rodents and other small mammals as well as cleaning up carrion in places where deer have overpopulated to the point of starvation. Farmers and ranchers are grudgingly learning to live with this wild dog, erecting predatorproof chicken coops and guarding sheep with the proven protection of sheepdogs.

Coyotes are responsible for most "wolf" sightings in places where there are no wolves. The confusion is understandable, but there are several differences between the two species. Coyotes are typically less than half the size of timber wolves, with an average adult weight of 30–45 pounds and a shoulder height of 23–26 inches, compared to 26–38 inches and 60–130 pounds for the wolf. Coyotes are also more trimly built, with a comparatively thinner waist and a narrower face that ends in a somewhat pointed snout tipped with a small nose. Both species have bushy, black-tipped tails roughly 1–1½ feet long, but note that gray wolves trot or run with tails held horizontally to the ground while coyotes tend to keep their tails fully down. Only among domesticated dogs and cats do we see tails held aloft; to do so in the wild would definitely alert prey.

Another source of confusion is the wide variation in colors and markings found among coyotes and wolves. Some are grizzled gray (particularly in winter), some are plain gray, some are reddish brown, and some may be a combination. Belly, chest, and legs are generally a lighter color, as with the wolf, and some coyotes do indeed resemble wolves from a distance.

Muddying the water still further is the "coydog," the offspring of a domesticated dog and coyote. Coydogs are generally sired by dogs that share at least some of the coyote's physical characteristics (pointed ears, bushy tail, thick fur, and so on), and the resulting gene combinations can create a real identity crisis—for us, not them. The coyote's willingness to interbreed with similar species may also hasten the extinction of the red wolf (*Canis rufus*), a small and very much endangered wolf of eastern Texas and Louisiana that may soon disappear through hybridization.

HABITAT AND RANGE

As proof of their remarkable adaptability, coyotes are found throughout North America south of the Arctic Circle, from Alaska to Mexico and even into South America. Coyotes have been sighted in all 49 continental states, but are rare in that portion of the United States southeast of a line extending from lower New York southwest to Louisiana.

The coyote's normal habitat is as varied as its range. Forests, desert, swamps, mountains, and prairies all support coyote populations, so long as they also support an abundance of prey animals. Coyotes may or may not be nomadic, depending on the food situation, but radio-collared individuals have been known to travel as much as 400 miles, most of it at an easy trot of 25–30 mph, in search of new habitat.

Note that, although no wild canid is a threat to humans, the coyote, being "top dog," as it were, has been known to overpopulate in some areas. And when a species overpopulates, nature typically culls out the

*Distribution of coyote (*Canis latrans*).*

weak with a fatal disease—one that may involve threats to humans. An incident that occurred near my home involved a thriving coyote population that over the course of two to three years virtually wiped out more than a dozen square miles of prime rabbit country—their own wintering grounds. Then for two consecutive Aprils there were incidents of a rabid coyote wandering through the yards and outbuildings of local residents (both animals were mercifully dispatched). An animal in the agonizing latter stages of rabies has no fear of anything and may attack if approached, transmitting the disease anew through its bite. The classic frothing mouth probably won't be seen, but any animal that shows no fear, seems disoriented and jumpy, or has a matted, greasy-looking coat should at least be given a wide berth and reported to local authorities.

FOODS

Like most wild carnivores, the coyote is an opportunistic hunter that may exploit almost any food source. Rodents are a mainstay of its diet, and the little wolf can exist on a diet solely of mice and voles if it has to (it rarely has to). Several people have told me about seeing coyotes "acting sick" in the middle of a snow-covered field or meadow, particularly during the lean months of February and March. They had actually witnessed one of the best mouse catchers in the world at work. Mice, moles, and voles travel under the snow through grass-lined tunnels, safe from most predators but detectable to the coyote's keen nose and amazingly sharp hearing. With more agility than a wolf, longer legs than a fox, and uncanny accuracy, the coyote listens for the sound of movement under the snow, cocking its head to pinpoint it first with one ear then the other. At the right moment it pounces, jumping high into the air to develop enough downward force for its front paws to punch through to the prey, pinning the victim hard against the ground. Foxes also hunt rodents this way, but their shorter legs limit their effectiveness as winter snows deepen.

With a top speed of 40 mph, the fastest running speed of all North American canids, coyotes may also hunt whitetails and mule deer or even pronghorns, but only rarely and under conditions of extreme hunger. Exceptions to this rule include newborn fawns in spring and weakened or injured adults driven into deep snow, which will support the lighter coyote but not its prey. In the latter case, coyotes almost always band together with a mate and, sometimes, adult offspring, but packs seldom number more than three to four animals. Coyotes may even try for a pronghorn calf, but pronghorn mothers are comparatively large and extremely protective, with sharp hooves and a running speed even coyotes can't approach.

Rabbits and hares are other staples of the coyote diet, and the canids often spend the latter part of winter almost entirely within the swamps and brush country where these animals live. Rabbits and hares are nimble and able to turn on the proverbial dime, but their 30-mph running speed is no match for God's Dog. The old rabbit trick of diving into water, so effective for eluding bobcats, seldom deters a coyote, which can leap more than 14 feet to snatch it from the water. In desert or prairie country, rabbits and hares are simply run down before they can reach the safety of a hole or burrow.

It was the coyote's cleverness in stealing food from other species that prompted Native American tribes to call it "the trickster." An old myth has it that badgers and coyotes sometimes work together digging rodents from their burrows, but in fact this arrangement is all the coyote's idea. While the powerful badger digs into a burrow's entrance, the coyote stations itself at the rodent's escape hole, ready to snap up whatever pops out. Otter holes on frozen lakes or rivers often have coyotes patiently waiting nearby, ready to snatch away any fish an otter brings onto the ice. They also raid the caches of bears and puma, stealing as many bites as possible before the owner—which they can outrun—charges in to stop them. Beaver dams are frequented by coyotes that arrive to drink, catch frogs and snakes, gobble newly hatched turtles (June–July), and maybe grab an adolescent beaver (adults are too much for a coyote to handle). Turkeys, ducks, and grouse are also taken, particularly during their mating seasons, and like wolves coyotes routinely cast an eye skyward for the telltale sign of crows, ravens, or vultures circling a dead or dying animal.

Most meat eaters enjoy at least a little sugar and fiber in their diets, and the coyote is no exception. Raspberries, wild cherries, rose hips, and blueberries are among seasonal favorites, and a variety of nuts, grasses, and plants may also be eaten. A few hunters have even had the "deer candy" they put out to attract whitetails stolen by sweet-toothed coyotes during the night.

MATING HABITS

Coyotes mate from late February to April, with breeding periods beginning later in the North than in the South. Females mate as early as one year of age, males at one to two years. Pairs may mate for several years to life in areas where the population is low, with adults becoming more polygamous as the gene pool grows. Lifemates constitute a small pack, sometimes supplemented by one or two grown offspring, which gives them the combined strength necessary to hunt larger animals such as deer.

In contrast with many other species' violent mating battles, male coyotes seldom fight among themselves, partly because of their more or less monogamous natures and partly because females outnumber males by roughly four to one. Pairs join together several months before the mating season, generally in late summer or early fall, giving them time to get used to each other. Once formed, the bond between male and female is virtually unbreakable until at least the following spring, and few males attempt to challenge it. Breeding is initiated by the female; males are sterile for eight months, from May through December. She signals her readiness with a hormonal scent and by pawing at the male's flanks, either to stimulate him or to aggravate him into compliance.

Females den in early April or May to give birth to a litter of 1 to 19 pups. Large litters are indicative of a well-fed mother, while small litters generally mean food is scarce. Dens may be sheltered rock crevices or small caves, but are usually excavated into the lee side of a hill, sometimes by enlarging an existing badger or fox den. Dens may extend inward more than 5 feet, with a deceptively small entrance opening into a larger birth chamber. The male is never far away while his mate is denned, and brings her rodents and whatever food is available from the surrounding area. Bears and especially mountain lions sometimes prey on newborn pups, but both adults will put up a fight vicious enough to discourage even large predators.

At about one month, pups venture from the den to play, learn, and grow, and at least one adult, sometimes a grown sibling, will be with the pups at all times. When pups are weaned at summer's end, they'll already be proficient at catching rodents, frogs, and other small prey. At one to two years, pups strike out to find mates, and the cycle begins again.

SEASONAL HABITS

Even though they may range several hundred miles to follow the availability of prey and other foods, coyotes tend to be very territorial about the place they're staying at the time. They prefer not to make trails, but usually travel already established pathways of deer, bears, and even humans. Scat deposits left along regular trails, especially at intersections, serve as warnings to other coyotes that an area is taken. So do scentposts, periodically freshened with urine and identifiable in winter as yellow stains atop the snow. Boundaries are generally respected by other coyotes, but hunger may prompt individuals to raid another's cache when times get lean. Fighting can ensue, with males doing most of it, but intruders seem unsure of themselves in another's territory and normally withdraw.

Coyotes never den except to give birth, preferring to remain in the open where their keen noses can constantly sample the breeze for predators, prey, or mates. The classic image of the lone coyote sitting high atop a hill is accurate, because mates may split up to cover more ground, and keeping to the higher elevations offers a better vantage point. If carrion or large prey is detected, the lone coyote will call for its mate with a howl.

TRACKS

Coyote tracks are, or course, doglike, having four toes tipped with nonretractable claws on each foot, but the heel pads of the front and especially the hind feet have shapes that are uniquely coyote. Like those of all canids, the coyote's front feet are noticeably larger than its hind feet, averaging 2½ inches long by 2¼ inches wide for the forefoot, claw to heel, and 2¼ inches long by 2 inches wide for the hind foot. The front heel pad, which may print only faintly, has three backward-pointing lobes across it, the outer two being narrower and extending farther back. This arrangement is unlike that of the wolf or red fox, and can be distinguished from the gray fox's by the coyote's larger heel pad. The coyote's front track is very similar to the hind track of a gray wolf, but about half the size.

The hind foot of a coyote is also unique. Its heel pad prints as a roughly circular shape, with two forward-pointing crescents emerging from either side at the middle, like the wings of a handlebar mustache. No other wild canid leaves such a track, and since most of the coyote tracks I've seen have been rather flat footed—surprising for such a fast runner—the distinctive pattern may register even on packed dirt.

At a casual walk, all four feet register independently in a slightly zigzag form. The stride is 14–15 inches, with a straddle of about 4 inches. At a 30-mph trot, which a coyote can maintain for miles, the track pattern changes to show the front and hind feet from opposite sides printing together in pairs, the hind foot ahead of the front; the stride runs 15–17

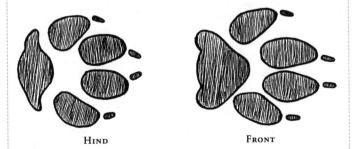

HIND   FRONT

Coyote tracks; 2 to 2½ inches long. Note uniquely winged lobes at either side of hind heel pad.

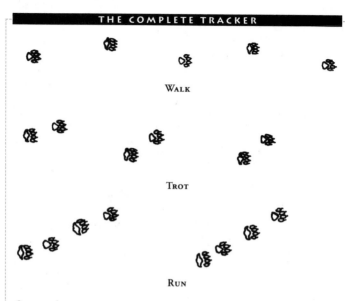

WALK

TROT

RUN

Coyote track patterns.

inches between pairs. At a 40-mph dead run, both hind feet print in staggered pairs ahead of the front feet, which print one behind the other. All four prints register as a group, with 8 to 14 feet between sets.

SCAT

Coyote scat sometimes defies positive identification. When the diet consists largely of rich venison or berries, scat may be a black liquid or semisolid mass, sometimes containing seeds or cherry pits. With a more normal diet of rodents and small animals, which are eaten whole, scat will be cylindrical, segmented, and filled with hair and perhaps a few small bone fragments. Individual scat measures 3 to 4 inches in length with a diameter of about 1 inch.

Unfortunately, the same description can apply to the scat of small wolves, foxes, and even bobcats, all of which share similar diets and often produce identical deposits. A scattering of such droppings of various ages along an established trail (usually not of the coyotes' making), especially at trail junctions, probably indicates an active coyote territory, but positive identification will most likely require finding tracks or other sign.

SIGN

The coyote's most important sign, the scentpost, is invisible to the human nose and eye unless snow covers the ground, but not undetectable in any season. Prominent trees, rocks, and even hiking-trail signs along an active coyote trail may become regular scentposts, where the dominant local male routinely asserts his ownership claim with urine. Like all canids, coyotes "wipe" their feet after urinating or defecating to remove traces of scent. These scratch marks, with the loose grass and sod thrown behind them, will usually be found 5 to 6 feet from an active scentpost.

A scattering of flight and down plumage from birds, usually without the feet or head, is a sign left by coyotes and foxes. Blue jays and other small birds careless enough to roost within jumping reach are plucked from branches by foxes, but the remains of large birds such as turkeys and geese more likely indicate the work of coyotes or bobcats, depending on terrain.

Piles of rabbit fur and, more rarely, porcupine quills are probably the work of coyotes, although bobcats and hungry foxes also prey on these animals. Again, head, feet, and even hide are eaten, leaving only a scattering of fur (contrast this with the black bear's habit of leaving a prey animal's hide with feet and head attached). Deer carcasses with heavily chewed rib ends and joints showing the puncture marks of canines, as opposed to the scrape marks of rodent teeth, are a definite sign of canid gnawing. Piles of deer hair left atop the snow, sometimes with hooves present, indicate that several animals dismembered a carcass and spirited off bones that were later cracked open to get at the fatty marrow inside.

VOCALIZATIONS

Coyote howling is much higher pitched than that of the timber wolf, with a distinctive yapping not made by wolves. Sharp barks threaten intruders that come too near a claimed kill or den site.

Like wolves, coyotes begin their nightly forays with a howling session that seems open to all within hearing distance. Unlike the low monotone moaning of a gray wolf, high-pitched coyote howls are preceded by yapping and barking, breaking into a prolonged howl that ends with an almost trembling quality, sometimes picking up again to a howl. Howls are also used by foraging mates signaling one another that carrion or easy prey has been found.

GRAY FOX
(*UROCYON CINEREOARGENTEUS*)

The gray fox is our largest native fox (the slightly larger red fox is a European immigrant), with a shoulder height of 14–15 inches and an adult weight of 7 to 13 pounds. Coyotes are nearly twice as large and have comparatively longer legs. The gray fox can resemble the red fox, especially when the latter is in its black-and-rust "cross-phase" or black-and-gray "silver phase," but grays are distinguished by a grizzled gray coat over the back, sides, face, and upper portion of a long (8- to 17-inch) bushy tail. A large white patch under the chin is broken by a band of rust-colored fur that forms a narrow border between the white chest and belly and the darker back.

The gray fox is unique among canids for its ability actually to climb trees, using nonretractable, catlike claws. It isn't agile enough to pursue

Leonard Lee Rue III

Gray Fox

prey through a tree's branches, nor does it pounce from them onto victims; rather, it uses its climbing ability to elude feral dogs—probably its main predator—and other carnivores that consider it food. It seldom climbs vertically, but can scamper swiftly up a leaning trunk and sometimes will nap well out of reach of other predators.

HABITAT AND RANGE

Gray foxes are found mostly in the eastern United States, and are common in southeastern states where coyotes are rare. Adapted to life in forests, brushlands, and swamps, they avoid open prairie, desert, and high mountains, and are scarce or absent from Washington eastward to Minnesota and from North Dakota southward to Oklahoma. Except for Washington and Maine, gray foxes are found in every border state, but their northerly range stops almost precisely at the Canadian border. The southerly extends well into Mexico.

Mostly nocturnal, the gray fox keeps to concealing undergrowth and is never far from trees it can climb to escape pursuit. Its range is determined by habitat and the seasonal availability of food, but the gray fox isn't nomadic and stays within the same 3 to 4 square miles if food permits. Probably owing to its climbing ability, it can run neither fast nor far. When the noble pastime of fox hunting on horseback was brought to the New World, its participants found little sport in chasing prey that climbed the first tall tree it came to. In the mid-1700s, the European red fox, which cannot climb trees, was imported to remedy this evolutionary inconvenience, and has since become even more widespread here than the gray fox.

All canids have some vegetation in their diets, but the gray fox is the most omnivorous among them. Berries, cherries, and grapes are seasonal

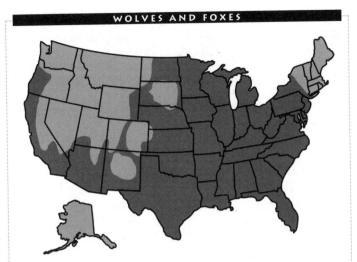

*Distribution of gray fox (*Urocyon cinereoargenteus*).*

favorites, and areas where these fruits are ripening are likely places to find gray foxes or their sign.

FOODS

As with bears, it would be quicker to list what gray foxes won't eat. They're good hunters, pouncing on rabbits from hiding, snatching birds from branches, digging out rodents, and, of course, eating any carrion not yet claimed by larger carnivores—many of which also eat gray foxes. But meat may be only a small part of this little canid's diet, particularly in summer and fall, when fruits, nuts, and berries become abundant. Because it can, the gray fox often forages in the upper branches of fruiting trees to get at foods inaccessible to most competitors. Black cherries, American plums, pincherries, and serviceberries are wild favorites, but orchards and vineyards may also be visited for apples, grapes, pears, and other fruits. Wild vegetation eaten by gray foxes includes a variety of grasses, clovers, berries, and flower tops.

MATING HABITS

Gray foxes mate in February and March. Males and females are polygamous, particularly where populations are strong, joining together in autumn and parting when kits (pups) are about four months old, in late July and August; both adults then seek out new mates. Females outnumber males by about three to one, so fighting over mates is rare.

Pregnant females den just prior to bearing two to seven blind, helpless young. As with wolves and coyotes, the male doesn't den with his mate but rather stands constant guard over her during this especially dangerous time, bringing rodents and other food from nearby while the new mother is occupied with nursing. Gray foxes usually have several dens in a single area, ready to move into kits and all, if the original den is disturbed.

At one month, fox kits leave the den; they're weaned at three months and by four months hunt well enough to feed themselves. When males and females go their separate ways in early autumn, the mostly grown kits begin to wander on longer forays away from their mother until finally, in late fall, they strike out to establish their own territories. Those still running with the mother when she's ready to breed again are driven off. Kits that survive the first 10 months of emancipation will likely find mates the following autumn.

SEASONAL HABITS

Aside from their ability to climb trees, gray foxes are notable for denning throughout the winter. Again, dens may be excavated into the side of a dirt hill, usually from the existing den of another animal, but will most likely take the form of a hollow tree, rock crevice, or a hollow under the roots of a large standing tree. Culverts and other man-made shelters may also be used in places with light human activity during the winter. An individual startled from its den may not return there, and most adults seem to have several alternates scattered about in an area. A gray fox spends the toughest days of winter curled into a ball, its bushy tail over its nose, inside a snug den; most of its normal winter prey will have gone to ground anyway, making hunting pointless, so they gray fox weathers rugged storms in a calorie-saving slumber, as do raccoons.

A gray fox's territory changes with the seasons to allow it to follow available foods. From spring through summer, when its diet consists of new plants, frogs, grasshoppers, rodents, and an occasional squirrel or young rabbit, it patrols open meadows where the snow has melted and hungry rodents are in a feeding frenzy. From late summer through fall, its diet consists largely of ripening berries and other fruits, so places where these foods grow are likely to become gray fox territory. In early winter, when the berries and fruits are gone, its diet changes to rodents and an occasional squirrel, so fields, marshes, and swamp edges offer good foraging possibilities. In deep winter, the gray fox's diet becomes strictly meat in the North, but includes at least some vegetation in its southern range.

TRACKS

Gray fox tracks are typically doglike; the animals have four toes on each foot, fixed claws, and large heel pads. Most striking are the sharp, catlike claws at the end of each toe. Because of their downward curvature, gray fox claws normally print closer to the toes than do those of other canids. The front paws are obviously larger than the rear, measure about 2 inches long by 1½ inches wide for the former and 1½ by 1¼ for the latter.

The front tracks of the gray fox look similar to those of the coyote, with three distinct rounded lobes at the rear, but are about half the size. The heel pad of a gray fox's front foot is comparatively smaller, printing

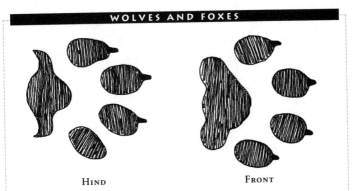

HIND   FRONT

Gray fox tracks; 1½ to 2 inches long. Note uniquely winged lobes at either side of rear heel pad.

with a wide gap between it and the outer toes, whereas the coyote's front heel pad prints very close to its outer toes. There's little danger of confusing gray fox prints with those of the red fox, which generally has shorter toes, different-shaped heel pads—with a distinctive ridge across each—and more fur on the feet.

The gray fox's rear heel pad is also unique. Like a coyote's, it has three prominent rounded lobes at the rear of each hind foot, and like the coyote's, the outermost two normally print only a partial outline, appearing as crescent-shaped "wings" on either side of the center lobe. This type of heel pad print is unique to the gray fox and coyote, but the crescents in a coyote print point forward, toward the toes, while those of a gray fox point rearward. On hard ground, crescents may not appear, and the heel pad may print only as a dot.

The track patterns of a walking gray fox reveal a rather long, 10- to 12-inch stride between the front and hind prints. They appear in a slightly zigzag line, with the hind prints registering ahead of the opposing front prints. The front claws show clearly, registering closer to the toes than with other canids. The straddle is a narrow 3 to 3½ inches.

At a trot, the front and hind feet print in distinct pairs, with the hind tracks registering just ahead and to one side of opposing foreprints. The stride, or distance between pairs, is 10–12 inches. The toes are dug in especially deep, often with a small fan of kicked-up soil behind, and heel pads may register lightly or not at all.

At a full run, a gray fox's track pattern is typically canine, with the hind feet printing in staggered pairs ahead of the front feet, which print one directly behind the other. The distance between sets of front and rear tracks shows leaps of 4 to 6 feet, with dirt or snow kicked up behind.

Gray fox walking.

When tracking the gray fox, bear in mind that it's a small, lightweight animal, about a quarter the size of a coyote, and newly emancipated young weigh only about 7 pounds. Prints will be light even on wet sand or thick mud, and tracks left in dew-wet dirt or sand will disappear within a few hours of sunrise.

SCAT

Since all canids, as well as bobcats and lynx, share very similar diets—consisting largely of rodents at any time of year—they also share nearly identical scat characteristics. Other than through obvious size differences (wolf scat would never be mistaken for kit fox scat), at times it's impossible to tell gray fox droppings from those of a red fox, swift fox, small coyote, or even bobcat. In all cases, the scat may be cylindrical, about 2½ inches long by ½ inch wide, and is often tapered to a point at one end, segmented, and filled with fine fur. The toughest identification puzzles are most common from winter into spring, when diets consist mainly of mice and voles, but they can usually be solved by reading tracks and other sign left in the area.

From summer through fall, the largely vegetarian gray fox feeds on a variety of plants, berries, fruits, and nuts as they ripen, and traces of these are often present in scat deposits. Grass and other plant fibers, seeds, and recognizable plant material are typically present to a greater degree in gray fox scat than in that of other canids. In areas where the fox diet consists mainly of berries from midsummer to autumn, its scat will likely be a black liquid containing seeds of fruits and berries—species the fox inadvertently helps propagate.

SIGN

Since even its larger canine cousins prey upon it, a gray fox has reason to keep a fairly low profile. It does identify its territory through scat deposits along regular trails, especially at boundaries and intersections, but again, they may be indistinguishable from those of other carnivores.

Scentposts along regular routes are recognizable in snow country as yellow stains melted into the hardpack, usually at the base of a tree, rock, or signpost. Foxes intruding on another's territory, particularly males, may announce their presence by simply squatting and urinating as they pass through. Wherever they are, scentposts are nearly always accompanied by obvious scrape marks on the ground where the animal wiped all four feet to remove traces of odor.

Gray foxes may also mark scentposts with their claws in the manner of cats, and maybe for the same reasons. If present, claw marks can be vertical, diagonal, or occasionally horizontal, but are always furrowed down or back toward the animal.

Gray fox dens are conspicuous, especially in winter, when tracks and other marks record the animal's passing in snow. Fresh dens can be identified by a spray of loose soil spreading from the entrance. Established dens normally will have a number of gnawed bones, feathers, and bits of fur around the entrance, but feces and urine are always kept at least several yards away.

Foxes, both gray and red, are also known to cache prey too large to eat in one meal by partially covering the carcass with dirt, snow, or pine needles—much as a bear might try to conceal a deer. The fox will remain close to its prize, eating from it until it's gone or until a larger predator comes along to claim it.

VOCALIZATIONS

Foxes don't howl like coyotes or wolves, but they do communicate with a wide variety of high-pitched yaps, barks, and growls. In accordance with its low-profile lifestyle, the gray fox is one of the least vocal animals in the forest, one that only the most dedicated tracker is likely to hear. Spring dens are good places to listen to the yelps and barks of an adult pair communicating, as well as kit calls and the sharp barks a mother uses to command them to safety. Newly joined pairs may play noisily, probably more so as the late-winter breeding season draws near, but such carefree behavior is likely restricted to remote wilderness.

RED FOX (*VULPES VULPES*)

Better known than the gray fox, the red fox is fabled as the embodiment of all that is sly and cunning. For centuries, children have been taught in fairy tales and cartoons to regard red fox characters with suspicion and distrust, and even well-intentioned kids' programs and literature can't seem to resist typecasting foxes as shifty villains.

Leonard Rue Enterprises

Red Fox

In truth, the red fox is no more crafty than other wild canids, and certainly less so than the coyote. Its reputation for cunning came from the Old World "sport" of hunting foxes with hounds while on horseback. Being a strong runner, with superb agility and canine intelligence fired by the terror of pursuing dog packs, the red fox provided a merry chase to the ruling gentry. But when noble adventurers to the New World tried hunting the native gray fox, they found it a disappointing game. Unique among canines, North America's gray fox can and usually does climb trees to escape pursuit, which made for a short chase in untamed wilderness. Such impudence from a fox was intolerable, and in the mid-1700s red foxes were shipped over from England to remedy the situation. These immigrants found the New World to their liking and promptly escaped into the wild, where they've been thriving ever since.

While shy and mostly nocturnal, red foxes are bolder than grays, and farmers long ago coined the phrase "a fox in the henhouse" to describe any situation in which a predator wanders freely among trapped, helpless victims. Red foxes were labeled poultry poachers mainly because they weren't very good at it. Foxes lack the manual dexterity needed to cope with the intricacies of chicken wire and latches and frequently got caught in the act, while more successful chicken thieves, such as weasels and (especially) raccoons, were seldom seen.

With large males weighing up to 14 pounds and standing 16 inches at the shoulder, red foxes are only slightly larger than their native gray cousins. Both have lithe bodies and long, bushy tails, but the red fox is aptly named for its thick, rust-colored fur, broken by a pronounced strip of white that extends from the underside of the muzzle, down the chest, and along the belly to the tail. Gray foxes also have white undersides with some red fur, but their coloring is predominantly grizzled gray. An uncommon coloration that causes confusion is the "silver phase," in which a red fox inexplicably grows a light, silver-gray coat contrasted by prominent black ears and a darker underside. Even more confusing is the "cross-phase," in which gray, red, and black fur are interspersed over the entire body.

HABITAT AND RANGE

Since its introduction to the eastern United States nearly 300 years ago, the red fox has thrived, becoming even more widespread than either the coyote or the gray fox. A creature of the forest, it avoids the open prairies and deserts in an area extending south from western Montana to Arizona and east from California to Oklahoma. Excluding these areas, though, red foxes are found throughout the contiguous U.S., in all of Canada, and in all but the northernmost reaches of Alaska. With thicker fur than the gray fox and furry, snowshoelike feet, they're right at home in any northern forest, and their range overlaps all but the most frigid places in that of the arctic fox.

Habitat requirements are essentially the same for red foxes as for grays: trees, high ground for denning, water, plenty of cover, and a thriving

*Distribution of red fox (*Vulpes vulpes*).*

rodent population. Because its thick fur allows it to curl up and sleep on the snow like a husky, the red fox may range deep into frozen swamps and marshes to catch rabbits and feed on winter-killed deer (gray foxes, which den all winter, keep to higher ground). In such places they're likely to be very alert, because lean coyotes, wolves, and bobcats consider foxes food.

FOODS

As with other wild canids, rodents are a staple of the red fox diet at any time of the year, and open grassy areas where mice and voles live are always a part of its seasonal territory. A seasonal behavior prompted by human deer hunters is the tendency of foxes to associate gunshots with food (the entrails of a field-dressed deer); a few times, I've arrived at the carcass of a deer I've shot to find a red fox tugging at its hide. As with other canids, a hard winter favors red foxes because it kills off weak and injured herbivores, particularly yarded deer, which then become a feast. The little fox is no danger to any deer not already dead, and it will quickly relinquish any carrion to a larger predator, but deer yards are good places to observe red foxes in snow country.

Red foxes don't eat as much vegetation as gray foxes do, but they're fond of berries, fruits, acorns, and other nuts, and where these seasonal treats are found you'll likely see sweet-toothed reds. They may also visit such areas to get prey animals attracted by the fruit. Rabbits are stalked and pounced upon from hiding, and the red fox is known for its amazing ability to catch birds.

MATING HABITS

Red foxes mate over a period from January to March, with those in the South mating earlier than those in the North. Pairs meet in early autumn and get to know one another for a period of several weeks before actually mating. Pair members of either sex may be only six to eight months old, having been born the previous spring. Like gray foxes, a pair may mate for several years running in places where populations are low, but in most cases a pair stays together only until the children are grown.

Red fox kits are born after a gestation period of just 52 days. A suitable den is prepared several days beforehand, often from an existing badger or other earthen den. Dens are usually sited in terrain where vegetation is sparse, an indication of the red fox's visual acuity; dens usually have several smaller escape holes. Caves, crevices, and, less frequently, hollow logs are also employed. Litter sizes range from 1 to 10 kits, with 6 being average, and the number of young born is probably determined by the availability of food—better-fed parents are, of course, healthier.

Kits remain in the den with the mother for about one month, nursing continuously while the father hunts for food to bring back to the den, usually regurgitated from his own stomach contents. After recovering from giving birth, the female may join her mate on local forages, but she remains close to the den, as does the father.

At four months, kits weigh 7 to 8 pounds and have grown large enough to fend for themselves. By September, all are driven off or simply abandoned by the parents, who also split up in most cases. Young males may wander as far as 150 miles before establishing their own territories.

SEASONAL HABITS

While red foxes are generally considered solitary creatures, adults actually spend most of their time with companions. If a pair meet in October, breed, and disperse along with grown kits in August, they'll have spent 10 months together. The solitary period only lasts about two months, until another mate is found for the coming year.

Unlike the less well-furred gray fox, red foxes rarely den in winter, and any that do are likely very old or injured. Instead, they weather storms in snow country by curling wolflike into a ball, bushy tail over nose, and letting an insulating layer of flakes cover them. In the South, habitat and habits change only slightly with the seasons; daytime beds are typically located in places that provide enough cover to hide but at the same time offer a panoramic view that allows danger to be seen while still a long way off. All foxes are nocturnal, but the red fox seems most willing to expose itself in daylight, and is often seen prowling fresh-cut hayfields at dawn and dusk in search of newly homeless mice.

TRACKS

The tracks of the red fox are characteristically canine, with four toes, fixed claws, and a large triangular heel pad on all feet. The front paws are larger than the hind, measuring about 2½ inches long by approximately the same width, while hind paws are 2 inches long. The most distinguishing feature of red fox prints is the forward-pointing, V-shaped ridge that runs

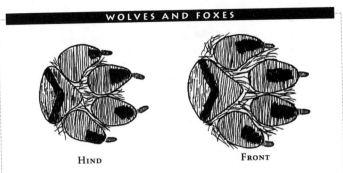

HIND   FRONT

Red fox tracks; 2 to 2½ inches long, front paws larger than hind. Note inverted V-shaped ridge across heel pads of front and hind paws, and heavy fur.

horizontally across all four heel pads. This ridge normally shows in any defined tracks (snow, mud, or wet sand) and is unique among North American canids.

At a normal walk, the red fox has long been noted for its "dainty" tracks, which print almost in a straight line. The front and hind feet print in pairs, hind foot ahead of forefeet, and the distance between tracks in these pairs ranges from 10 to 12 inches. The stride, or distance from one pair to the next, is 17–19 inches. The straddle is narrower than with other canids, ranging from 2 to 3½ inches and justifying the red fox's reputation for leaving a single row of dotted prints, much like the perforations on a stamp.

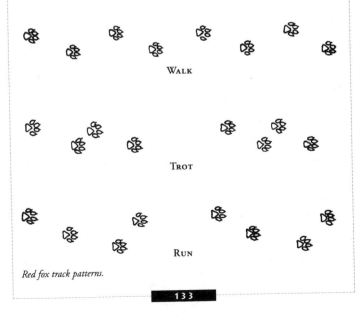

WALK

TROT

RUN

Red fox track patterns.

Remember that red foxes have exceptionally hairy feet—especially front feet—that protect their pads from cold and increase the area covered by each paw, in effect giving them snowshoes. Arctic, kit, and swift foxes also have hairy feet, but lack the distinctive ridge found across a red fox's heel pads. The result of such hairy paws is a track that may seem blurred, with distinguishing characteristics muted or in some cases obscured altogether. A closer look at such tracks will usually reveal lines imprinted by the hairs, and sooner or later that identifying heel pad ridge will appear.

At a trot of 6 to 8 mph, which an adult can maintain all day, track patterns change to show distinct sets of four prints, with each set separated by short leaps of 1 to 2 feet. The foremost track, a hind print, registers in an almost straight line with the rearmost track, a front print of the opposite side. The other two front and hind feet, again from opposite sides, print close together, sometimes overlapping, in the center of the pattern.

At a full run, about 20 mph, both hind feet register ahead of the forefeet, with each track printing individually in a staggered line. This is the "rocking horse" gait typical of most four-legged animals. Leaps of 4 to 5 feet separate each set of four tracks, and toes in each print dig deeply, often with a spray of snow or soil behind.

SCAT

The difficulty of differentiating among scat deposits within the canine family continues with the red fox. With a balanced diet of rodents, birds, berries, and vegetation, scat appears as roughly cylindrical but irregular in shape. Its diameter runs about ½ inch and it's about 4 inches long, with much shorter segments being common, some tapered to a sharp point. Massed rodent hairs are generally predominant, sometimes along with the coarser hairs of deer, small feathers, and bits of bone. Seeds and pits of berries and cherries are also common in season, but not usually as common as in gray fox scat. When the diet consists mostly of carrion—an unclaimed deer carcass, for example—deposits may be nearly black with a pronounced lack of hair. The commonly held belief that red fox scat is lighter in color than gray fox scat because the latter species eats more cherries and berries is a good rule of thumb, but isn't always reliable.

Red fox territories are determined by the availability of food, so you can expect a fox you've been seeing for months to simply disappear because berries are ripening somewhere or because winter has provided a good supply of carrion in the deep woods. Regularly patrolled trails are established to lay out the boundaries of seasonal territories, and these trails are marked at intervals with scat deposits, especially at intersections.

SIGN

Red foxes are notoriously good bird catchers. They pounce on grouse hidden under fresh snow, grab nesting ducks, and seem especially good at snapping up blue jays. Coarse wing and tail feathers are pulled off with the teeth and discarded, sometimes along with the feet or beak. Birds are often carried to a different location before they're eaten, so a pile of feathers doesn't always mark the kill site.

Tufts of rabbit fur may also mark the feeding, if not the kill, site of a red fox, but remember that gray foxes, coyotes, and bobcats also prey upon rabbits. Identifiable tracks are sure to be present in an area with so much activity.

Denning sites are also scattered with bones, fur, and an occasional feather from prey brought by the parents. Red fox dens are noted for having several small mounds of dirt around their entrances in no discernible pattern. Small holes where food was cached will also likely be present; the mounds may serve as some kind of scentpost. Less often, gray foxes may have similar mounds near their own dens.

Keep in mind that the red fox's white-tipped tail is bushier than that of other canids, and sometimes drags in deep snow or mud. The same is true of the gray fox, but the markings are less conspicuous.

VOCALIZATIONS

Vocally, the red fox is typically canine, uttering a variety of barks, growls, and even a scream. It isn't nearly as vocal as the coyote or wolf, but individuals do make more noise than the gray fox.

Most commonly heard is the red fox's bark, a sharp soprano that sounds much like the barking of a small dog. Different barks appear to have different meanings; it seems pretty certain that red foxes use barking to signal their position to mates or wandering kits, much as coyotes and wolves use their own howls.

You'll hear a variation of the bark if you approach an active den too closely in spring. This call, which obviously indicates distress, begins as a high-pitched bark but ends in a prolonged scream that some hikers have said scared the pants off them. Maybe that's what it was meant to do.

WILD CATS
(FELIDAE)
12

AS MY 12-YEAR-OLD NEPHEW and I stepped from the cedar swamp onto an abandoned railroad grade that first week of April, we did so cautiously, having learned that many normally reclusive animals traveled its more remote stretches out of convenience. With standing water still frozen and trees barren, our long-range human eyesight was for once an advantage—particularly when aided by a mini-binocular.

As it turned out, optics were unnecessary; as soon as I had a clear view down the grade I could plainly see a large, buff-colored animal with its nose to the ground, not 200 yards distant. The loose, rolling gait identified it as a cat, and when it trotted to within 150 yards of our hiding place there was no doubt that it was an adult mountain lion. As it turned to enter the swamp, clearly showing its long tail, Josh exclaimed, "That's a mountain lion!" He hasn't stopped talking about it since, and I've no doubt the tale of our sighting will be told—with inevitable embellishment—long after I've departed.

Like wild cats the world over, North America's seven native feline species—the jaguar, puma, bobcat, lynx, ocelot, jaguarundi, and margay (listed in order of size)—are superbly equipped to live by preying upon other animals. They can sneak up undetected by the sharpest senses, take down prey larger than themselves, and climb trees effortlessly, and they have perhaps the most effective arsenal of natural weapons of any mammal. Powerful, lithe bodies are characteristic of all cats, as are coarsely textured tongues whose main purpose is to rasp meat from bone. "Catlike agility," "cat's eyes," and "cat-footed" are just a few of the many phrases we've chosen to express our awe of feline traits.

Like canids, felines have four toes on each foot, but whereas canine tracks always show claws, cats keep their most potent weapons sheathed by retracting them into the toes, an ability few other animal families possess. Not only does this keep the claws sharp, but it also eliminates the scraping noises characteristic of fixed claws. Cat claws curve sharply downward and end in very keen points, even on large animals. Few enemies are willing to face these natural sabers, but their designed purpose is to hold prey firmly while a lethal bite to the neck is delivered with the elongated upper and lower canines—which are also curved inward to provide a surer grip.

Wild cats share a disdain of eating animals already dead, so baiting them into camera range by using carrion or slaughterhouse scraps may not work, except perhaps on old or injured individuals. Most other flesh eaters (bears, coyotes, weasels, and so on) will respond to the smell of dead meat, but cats prefer to kill their own food, a trait possibly developed to safeguard against food poisoning.

The feline ability to see in all but total darkness is well known. Most prey animals have eyes that face to the side, but cats have eyes that face forward, giving them binocular vision and the depth perception necessary to accurately judge distance. All cats have good noses at moderate distances, but their hearing, while directional and very precise at close range, isn't as keen as a coyote's or a whitetail's at longer distances. Long whiskers, another common trait, are thought to help cats navigate through dark, confined areas and perhaps determine wind direction, but all we can really know is that cats seem disoriented without them.

The three wild cats covered in this chapter—the puma, lynx, and bobcat—are most common in the United States and Canada. It may take time and patience to find and observe these reclusive, mostly nocturnal animals, but you should have no trouble identifying the species when you spot one. Aside from being much larger than the other two, the mountain lion is the only species with a long tail, proportionally much like that of a house cat. Bobcats and lynx have only residual "bobbed" tails, 2 to 6 inches long. Lynx are slightly smaller than bobcats and are better suited to life in the extreme North, having very thick fur and large furry feet that work like snowshoes in deep snow. The bobcat's tawny coat is lighter than that of the grayish lynx and mottled with darker brown spots, although these aren't always noticeable, and it lacks the long tufts of fur that stick up like antennae from the lynx's pointed ears. Tracks, too, can be identified with some certainty. (Refer to the tracks section of the species in question for details.)

MOUNTAIN LION OR PUMA (*FELIS CONCOLOR*)

Also known variously as the cougar, painter, panther, and catamount, the puma is officially the second-largest cat in North America. Its bigger cousin, the jaguar (120–300 pounds), hasn't been sighted north of Mexico since World War II. With an adult body weight of 75–275 pounds and a body length of 6 to 7 feet, the puma is a formidable predator upon larger game, especially whitetails and mule deer. Its heavy, black-tipped tail averages 2 to 3 feet long and serves as a balancing aid when footing is precarious.

HABITAT AND RANGE

At one time there were mountain lions throughout the wilderness areas of

Leonard Lee Rue III

Mountain Lion

North America, but unrestricted hunting and the species' own inability to coexist with civilization have made it virtually extinct east of the Rockies. Today, mountain lions inhabit roughly one-third of the western United States, ranging from the southern tip of Alaska into Mexico and spreading inland to the Rocky Mountains and throughout southern Texas. There are isolated populations in Louisiana, Alabama, Tennessee, and the southernmost tip of Florida. The range to the north includes most of Manitoba and possibly extends southward into northern Minnesota.

As this range shows, few wilderness areas are geographically unsuitable for the versatile puma, but populations are definitely limited by the expansion of humankind. The cats have on occasion been known to regard small, lone humans as prey, and when suburbia intrudes into their domain, such problems have historically been resolved to pumas' detriment. As a result, most mountain lions are found far off the beaten track in terrain where people seldom go. Hollywood's image of a puma lying in wait on a rocky outcrop in mountainous country is accurate, but these opportunistic hunters are equally at home in hardwoods, swamps, and almost anyplace else where they can eat regularly and not be bothered.

I must also mention that in recent years the mountain lion's range has increased unnaturally at the hands of well-meaning but misinformed humans. After a few tragic encounters between native puma and encroaching humans in northern California and Oregon, it was decided at an official level to reinstate a legal hunting season on the cats. In response, some animal-rights types illegally live-trapped an unknown number of pumas and transported them to different states (Minnesota, Wisconsin, Michigan, and probably Pennsylvania), where they were released, all or most of them alone. Accredited biologists agree that such unsupervised transplants generally do more for the human conscience than they do for displaced mountain lions.

*Distribution of mountain lion or puma (*Felis concolor*).*

FOODS

Discounting the jaguar, mountain lions are the only predators in North America capable of tackling a healthy adult whitetail or mule deer with a real chance of success. With a sprint speed of 45–50 mph, an adult mountain lion can outrun a healthy deer, but the chase must begin at close range and the deer must be brought down quickly, or the cat will tire and be left behind. Small deer are the cat's main prey, and, like all predators, they tend to take down animals that are too injured or weak to put up a fight. By culling the weak and leaving the strong to breed again, puma, like wolves and coyotes, actually contribute to the health of a herd. Contrast this with the human philosophy of killing the strongest and leaving the weak.

Mountain lions may take an elk or moose calf if the opportunity presents itself, and spring birthing places for deer of all types are likely to attract the big cats from far away. They'll also kill and eat a variety of smaller animals, such as marmots, foxes, coyotes, an occasional beaver, and even porcupines, if times are lean. Small rodents are eaten as are grasshoppers and other insects in season, but the panther is designed for deer hunting, and deer make up most of its diet.

As mentioned earlier, cougars and cats in general tend to avoid eating carrion unless an individual is too weak to hunt for itself. A strong instinct to hunt is necessary when the prey is sometimes larger than the predator, and nature has seen to it that cats derive special pleasure from the experience. Rare, "unexplained killing orgies," in which mountain lions have killed several penned sheep or newborn fawns without eating them, are most likely examples of this hunting instinct gone wild upon prey that was simply too easy.

MATING HABITS

Mountain lions of both sexes lead solitary lives, except during a brief two-week mating season when pairs meet, breed, sometimes play and hunt together, then go their separate ways after the female becomes pregnant. Mating generally takes place in February and March, although there's no defined breeding time when all cougars are fertile. Beyond breeding, no bond exists between mates; females decisively drive males away when their part in procreation is done, and males go off to seek out new mates as opportunistically as they do game.

One to six kittens are born in May or June in a grass- or moss-lined den located well away from potential dangers. Because most of the puma's current range encompasses rocky terrain, dens are typically found in isolated crevices or small caves. When the habitat is a lowland forest or swamp, dens may be sited in large hollow trees, in bear dens from the previous winter, or in secluded thickets. Never approach a suspected puma den closely until after August.

Newborn puma kittens are small, blind, and helpless, with yellowish tan fur and black spots that make them resemble miniature jaguars. Like all of the more intellectually advanced species, baby cougars develop slowly and are wholly dependent on their mothers for food and protection for their first year. Kittens are weaned at one to two months and roam with their mother thereafter. By six months the spotted baby coat has been replaced by the tawny fur of an adult, and young will have learned to catch small prey. Adult mountain lions need fear only humans, but until kittens are a year old and weigh 75–100 pounds, they may fall prey to bears, wolves, coyotes, and even eagles and hawks. At one year, males typically strike out to establish their own territories and find mates, but female young may remain with their mother for two years. Hangers-on are driven off before the mother mates again.

Since females outnumber males by roughly three to one, competition for mates is seldom heavy, and fights between individuals for any reason or in any season are rare. A preference for killing their own prey prevents food fights, and if two adult males should meet over a female in heat, dominance is nearly always established through body language, such as an erected mane of hair along the spine, a showing of fangs and claws, and perhaps a few swipes at the air to instill fear in an opponent. All species of cats are loathe actually to fight one another, because combat between two such well-armed adversaries is likely to prove fatal for both in the unforgiving wilderness.

SEASONAL HABITS

As with other large predators, the puma's seasonal range and habits are determined in large part by weather and the seasonal movements of its main prey, deer. In early spring, when deer in the North are weak from a long, lean winter and flock to open places for the first taste of green vegetation, you can bet that resident mountain lions will be patrolling somewhere between their bedding and feeding areas. And when deer move to their isolated winter yards, the big cats follow. Most hunting is done at night, because deer tend to be nocturnal, but both the cats and their prey may be active at any time of day in places relatively free from human intrusion.

Unlike wolves and coyotes, mountain lions don't actually trail prey by scent but rather wander freely between places frequented by these animals, sometimes covering as much as 25 miles in a single night. When a young or otherwise weakened deer is located by airborne scent, the cat stalks to within 30 feet with a low, slinking crouch. From there, the puma takes two leaps of as long as 20 feet to land on its victim's back, where sharp, curved claws dig firmly into flesh to provide a sure grip while long fangs deliver a fatal bite to the neck. Kills must be made swiftly, because, although a cougar can outrun a deer over short distances, the cat tires quickly, and if a fleeing deer makes it to thick cover it will probably be lost in a maze of trails and scents.

TRACKS

Each member of the cat family has a track with unique characteristics that serve to identify its species, and even a fairly undefined partial print can yield positive identification. Like those of most four-legged mammals, a puma's forepaws are noticeably larger than its hind, measuring 3 to 3½ inches long; hind paws average between 2½ and 3 inches. Claws never show in tracks unless the cat is nervous or agitated. Unlike those of deer, or even animals that cannot retract their claws, cat tracks are "soft," meaning they have very little impact on the ground and may be virtually invisible on packed earth, crusted snow, or, of course, rock. But not every track is thus; patience and an eye for detail, along with a solid knowledge of the species' normal habits and habitat, are the order of the day when tracking any wild feline.

HIND   FRONT

Puma tracks; front, 3 to 3½ inches long; hind, 2½ to 3 inches long. Note shape of front heel pad and lack of claw marks; front paws are noticeably larger than hind feet.

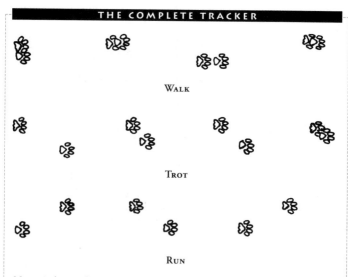

Mountain lion track patterns.

Typical of four-legged animals designed for speed, most of a puma's weight is held on its toes when it walks, especially while stalking, and its heel pads may not touch the ground. When they do, however, a mountain lion's front heel pad is unique (see the illustration), with three distinctive lobes to the rear and two smaller but equally distinctive lobes to the front, just behind the two middle toes. The hind heel pads also have three clearly defined lobes to the rear and two small lobes to the fore, but the heel pad itself is asymmetrical and nearly formless.

The walking track patterns of a mountain lion vary considerably with the type of terrain. Most regular in appearance (but rarest in occurrence) are paired tracks left on a flat, even surface, in which the hind feet print ahead of and to the inside of the opposing front feet. The stride between paired tracks runs to about 20 inches, with a straddle of roughly 4 inches, but either of these measurements is subject to extreme variation as the cat's almost rubbery gait conforms to changes in terrain.

A cougar carries its heavy tail in a wide U shape that curves back upward at the tip, and at a normal walk in several inches of snow, the lowermost portion may leave drag marks between each print. Since cougars are the only species in snow country with a tail long enough to drag, such marks are positive identification.

In deep, loose snow, where cats, like humans, find walking a real struggle, an animal may elect to move ahead in leaps, placing all four feet together and jumping forward as much as 20 feet to land with the feet together, then leaping again. In this pattern, the forefeet print one ahead of and one behind the rear feet, which print together between them. Conveniently, this pattern is also typical of the species' running gait.

Mountain lion scat, 4 to 6 inches long. Deer hair is predominant, sometimes with rabbit and rodent fur and bones.

SCAT

Mountain lion scat often closely resembles that of most species in the dog and cat families. In places where puma coexist with wolves, which also make venison a major part of their diets, scat from the two species may be identical. But mountain lions prey upon deer to a greater extent than any other predator. The scat deposits I've seen have contained an abundance of deer hair at all times of year, which means the cats were taking down relatively healthy midsummer deer when most other predators had turned their attentions to smaller, easier prey. The scat of coyotes, bobcats, and wolves always contains a greater percentage of rodent hair and bones, rabbit fur, and insect parts than the scat of cougars at any time of year. Nearly all deposits are found in places where loose soil can be scraped over the scat in a lazy attempt to hide its odor.

Mountain lion scat is generally cylindrical in shape, irregular, segmented, and tapered to a point at one or both ends. An average scat measures between 4 and 6 inches long by 1 to 1½ inches in diameter, and scat size is a good indication of the animal's size. Wolf scat is similar in shape and appearance, but, again, cougar scat contains an abundance of rough deer hair at all times of year.

SIGN

While mountain lions don't roam as widely as do coyotes or wolves, they have seasonal territories they patrol regularly. And as with other predators, the sizes of those territories are determined primarily by the seasonal movements of the cougars' prey, namely deer. Trails are regular and well used, particularly in deep snow or thick undergrowth where travel is restricted. Trails are somewhat trough shaped and between 10 and 12 inches wide; the gentle way grasses or other plants are pressed down at their bottoms reflects a very light tread. This can be important to a tracker, because, while deer leave high-impact trails that can remain visible for months, a mountain lion's trail may be overgrown a couple weeks after being abandoned.

Scat deposits are probably the most reliable way of determining if a trail is active, and scentposts where scat is deposited regularly are common along a trail's length. Older deposits bleached white from age alongside deposits still wet or even warm give a good indication of how long and how often a trail is used. Preferred sites are areas of loose soil, including cinder railroad grades and seldom-used dirt roads. You can also age scat deposits by the claw marks left during a cat's cursory attempt at covering them, and it should be noted that claw marks are generally made while the animal is facing the direction it intends to travel.

Claw marks left on trees and stumps are another sign marking a cat's territorial boundaries. These claw marks are, of course, larger and higher or smaller and lower depending on the size of the animal, but those left by an adult cougar will be 3–4 feet above the ground and about ¼ inch wide. Aspens seem to be the trees of choice, but hardwoods are occasionally clawed; evergreens are avoided because of their sticky sap. Bear claw marks are much higher, wider, and deeper, and not nearly so vertical as those of the mountain lion.

Claw marks are frequently accompanied by a spray of urine against the clawed tree or on a prominent landmark nearby. Both males and females mark their territories in this manner, and the odor of those urine-spattered scentposts is unmistakable to anyone who's owned a house cat. Depending on wind direction, temperature, and how recently the scentpost was anointed, you should be able to smell the generically pungent aroma of cat urine at several feet to several yards, and possibly follow it to a well-clawed boundary marker.

VOCALIZATIONS

Anyone who's ever been annoyed by domestic cats fighting for mates or territory in the middle of the night can attest to the amazing vocal range common to members of the feline family. The cougar has a deeper, more throaty voice than its smaller cousins, but all cats hiss, spit, purr, mewl, growl, yowl, and cry like a lost child. The classic mountain lion snarl heard in virtually every movie they've appeared in is just one of a kaleidoscope of feline vocalizations that scientists have only begun to decipher. The task is made even more complex by the fact that much communication is also done through visual sign (claw marks), scent, and body language.

We do know that purring is a voluntary sound made by a cat when it's content, but also when it's injured or in pain. A nursing mother will purr as her kittens suckle, but so will a mountain lion laid up with its ribs stove-in from a flailing hoof.

We also know that the "meow" sound common to felines is a distinct, two-part message. The first part, the "me," denotes something between friendship, as between a mother and her kittens, and cautious acceptance, as between prospective mates on their first meeting. The "ow" sound, sometimes used alone, drawn out to a wail, or in conjunction with a low growl, is a warning for intruders to keep their distance. A twitching tail is another sign of agitation, while laid-back ears, bared fangs, and a low crouch are warnings that the animal is prepared to defend its position.

Most sensational are the eerie wailings and spine-tingling moans that echo through the night during mating season, especially when competing males meet over a receptive female. All wild North American cats can sound downright spooky during their brief mating seasons, and puma wails have been likened to a child crying, a woman's scream, and the screeching of someone in terrible pain.

BOBCAT (*FELIS RUFUS*)

The bobcat or wildcat is easily the most resilient and adaptable species of North American feline. Despite encroachment by civilization, trapping, hunting, and the species' own aversion to humans, the bobcat has always found space enough to make a living and has never been endangered over most of its range.

Officially the third-largest cat in North America (if you count the jaguar), adult bobcats can weigh in at 15 to 70 pounds, with specimens becoming progressively larger the farther north you go. Shy and seldom seen by humans, the bobcat is as much a hunter as any wild feline, capable of taking down prey as large as whitetails and as small as mice.

As its common name implies, the bobcat has a short "bobbed" tail, 3 to 7 inches in length with two or three darker horizontal bars and a black tip on the upper side only; the underside is uniformly white. In summer the bobcat wears a reddish brown coat mottled with its trademark brown spots, but some individuals have rust-colored coats that appear to be one color. In winter its coat becomes thicker and darker, but retains a more red-brown hue than the gray-brown winter coat of the slightly smaller lynx. The black tufts of fur at the ear tips are much smaller and less prominent than those of the lynx. Some believe these tufts help enhance the cat's hearing, but if so, it's probably not in a way humans can comprehend.

HABITAT AND RANGE

Bobcats once roamed throughout the United States and western Canada, and despite the growth of civilization they still occupy most of this range. They're fairly common in the lower 48 states, except in southern Minnesota, Wisconsin, and Michigan; all of Illinois, Indiana, and Ohio; the interior of California; and the section of the East Coast from New Jersey to Maryland. Their northern range covers most of Alberta, with populations extending into all of Canada's southern provinces. Places now devoid of bobcats are said to have been overtrapped during

Leonard Lee Rue III

Bobcat

the fur boom, but it's probably no coincidence that these same places are highly urbanized.

It has also been said that the bobcat's original habitat was scrubland, but in truth the little wildcat is at home in virtually any warm to moderately cold environment offering good cover, a steady supply of prey, and enough room to avoid contact with humans. In some remote farming areas, bobcats have learned to prey upon unguarded livestock as large as sheep, but such forays are rare and have never posed a significant threat to ranchers.

A bobcat's home range is determined by available terrain and the abundance of prey within it—and the latter, of course, depends on the species of plant life present. Based on my own experiences with them in the North, bobcats require a minimum of 1 square mile, about the same as a whitetail. Being predators, the cats do follow the seasonal movements of prey, sometimes extending their range but seldom relocating altogether.

*Distribution of bobcat (*Felis rufus*).*

FOODS

A bobcat's main source of nourishment is fresh meat, and it's well equipped for hunting. In late winter it may take down an injured or starving snowbound deer much larger than itself, but most meals are smaller and less spectacular. Just as the bear has compensated for a powerful but clumsy body with the ability to digest almost anything organic, a bobcat makes up for its singular diet with hunting prowess matched by only a few land predators in the world. It may eat only flesh, but the fare includes grasshoppers, frogs, voles, squirrels, rabbits and hares, foxes, an occasional spawning fish, birds, and even cave bats. Grasses are occasionally nibbled, but sparingly, and probably only as a vitamin source.

Except in the most remote places, bobcats hunt only at night, leaving their well-hidden dens at dusk to travel established trails in search of opportunity and returning in the dim hours of early morning to sleep. The prey is mainly rabbits and hares, upon whose populations bobcats and especially lynx depend greatly, but almost any animal within bobcats' abilities may be considered fair game.

Like lynx, bobcats frequently lie in wait for passing prey on a tree branch several feet above the ground, usually near a well-traveled animal trail. Like other forest cats, a bobcat can sprint quickly enough to catch rabbits and young deer (does typically won't defend their young), but only over short distances. To hedge its bets, a bobcat relies mainly on stealth to get within pouncing range on the ground. In any case, once it gets its claws into a prey animal, the drama almost always ends with a fatal bite to the neck. Small prey such as mice or squirrels are eaten on the spot or, if the cat is a mother with young kittens, taken back to the den. Larger prey such as deer are partially—usually barely—covered over with snow or forest debris. Unless prey is very scarce, bobcats will not eat carrion.

While bobcats share a typically feline aversion to water, they're fast, excellent swimmers and don't usually hesitate to follow prey into a pond or marsh. In early spring and autumn, the remote lakes and ponds around my home in northern Michigan, most of them surrounded by thick cedar swamps and marshes, are alive all night with the cries of nesting or resting Canada geese, as bobcats prowl in search of opportunity. They'll also take a young beaver in late spring if they can, but both beaver parents are very protective, and an adult beaver, which may outweigh a bobcat, can be very dangerous when threatened.

MATING HABITS

Bobcats mate in early spring, in February and March, with cats in the North breeding later than those in the South. In the Deep South, where temperatures are mild all year, females may breed again in September or October, producing two litters of one to seven kittens a year (four is average in all climates). Gestation takes three months, with spring kittens born mostly in the last week of April and the first week of May. Denning places vary with terrain but include caves, rock crevices, large hollow logs, deserted coyote and black bear dens, and brushy thickets.

Kittens are born blind and, like all the most intelligent mammals, develop slowly, leaving the den for the first time at about six weeks of age, but staying close to the protection it offers until about three months. Until this time they may be preyed upon from many directions, but probably the greatest danger comes from owls, hawks, and other large birds of prey. Kittens stay with the mother for their first year (six months in southern climes, where two litters a year are born), wintering in a secluded den. Males are generally first to strike out on their own, but year-old females may have to find their own dens in fall because they, too, are pregnant.

Unlike his canine counterparts, a male bobcat plays no part in the procreation process beyond the act of breeding. In fact, males and females are downright unfriendly toward one another except when their hormones are raging. When a male, who is physiologically ready to mate all year, detects the scent of a female in estrus, he tracks her down and begins a so-called courtship ritual that may last several days before the female becomes comfortable enough to allow him to mount her. Mating takes place for two to three days, until the female, who seems to know instinctively when she's pregnant, ends the affair with bared fangs and a swipe or two of a well-clawed forepaw. Taking her hint, the disenchanted male sets out to find another mate before the season ends.

Competition for females among bobcats is light, primarily because females outnumber males by about three to one. If two adult males do meet over a single ovulating female, the contest is usually limited to posturing, bared teeth, and growls. Battles between such well-armed opponents would not be conducive to survival of the species. For one thing, the winner would probably be in no shape to mate.

SEASONAL HABITS

Aside from breeding and rearing young, bobcats of both sexes are among the most solitary and reclusive animals in the world and actually seeing one in the wild is an experience very few people ever have. As mentioned previously, the cats lie up in a safe place—sometimes on a horizontal tree limb—to nap away the daylight hours. At dusk they leave to patrol well-established routes, using trails not of their own making. (As you may recall from chapter 2, many species use the same trails out of sheer convenience.)

In summer, a bobcat's nightly hunting route most likely will follow well-worn deer trails, which are also used by rabbits, porcupines, and other animals that feed on the same types of vegetation in the same places. Routes may vary as opportunity dictates, but precisely the same places will be marked with urine, claw marks, and scat every evening to reinforce the fact that this territory has been claimed. Bobcats typically respect each other's claims but add their own scent as a sort of calling card.

When winter snows deepen sufficiently to send deer into the seclusion of their yards, smaller and lighter animals that can run atop the snow are forced to create their own trails. Starving or injured deer are killed in late winter, but rabbits and hares are a bobcat staple throughout the year, and the cats know to stake out places where sumacs, raspberries, and the other shrubs that make up a rabbit's winter diet are found. A bobcat's large, wide feet allow it to run on top of hardpack snow with almost the same ease as a rabbit or hare.

TRACKS

Like all felines and canines, bobcats have four toes on each foot (five if you count the single dewclaw on each ankle). The paws are generally more round than those of wild canids, with the toes more widely spread, and tracks lack claw marks. The front and hind feet are approximately the same size, measuring 1½ to 2 inches long, with the width nearly equal to the length.

Discounting size, bobcat tracks are very similar to those of the mountain lion, and in places where the animals' ranges overlap you may have to do a bit of investigating to make a positive identification. They have nearly identical heel pads on the front and hind feet (see the illustrations), but one big difference is that a cougar's forefeet are noticeably wider and longer than its hind feet. A lynx has similar heel pads, except that those of the forefeet have only two lobes at the rear while the bobcat has three, and, owing to its very furry soles, the lynx's heel pads normally print as an uneven circle.

At a normal walk, the bobcat's track patterns vary with changes in terrain. On even ground, the hind tracks print close to or inside the front

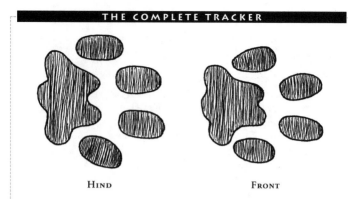

HIND   FRONT

Bobcat tracks; 1 to 2 inches long, as wide as they are long. Note that front and hind feet are approximately the same size, unlike lynx or puma.

tracks—a common and probably learned trait among animals whose survival depends on stealth. Being able to see the forefeet allows their precise placement where they'll make the least noise, and an ability automatically to place the hind foot on that same spot helps ensure near-silent walking on most terrain. The straddle is 6 to 7 inches; the stride 16 to 18 inches.

On uneven ground, which pretty much describes all of a bobcat's natural habitat, the walking track pattern becomes nearly patternless, with each foot printing in accommodation to terrain changes. Tracks may be superimposed upon one another, side by side, or one in back of the other. It follows, then, that the stride and straddle are also variable.

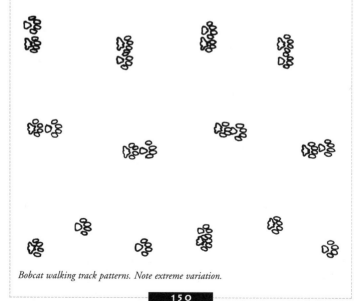

Bobcat walking track patterns. Note extreme variation.

Lynx and bobcat scat. Scat from either species is indistinguishable from the other due to nearly identical diets.

SCAT

Bobcat scat closely resembles fox or coyote droppings in shape and size, being generally cylindrical and segmented, but usually contains an abundance of rabbit fur. The scat of carrion-eating canids contain a wider variety of hair, including deer, rabbit, and rodent.

A typical bobcat scat measures from 2 to 6 inches long by roughly 1 inch in diameter. Because scat deposits also serve as scentposts to outline their owner's territory, where you find one, you'll probably also find several more of varying ages within just a few feet. Fresh deposits are dark brown to black, growing lighter with age, and finally bleaching to white just before disintegrating into the earth. Bones from small birds and rodents, which are swallowed whole, are prevalent throughout.

One sure way to tell bobcat scat from that of smaller felines is by the scratch marks left in the soil around its perimeter, which the cat makes in a perfunctory attempt at covering it. Some deposits may be covered over completely, again with the telltale claw marks next to them, but those left as scentposts are purposely left mostly uncovered. Unlike those of the cougar, which most often scratches from the direction it departed, bobcat claw marks tend to be from all directions and cannot be used as a direction-of-travel indicator.

SIGN

Like all territorial mammals, a bobcat marks its territory as a warning to intruders. But in this case the marks aren't obvious or sometimes even visible, because much of a cat's claim to territory is scent borne. Scat scentposts, described above, are one of the visible boundary signs bobcats use, but urine is also used by both males and females to further mark their territories. Bobcats (like all cat species) back up to a convenient tree, stump, or bush in their territories, raise their tails, and literally spray the landmark with strong-smelling urine. You won't actually see this type of scentpost unless it was freshened just minutes before or unless there's snow on the ground, but as any cat lover can attest, feline urine is extremely pungent. If I'm out trying to cut cat sign in warm weather—when finding a track on the forest floor is most difficult—I rely heavily on my nose to lead me to scentposts. Once I've located a strong-smelling scentpost, I know where to concentrate my efforts, because its owner's trail has to pass right by it.

Another visible but less obvious bobcat sign is claw marks in the trunk of a tree, usually a softwood such as an aspen or cottonwood, almost never a pine or cedar because of their gluey sap, or sometimes in a fence post. Bobcat claw marks are normally 2 to 3 feet above the ground and consist of three or four long, parallel scratches running almost vertically down the trunk. Unfortunately, the scratching posts of a bobcat bear claw marks identical to those of a lynx or even an immature mountain lion, and in places where these species overlap, scratching posts cannot be used for positive identification.

VOCALIZATIONS

For the most part, a bobcat makes the same variety of sounds as an ordinary house cat, a vocabulary made up of mewing, meowing, purring, hissing and spitting when threatened, growling, and yowling. As with other cats, its "meow" is actually two messages, each of which is sometimes used individually. The "me" portion is a statement of peaceful intent, while the "ow" part carries a warning that personal space should nonetheless be respected. The former is common between mothers and their kittens, while the latter, often prolonged into a growl, might be heard between a pair of rival males.

Most startling is the bobcat's scream, emitted when the animal is frightened or cornered and sometimes accompanied by what has been described as a "cough-bark."

But most eerie are the various yowls and wails heard—mostly from males—during the brief, late-winter mating season. These mating calls have been likened to the crying of a lost child, which aptly describes the ones I've heard, and many a novice camper has spent a sleepless night after hearing them echo mournfully through a dark woods.

LYNX (*FELIS LYNX*)

Wildlife biologists can't seem to decide what the scientific name of this close cousin of the bobcat should be: The cat has been known as *Felis lynx, Felis canadensis, Lynx canadensis,* and *Lynx lynx,* depending on whose word you take.

Human politics and semantics aside, the lynx is a fascinating wild cat that symbolizes the spirit and freedom of the wilderness as much as any animal on the planet. At 12 to 40 pounds, it's slightly smaller than a bobcat, but its longer legs, bigger paws, longer ear tufts, large tufts at the

Lynx

jowls, and gray-buff coat of long fur once prized by fur traders can make it appear larger.

But unlike the bobcat, whose populations have never been endangered and which appears actually to be increasing its range, the lynx harbors an absolute aversion toward civilization. As its physical characteristics indicate, the lynx has always had a more northerly range than the bobcat, although the species do overlap. Its most dangerous threat comes from human expansion. When I was growing up in northern Michigan, the lynx was a frequent neighbor at remote campsites (one actually came into camp one night), but now it's found only in the most inaccessible forests and swamps of the state's upper peninsula.

HABITAT AND RANGE

Even when the first explorers came to the New World, the secretive lynx was a rare sight, and if an adventurer wasn't hardy enough to endure long, bitterly cold winters with snow deep enough to make horseback travel impossible, he'd never see one. Lynx are strictly creatures of northern forests and swamps, where their abilities to withstand subzero temperatures and run atop deep snows match those of their main prey, the snowshoe hare.

Today, lynx are found in northern Wisconsin, Michigan, Maine, Vermont, New Hampshire, and upstate New York. To the west they're found only in Montana, Idaho, and Utah, where they keep to the high mountain forests. Farther north the cats become more plentiful, although never common, occupying almost all of Canada, except for southern Alberta and Saskatchewan and the west coast of British Columbia. In the Far North, lynx cover all of Alaska except the Alaska peninsula.

*Distribution of lynx (*Felis lynx*).*

FOODS

Like all cats, lynx are strictly meat eaters. Their prey is virtually identical to that of the closely related bobcat, but whereas the bobcat relies heavily on the snowshoe or varying hare (*Lepus americanus*) as food, the lynx is utterly dependent on the little hare for survival. Snowshoe populations are cyclical, peaking once every decade then plummeting as the stress of overpopulation causes a sharp curtailment in mating (a natural means of birth control seen in many other species). So closely linked are prey and predator that when snowshoe populations decline, lynx populations also fall due to starvation, lagging behind the hare by one year. And when snowshoe numbers rise again, the lynx population increases as well, again lagging behind by one year. No one is sure how or why this rather bizarre natural balance came to be, but it seems to work well for both species.

Lynx are more arboreal than bobcats, spending much of their time apparently lazing on overhead tree limbs waiting opportunistically for a meal. Owing to their longer legs, lynx can run faster than bobcats, reaching speeds of up to 30 mph or more, but only for ¼ mile or so. Winter-weakened deer, mice, foxes, and other prey animals are taken from time to time, but only the snowshoe hare provides a sufficiently steady supply of food to sustain the lynx.

Like all North American wild cats, lynx have a natural aversion to eating carrion, preferring to kill their own prey. If food is scarce, the cats may lower themselves to scavenging, although a solitary lynx may have to compete with packs of wolves and coyotes for a deer carcass.

MATING HABITS

Lynx mate over a period of about three weeks, from mid-March to early April. Mating rituals are essentially the same as for bobcats, with solitary adults coming together for breeding purposes only, then going their separate ways. Pregnant females search out a small cave, rock crevice, overhung rock ledge, or hollow log to use as a birthing den, while males continue to chase breeding females until mating season ends. As with other cats, the males take no part in rearing the young, and in fact may kill kittens left unprotected.

Lynx kittens are born in May through July. Litter size is usually two kittens, sometimes three if snowshoe hares are especially abundant, and sometimes none at all if the hare population is in a cyclical decline. Kittens winter with their denned mother for their first winter, nursing for one month then switching to meat brought back by the mother. At first, prey is brought to the kittens dead, but after three months the mother will begin bringing in rodents and other small prey that are merely injured. This may seem cruel by human standards, but it's a necessary exercise if the young are to learn to kill for themselves, and all American cats—including house cats—do this. A mother won't intervene on the kittens' behalf when live prey is brought to the den, and if an animal escapes she'll simply catch another and let them try again.

By spring, lynx kittens will be hunting with their mother but are still dependent on her for food until midsummer, when males typically strike out on their own. Female kittens may remain with the mother until early autumn, but are driven off forcefully if necessary to free her up to mate again. Kittens mate the following year.

SEASONAL HABITS

Lynx spend more time in the trees than other American wild cats, lying silently above animal trails on overhanging limbs for hours, a hunting technique adopted to conserve precious calories in their often frigid habitat. A lynx may pounce from its perch onto prey, especially newborn fawns or seriously weakened adult deer, but in most cases an overhead perch simply provides a superior vantage point, as does a bow hunter's treestand. When passing prey is spotted, the cat's usual method is to descend and stalk to within range. With longer legs than a bobcat, the lynx is a match for most prey in a short footrace, but, like all cats, it relies more on stealth than on speed.

At all times of year the lynx's main source of food is the snowshoe hare. From spring through autumn the cats roam open marshes, beaver ponds, and forest glades to catch hares feeding on green plants, and, of course, any rodents, fawns, red squirrels, or beaver kits they may happen upon. The same big feet and long legs that make them fast runners over snow also make them powerful swimmers, and lynx don't hesitate to enter water in pursuit of prey. Unless an individual is very old, sick, or injured, lynx will not eat carrion in summer.

In winter, when deep snow forces many animals to restrict movements to a few packed trails, both the lynx and the snowshoe hare can travel relatively unhindered because of their broad, snowshoelike feet and long, powerful legs. Even on deep hardpack, an adult lynx can overtake the hare's top speed of 30 mph, although both animals are short-distance runners. A snowshoe can turn on the proverbial dime, however, instantly changing direction with leaps of 12 feet or more, and not every chase ends with a fatal bite to the hare's neck.

As snow deepens, the cats frequent brushy areas, again following the hares as their diet turns to buds and bark of staghorn sumac, raspberry, willow, and cherry. In late winter, when the weakest deer are on their last legs, lynx include whitetail and mule deer yards in their daily patrols, but the 40-pound feline won't tackle such large prey unless it's nearly dead.

TRACKS

Lynx have four toes showing on each foot, but unlike the case of bobcats, their front paws are obviously larger than their hind (see the illustration). Although an adult lynx is 25 percent smaller than a bobcat, its feet are nearly twice as large. The paws are as wide or wider than they are long, because of the widely splayed toes. The claws are normally kept retracted unless the animal is agitated, and tracks are usually obscured to some degree, even on mud and snow, by the heavily furred soles.

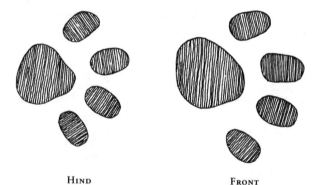

HIND   FRONT

Lynx tracks; 3 to 4 inches long. Front feet are larger than hind; both feet have widely splayed toes and almost formless heel pads. Tracks in snow sometimes obscured by thick fur on soles.

In many instances, the track patterns of a lynx will exhibit an unpredictability common among cats, all of which place their feet in accordance with terrain and stealth. At a normal walk on even ground, the lynx's stride and straddle are virtually identical to a bobcat's, at 14 to 16 inches and 6 to 7 inches, respectively, despite the fact that the lynx has longer legs. And while many animals increase their stride length in deep snow to compensate for the more difficult walking, a lynx's stride remains virtually unchanged, an indication of the ease with which it can travel over snow.

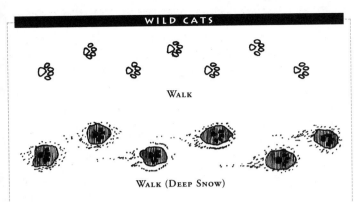

WALK

WALK (DEEP SNOW)

Lynx track patterns as they might appear at a normal walk through mud (top) and snow (bottom).

At a run, the hind feet print nearly beside one another horizontally, with the forefeet printing behind in a nearly vertical pattern, one ahead of the other. The distance between each set of four prints averages 4–6 feet.

SCAT

Lynx scat is virtually identical to the bobcat's in size, shape, and texture, being roughly cylindrical, segmented, and filled with fur throughout. Small rodents are swallowed whole, and their undigested bones may be in evidence, but rabbit hair is predominant in all scat samples. In the few places where bobcat and lynx populations overlap, positive identification by scat alone is almost impossible; the only small difference is that lynx eat more rabbits and hares, and their droppings reflect this.

SIGN

Once again, lynx and bobcat sign are nearly identical. Most obvious to a human tracker are a cat's scratching trees, where it sat back on its haunches and clawed the trunk as a territorial marker, much as does a house cat. Selected trees are usually softwoods such as poplar, aspen, and birch, because claw marks are meant to be visible markers, and these trees display them better than do rough-barked varieties. Conifers are never used as scratching trees (at least not more than once) because of their sticky sap. Claw marks start 3–4 feet up a trunk and extend several inches to more than a foot downward in parallel sets of four, although the outermost claw may make only a faint scratch.

Lynx also mark their territories by spraying trees and bushes with strong-smelling urine, usually near trees they've clawed but seldom on the same trunk. In winter, such sprayings are visible as yellow stains on the snow, but in summer they can best be detected by a strong, musky feline odor.

Lynx eat small prey on the spot unless it's being taken back to denned kittens, but larger prey is cached by covering it haphazardly with forest debris or snow and marking the surrounding area with urine. Tracks surrounding a partially consumed carcass identify its owner, which will return periodically to finish eating it unless deposed by larger carnivores.

VOCALIZATIONS

Lynx calls approximate those of a domestic house cat but are correspondingly louder and deeper. Don't expect to track one down by following its cries, however, because the cat spends most of its life in silence.

One exception to this rule of silence is the brief, early-spring mating season. During this time, mating adults can be downright noisy, particularly the males. If the cry of a mating bobcat sounds like a lost child wailing, that of a mating lynx sounds like the rest of the child's family joining in. It's tough to describe these yowls, growls, and wails, except to say that you'll never forget them once you've heard them.

Another interesting feature of the lynx's voice is its ability to sound as though it's coming from somewhere else. The lynx is nature's own ventriloquist, and more than a few old-timers have admitted to having the dickens scared out of them by wailing cats that seemed to be everywhere at once.

WEASELS
(MUSTELIDAE)
13

THE WEASEL FAMILY IS A diverse group of animals whose members include such unlikely relatives as skunks, otters, wolverines, and badgers. Sizes within this family vary considerably, from less than 2 ounces for the least weasel to more than 40 pounds for the wolverine. All are mostly or entirely carnivorous and well adapted to their habitats, but some, such as the black-footed ferret of our western plains and the wolverine of the northern forests, have been poisoned, trapped, shot, and generally persecuted into extinction over much of their original ranges.

Weasels have five clawed toes on each foot, small round ears, short legs, and low-slung, humped bodies—some longer or stouter than others. All species have a pair of anal scent glands that secrete powerful odors used in social and sexual communication, hence the family name, "Mustelid." Among skunks, these glands have evolved into effective distance weapons (history's first tear gas aerosol) that only a few swift birds of prey can overcome.

For as long as there have been farmers in the New World, weasels have had an often justified reputation as killers of livestock—a problem that has largely disappeared with modern predatorproof construction methods. When farmers began pushing back virgin forests, wolverines saw little reason to pursue fast, sometimes formidable prey with all those helpless sheep and goats available. Smaller weasels apparently felt the same way about chickens. Blameless individuals such as the badger, pine marten, and fisher were trapped for their useful pelts, and the black-footed ferret of our western plains was nearly poisoned out of existence in our unsuccessful war to exterminate coyotes.

WOLVERINE (GULO GULO)

This most infamous of weasels is the family's largest member, with an official weight of 18–42 pounds. Its scientific name means "glutton," an allusion to the insatiable appetite of this typically hyperactive weasel. Some Native American tribes called it "skunk bear," because of its musky odor and the two wide, yellowish stripes running horizontally along each side of its body. The classic Stutz Bearcat automobile derived its name from a description common among white trappers, who hated wolverines

Leonard Lee Rue III

Wolverine

for their cunning in stealing bait from traps—even traps meant for them—without getting caught. Even less endearing was their habit of eating already-trapped animals, marking anything they couldn't eat with foul-smelling urine that not only destroyed the pelt but also made it necessary to boil every tainted trap before it could be used again. But no animal is more diabolical than man, and a great many wolverines contributed their thick, oily fur to make water-repellent parkas.

HABITAT AND RANGE

When I was a boy and camped alone in the deep woods of northern Michigan, I can recall spending an anxious night after hearing on my transistor radio that local conservation officers had reported a pair of mating wolverines headed in my general direction. Twenty years later, a prominent Detroit newspaper carried a full-page excerpt of some fellow's doctoral dissertation for the University of Michigan, which argued that the Wolverine State had never been home to wolverines because the habitat was "wrong."

The truth is, wolverines once inhabited most of the northern United States and Canada, before trapping, poisoning, and the whine of chain saws drove them into the most remote northern regions. Although they've always preferred a colder climate, the primary reason for their continued disappearance is loss of habitat. A single adult wolverine requires up to 1,000 square miles of undisturbed wilderness in which to live, and such vastness is getting scarce in modern North America.

Today, wolverines are found in few of our lower 48 states. There are small populations in northern Washington, central Oregon, and eastern

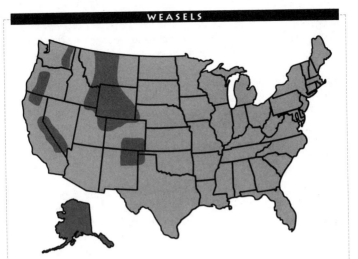

Distribution of wolverine (Gulo gulo*).*

California; slightly stronger populations inhabit the Rocky Mountain range from Montana down through Wyoming and into Colorado. In the Northwest, there are good numbers of them north through British Columbia, the Yukon Territory, and all of Alaska, and they extend east through most of the Northwest Territories, northern Ontario, and northern Québec. It's no coincidence that these are also the most untouched and vast regions of wilderness on the continent.

FOODS

Although wolverines are primarily carnivores, their gluttonous and opportunistic diet also includes insects, fruits and berries, eggs, and roots dug up with their powerful, semiretractable claws. Frogs, snakes, rodents, and spawning fish are eaten as they're encountered, and even an occasional bird will fall prey to always-hungry bearcats.

As a hunter, the wolverine is less than impressive. Its shuffling run of about 20 mph isn't sufficient to chase down most prey, its eyesight is poor, and its hearing is only fair. It balances these deficiencies, however, with an extremely sensitive nose, a powerful body, vicious claws and teeth, and a ferocious willingness to fight that's unmatched among North American animals. It can't catch a deer under normal conditions, but it will eat carrion, and an adult wolverine has both the will and the weapons literally to take kills away from far larger carnivores such as mountain lions and even brown bears. Tangling with a determined wolverine is like fighting a buzz saw, and few large predators are hungry enough to risk certain injury over a kill.

In deep snow the wolverine comes into its own. Its big feet allow it to run atop snow deep enough to bog down hoofed animals, and when its tireless nomadic habits bring it upon a snowbound deer, elk, or even moose, chances are good the wolverine will make a kill. While it might seem incredible that a 40-pound bearcat could kill a moose 30 times its size, remember that a snow-stricken deer's most potent weapons, its hooves, are trapped. In such cases a wolverine eats all it can, then taints the remains with foul-smelling urine that repulses other carrion eaters. It may return to feed again, immune to its own smell, but will probably continue on its way before the corrupted carcass has been consumed, which accounts for its reputation as a wasteful killer.

MATING HABITS

For most of the year a wolverine is as solitary as any animal, but even the orneriest species has to mate to survive. A single male shares his vast territory with two to four females, and with so much real estate to cover, pair members need considerable time to find one another. For this reason the species has an unusually long mating season, which runs from April to September.

The actual mating of a pair is brief, lasting only a few days before the two part. The male will then set out to find another mate, taking no part in the rearing process. The impregnated female simply continues about her business; the fertilized egg remains alive but in suspension inside her uterus, and delayed implantation occurs in January. If food is scarce and the would-be mother isn't sufficiently well fed, the pregnancy will spontaneously abort.

Once implantation occurs, embryos develop rapidly, and the expectant mother must find a secluded birthing den where she and her young can be safe during their short period of vulnerability. Den sites vary with terrain, but may be under the roots of blown-over trees, in rock crevices or small caves, inside large standing stumps, or in abandoned black bear dens. Sites are chosen with defense as well as shelter in mind and have only one entrance.

Gestation takes about three months, with two to five young born from late March through April. Indicative of a highly developed species, wolverine young mature slowly, staying with their mother for two years before striking out to establish their own territories; young males are usually the first to leave. Predation is light, owing to a wolverine mother's fierce protectiveness, with the greatest danger coming from large birds of prey.

SEASONAL HABITS

Wolverines are constantly on the move in search of food, mostly carrion, and can cover up to 200 miles in a single day, a nomadic lifestyle that makes trailing these reclusive animals very difficult. Unlike the cases of many other species, an abundance of food isn't sufficient to keep wolverines in one place for long, and the drive to move on in search of more food is strong, which probably indicates an evolutionary process that included much starvation.

While a wolverine is too slow to be a hunter in the conventional sense, it's also the most powerful animal for its size on the continent, very intelligent, and a strong climber. In winter especially, it will climb trees or rock overhangs above prey trails and lie in wait like a lynx, except in this case the usual tactic is to leap directly onto a passing deer or other animal and dig in with long claws while delivering a fatal bite to the throat. Once again, the species owes its success to an almost unnatural willingness to fight viciously, although even a wolverine will retreat if it appears an opponent might inflict serious injury.

Except for pregnant females, wolverines don't den, regardless of weather. Travels are interrupted with alternating periods of rest every three or four hours, and sleeping places may be almost anywhere, thanks to the protection given by the animals' thick, oily fur. The hours of activity vary as well, largely because human presence is a major factor in making animals adopt nocturnal habits. Still, wolverines seldom exist in places frequented by humans.

TRACKS

Like all weasels, wolverines have five toes on each foot, although the small toes on the insides of both the front and hind paws—opposite our own arrangement—may print lightly or not at all on firm ground. The front paws measure from 4 to nearly 8 inches long, hind paws 3 to about 6 inches, with a broad toe spread making all paws nearly as wide as they are long. The semiretractable claws always show in tracks, but when only four toes print, you might mistake them for wolf tracks at a quick glance. A closer look at the wolverine's uniquely shaped heel pads should clear up any doubts about an animal's identity (see the illustration).

At a walking or trotting gait (the latter is most common), track patterns vary as the terrain demands, but on regular surfaces the pattern tends to

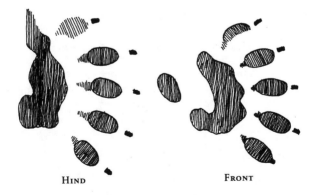

HIND

FRONT

Wolverine tracks; front, 4½ inches long; hind, 3½ inches long. Heel pad may not register on firm ground. Note widely splayed toes and long claws.

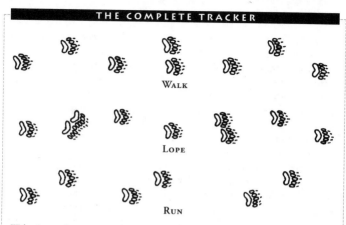

WALK

LOPE

RUN

Wolverine track patterns.

be one forefoot printing 3 to 12 inches behind one hind foot, followed by a side-by-side pair of front and hind tracks 3 to 12 inches ahead of that. The straddle, measured from the outside of one track to the outside of the next, averages 7 to 8 inches. As you can see, even on flat ground there's considerable variation among track patterns at a casual gait.

At a fast trot, track patterns generally show the front and hind feet printing in slightly staggered pairs, the front foot ahead of the hind. The straddle remains about 8 inches, but the stride, or distance between track pairs, varies from 5 to 35 inches.

Moving at an easy, mile-eating lope, which the animal can maintain for hours, the pattern shows one forefoot printing behind paired front and hind tracks, with the last hind foot printing ahead of the pair and the pattern repeating itself every 18 inches or so.

The full-speed gallop of a wolverine shows all paws registering individually in a staggered line, with both forefeet printing behind both hind feet. A complete set of all four tracks measures about 40 to 65 inches long, with more than 3 feet between sets. The stride runs 8 to more than 12 inches.

Even without clear tracks, the wolverine's trail is indicative of its species. Perhaps more than any other animal, wolverines tend to meander, following their keen noses to almost anything that might be food, digging here, scratching there, and ultimately continuing on in the original direction. Remember, the wolverine has been designed by nature to be a supreme scavenger, and the only place it really has to go is in the direction of food.

SCAT

Wolverine scat might easily be confused with that of the gray wolf or mountain lion: All are roughly cylindrical, segmented, tapered to a point at one or both ends, and exhibit bits of bone with copious deer and

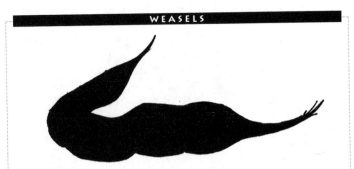

Wolverine scat, 4 to 6 inches long. Contains a variety of fur, hairs, and small bones.

rodent hair. The length averages 4 to 6 inches—often longer, sometimes shorter—and the diameter roughly 1–1½ inches.

Unfortunately, this same description applies not only to wolves and cougars but also to lynx, bobcats, and coyotes. One clue is that wolverines have too large a territory to patrol on a daily or even weekly basis. (Wild felines and canids have established routes that they patrol nightly, usually leaving a scat deposit at the same place or places on each trip.) Also, wolverines don't bother to hide their scat, probably because they won't be back the same way for some time, so partially covered dung with telltale scratch marks doesn't belong to a wolverine. As always, your best strategy is to link scat with tracks and other sign.

SIGN

Aside from its tracks and the evidence it leaves at animal carcasses, a wolverine has one of the lowest profiles of any wild animal. Since it doesn't claim a territory in the same sense as less nomadic predators, it has no need to mark or guard an area against other wolverine competitors. Doubtless its scat and strong-smelling urine warn others of its passing, but a wolverine rarely stays in one place long enough to defend it.

One unmistakable wolverine sign is half-eaten remains of a deer or other large animal tainted with a strong, skunklike odor. I don't recommend approaching any dead carcass, however—that's why a tracker carries a binocular. A wolverine may hang around after claiming a kill, or the carcass might belong to a bear, puma, or some other possessive carnivore.

VOCALIZATIONS

If wolverines have even a rudimentary language, it's unknown. Their calls seem to consist of little more than snarling and growling interspersed with grunts and snorts.

BADGER (*TAXIDEA TAXUS*)

Although half the size of a wolverine, the 8- to 25-pound badger has nearly the same feisty disposition and natural weaponry, and exudes the same, if slightly less potent, skunklike aroma from paired anal musk

Leonard Lee Rue III

Badger

glands when agitated. I once saw all three characteristics close up while driving a remote dirt road, where I encountered a female with a pair of two-month-old babies, just standing to one side as if expecting a bus. Naturally, I pulled right up beside them, and the four of us started at each other across a distance of less than 10 feet. The youngsters standing on either side of their mother were her miniature replicas, and I was impressed by the way all three stood their ground and obstinately refused to go around my car, even though they obviously intended to cross the road. We stared for what seemed like several minutes, and not one of the trio so much as blinked. Finally I could resist no longer; I leaned slightly out my open window, bared my teeth, and hissed loudly.

The reaction was astounding. Mother and young all laid back their lips (the babies barely had teeth) and snarled ferociously, literally jumping up and down in anger although staying in the same place. I laughed so hard tears ran down my cheeks, but you couldn't have paid me to get out of my vehicle.

The American badger gets its name from a smaller European cousin that wears a similar "badge" of white markings on its black face, one on each side emphasizing the eyes and a white stripe running lengthwise from the top of its head to its nose. "Badgering" with trained hounds—bassets were bred for the task—was a popular pastime in the Old World, but immigrants to the New World quickly learned that American badgers are both willing and able to take the fiercest dog apart. The "sport" was discontinued.

Physically, the badger is unique, with powerful but stubby legs holding up a very wide, squat body. Its thick fur, once prized for shaving brushes, is buff colored on the back and interspersed with grizzled gray vertical stripes extending in a random pattern down to a completely grizzled underside. Most distinctive are the black-and-white striped face, short round ears, and pointed, slightly upturned snout.

HABITAT AND RANGE

While most mustelids adapted to life in the forest (otters took to the water), the badger developed a powerful body, long sturdy claws for digging, and a disposition that demands respect from even much larger carnivores. Thus armed, it left the trees and learned to make a living in wide open spaces, where its ability to dig several times faster than a man with a shovel not only enabled it to escape potential enemies but also made it a formidable predator of ground squirrels and other burrowing animals. Able to disappear underground in a spray of flying dirt within seconds, the badger has long been cursed by horsemen of the western plains, who must keep a constant eye out for the holes it leaves, lest they and their mounts go sprawling.

Although badgers are ground dwellers, they also live in forested areas, but only where there are open meadows or fields and the water table is low enough to permit burrowing at least several feet deep. Home territories are generally quite small, because this large weasel isn't well adapted to traveling; territories range from just a few acres to about 1 square mile.

The badger's home range appears to have changed little over the centuries, despite encroachment by civilization. Today, it occupies more than half of the United States from Michigan down through Ohio in the East, west to Illinois, and south through Texas. Its western range includes every state except the heavily forested areas of Washington and Oregon. In the North, it ranges across the southern portions of British Columbia, Alberta, Saskatchewan, and Manitoba.

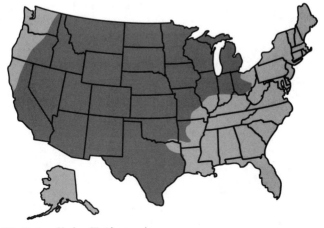

*Distribution of badger (*Taxidea taxus*).*

FOODS

One of the more interesting legends about the badger is its apparent partnership with the coyote, which often shadows the burly, clown-faced weasel as it digs out burrowing rodents, stationing itself at an intended victim's escape exit as the badger excavates the front entrance. In truth, while there's no animosity between the two species—which nonetheless avoid close contact—they're not partners; coyotes have simply learned that this practice often nets them a free meal.

Badgers probably include some roots, fruits, and berries in their diets, but, like all weasels, they subsist primarily on flesh. The species is virtually incapable of climbing trees, but it does sometimes capture birds, and is a strong enough swimmer to pursue waterfowl and their eggs. A nesting goose or swan feisty enough to defend its eggs will probably become a meal itself.

Snakes of all varieties are also a favorite seasonal food, and badgers are renowned for the capacity of their tough, loose hides to absorb rattlesnake bites with apparent impunity; the animals are only vulnerable to bites on their unprotected noses. Insects, frogs, and fat-rich grubs are also eaten in season.

In winter, badgers continue to subsist mainly on rodents, but they won't turn down an easy meal of carrion and are capable of appropriating deer or other carcasses from smaller carnivores. Badgers cache uneaten prey or portions of large prey by burying them under earth or snow.

MATING HABITS

Solitary most of the year, badgers mate in late summer, usually July and August but perhaps as late as September in the Deep South. Males seek out females, the farthest they may ever travel, but fights between rivals are rare and seldom violent, because females outnumber males by roughly three to one. Actual breeding may last only a few days before the two part, with ejected males leaving to find another mate before the rut ends and females foraging voraciously to put on body fat to help nourish the babies. The fertilized eggs remain in suspension before attaching themselves to the uterine wall in January (delayed implantation), where they then develop quickly. If an impregnated female isn't sufficiently healthy and well fed, the eggs will abort. Gestation lasts three months, with two to five blind but fully furred young born in a deep, underground winter den in March or April. The litter size depends largely on how well fed a mother is; the largest litters are born to the healthiest mothers.

Male badgers play no part in the birthing or rearing of their young, but badger mothers are among the best in the animal world. Babies nurse for their first two months and mothers are fiercely protective. After being weaned (which understandably coincides with the development of teeth), babies accompany their mother on foraging excursions, learning to dig, hunt, and kill by watching what she does. Young stay with their mother until late summer, dispersing in late August or September. Males are typically first to leave the family group, striking out to establish their own territories, but they probably won't breed until their second year, especially if there are many other adult males in the region.

SEASONAL HABITS

Badgers are active throughout the year, although in very cold winter weather or blizzards they may lay up in snug dens for several days at a time. As the most powerful and capable digger in North America, the badger is merely inconvenienced by deep snows or frozen ground. An established territory is generally well dotted with previously excavated burrows—something horseback riders know only too well—so easy shelter is always available.

Badgers living in snow country have an advantage not enjoyed by most other carnivores that remain active through winter, in that they have the natural tools necessary to reach hibernating ground squirrels, marmots, and rodents in their deep subterranean dens. In crude terms, these hibernating animals provide a steady, easily obtained supply of fresh meat until spring. Carrion is also eaten, but, although a badger can hold its own against most aggressors, it seldom picks a fight unless very hungry.

One exception to this rule occurs in spring, when hungry badgers sometimes invade the dens of smaller animals, including foxes, to prey on helpless young. Frequently they even occupy dens vacated by owners off on foraging trips, waiting patiently until the unsuspecting prey returns then pouncing on it. Their strong musky odor probably makes this an ineffective hunting method.

Left undisturbed, badgers may be active at any time of day or night, but in places frequented by humans, they're normally mostly or entirely nocturnal. They pose no threat to humans unless provoked (and even then you can simply outrun the clumsy weasel), but pet dogs have been known to make them extremely aggressive.

TRACKS

As much as those of any animal, badger tracks are distinctive, both in shape and pattern. Like all weasels, they have five toes on each foot, and the front paws are noticeably longer and wider than the hind. Measured from claw tips to heel pad, the front paws are 2½ to 3 inches long by about 2 inches wide. The hind paws average 2 to 2½ inches long by 1½ inches wide. The toes of the front feet are nearly twice as long and wide as those of the hind feet, with the smallest toes inside, opposite our own arrangement. The claws of the front feet are exceptionally long—up to 1 inch or more for the three center toes—and distinctly angled toward the inside, or smallest, toe. The claws on the hind feet are much shorter, usually less than ½ inch. All toes and claws generally print in any identifiable track, with the least weight being applied to the innermost (little) toe.

The heel pads of the front feet are boomerang shaped, with the apex pointing forward, toward the toes. Those of the hind feet are unique,

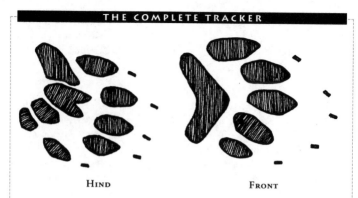

HIND   FRONT

*Badger tracks; front, 2½ to 3 inches long; hind, 2 to 2½ inches long (minus claws).
Note claws run diagonal to toes, a result of the badger's toed-in walk; rear heel pads are
segregated.*

showing four separate sections, with the largest center section appearing in a rough heart shape (see the illustration). The areas between the pads and the toes are well furred, a feature that often shows in tracks.

Badgers have only two gaits: a normal walk and a clumsy, shambling trot of about 10 mph, which they can maintain for short distances. Both gaits exhibit an extreme toe-in pattern for all four feet that's unlikely to be confused with that of any other animal in North America.

The badger's track pattern is noted for being quite variable, but a prototypical pattern left during a casual walk on a level surface, such as hardpack snow, shows front and hind paws on the same side printing atop one another, sometimes with the front track superimposed on the hind, sometimes the reverse. The toe-in angle of all four feet averages 25–30 degrees.

Most of the time, a badger's track patterns are far less predictable, regardless of gait or terrain. Front and hind feet may print atop one

*Badger walking track patterns, hind feet registering in and slightly behind front prints.
Note extreme toe-in walking pattern.*

another in either order; one ahead of the other in either order; side by side; individually; or in any combination. The stride and straddle also reflect this variability, ranging from 6 to more than 12 inches for the former, 4 to 7 inches for the latter.

Remember that the short legs and waddling gait of a badger cause it to leave a sometimes easily identified trail through grass, and especially through snow. Even without clear tracks, though, the animal's toe-in stance and long front claws may be evident, and its low-slung body leaves a trough-shaped trail similar to that of the porcupine, but lacking the broomlike brush marks made by a porky's swinging tail.

SCAT

While badger trails are distinctive, badger scat is not. I wish it were otherwise, but badger droppings are identical to those of many other carnivores with similar diets and body weights. Individual deposits may range from 2 to more than 6 inches in length, have diameters of roughly 1 inch, and contain masses of rodent hair with bits of bone.

Nor do the locations of scat provide certain identification, although it appears to me that badgers don't share the habit of foxes and bobcats of defecating in precisely the same place repeatedly. The only real difference is that badgers tend to be meticulous about burying their scat, while bobcats make only a perfunctory effort to conceal it and foxes none at all. In any case, positive identification can be made only in concert with other badger sign.

SIGN

The most identifiable badger sign is its den, or the excavated burrows of its prey, which may at times be one and the same. Entrances to these burrows conform to the shape of their maker, being roughly oval shaped and wider than they are long. The size, of course, varies with the badger, but den entrances average about 8–12 inches wide, with a height of slightly more than half the width. More so than foxes and other burrowers, badgers tend to pile excavated earth in a single mound in front of their den entrances, and usually there will be recognizable tracks in that loose soil.

Beyond its elliptical doorway, a badger den can be positively identified by rattlesnake rattles scattered around the entrance. This is, of course, no help in the many badger habitats where rattlers don't exist; then, other clues include bones, fur, broken eggshells, and other inedible castoffs scattered around the den's front.

VOCALIZATIONS

Badgers are typically silent unless threatened, and most creatures have little inclination to threaten them. The only sounds that I'm aware they make are the variety of hisses, growls, and snarls mentioned at the beginning of this section.

RIVER OTTER (*LUTRA CANADENSIS*)

I met my first river otters several years ago while hacking a trail through dense willow and cedar branches on the bank of a wide stream running through thick swampland. It was a hot day, and sweat made the many scrapes and scratches I'd received sting like the devil. The going would've been easier farther away from the thick undergrowth that always borders wilderness waterways, but I knew that my best chance of seeing something really cool would come from sticking to the streambanks.

Sure enough, I was squirming between abrasive young cedars when I heard splashing directly ahead. I dropped to hands and knees to crawl forward cautiously, but my cover was already blown. When I peeked up over the waist-high sawgrass, I was greeted by five river otters sitting upright on their haunches in the shallow water, staring right at me. I wasn't quite fast enough to get a photograph before all five simply vanished beneath the water, but I sure took home a terrific memory.

Leonard Lee Rue III

River Otter

HABITAT AND RANGE

While most weasels are land carnivores, the river otter and its much larger seagoing cousin, the sea otter (*Enhydra lutris*), have adapted to an amphibious life with a vengeance. The difference in size—11 to 30 pounds for the river otter versus 25 to 80 for the sea otter—is most likely an adaptation to different environments, prey, and enemies. Aside from their habitats and sizes, the most obvious difference between the two is coloration: a silvery gray throat and longer tail for the river otter, and a yellowish or grayish head and neck for the sea otter. Similarities include

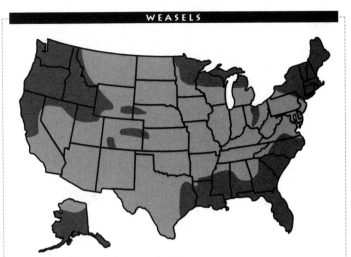

Distribution of river otter (Lutra canadensis).

the thick, dark brown fur once prized by trappers, prominent gray-white whiskers, webbed feet, small round ears, and a black button nose.

True to their name, river otters are found mainly around remote streams and rivers, but you may also find them around relatively undisturbed inland lakes, watery marshes, and beaver ponds. Territories are extremely variable, ranging from less than 1 square mile to more than 50, depending on the availability of food, human intrusion, and the species' own population density. While unregulated trapping took a heavy toll on otters until the 20th century, these days toxic air and water pollutants—especially mercury and other heavy metals that collect in fish—are blamed for wreaking havoc on some populations. The good news is that river otters seem to be making a comeback, and some think they may be evolving a resistance to man-made poisons.

Today, river otters are gone from most of the interior regions of the lower 48 states, although there are small, isolated populations in a few places. Large, established populations are found in the Northwest from northern California through Washington, extending eastward through Montana, Idaho, and Wyoming. To the northeast, otters are found in northern Minnesota, Wisconsin, Michigan, and up the East Coast from New York to Maine. Their southern range includes Louisiana, Mississippi, Tennessee, Alabama, Georgia, Florida, South Carolina, North Carolina, and Virginia. Otters occupy most of Canada, except for Alberta, Saskatchewan, and Manitoba. Their range also extends to all but the northernmost portion of Alaska.

FOODS

Otters are strictly carnivorous, and their reputation for hunting expertise is due at least in part to their being perhaps the most playful land animals in the world. While other predators must spend all or most of their waking hours in pursuit of prey, river otters are such efficient hunters that getting a full belly occupies only a small part of their days, leaving plenty of time for amusement. Fish make up most of an otter's diet throughout the year, and only the very largest, such as salmon or sturgeon, are immune to the otter's sharp teeth and incredibly fast swimming speed. "Sport" fish such as bass, pike, and trout are occasionally eaten, but slower-moving "trash" fish—suckers, carp, chubs, and bullheads—are more easily caught and thus favored. Based on my own observations, sport fishermen who blame otters for depleting gamefish populations will find the true culprits in a mirror. Small catches are typically eaten while the otter floats on its back, while larger fish are hauled onto shore or the ice of a frozen lake to be eaten.

Crustaceans such as clams, snails, and, especially, crayfish also make up a large part of the river otter's diet. Unlike the sea otter, which often uses a rock to crack open mollusk shells, river otters usually open fresh-water clams by simply pulling the halves apart. Crayfish are eaten whole, as are frogs and snakes.

Mammals are preyed upon as well, and otters constitute the only seri-ous threat to beavers. Adult beavers, which may weigh up to four or five times as much as an otter, are safe enough, but beaver young (kits) are fre-quently snapped up in lightning-fast attacks if they venture too far from the protection of parents or older siblings. Even the feisty muskrat keeps its distance, and will probably sit tight in its streambank den when otters are in the area.

On land, the otter isn't nearly so nimble as its smaller cousins—the fisher, mink, and ermine—but it can run quite well despite its webbed hind feet. Rodents are snatched from hiding places under logs, waterfowl nests are raided for eggs in spring, and ducklings, goslings, or swan cygnets are safe only when far from the water. Even chipmunks and red squirrels are sometimes driven into the water, where they become easy prey for the torpedo-like otter. In a nutshell, an otter considers almost any creature small enough to be handled as prey, if it can be caught.

MATING HABITS

Where populations are stable, otter pairs may mate for life. Two to three otter young are born in an enclosed den during March or April. Immediately after giving birth, females mate again, carrying their fertil-ized eggs in a state of suspended animation until January, when they attach themselves to the uterine wall and begin developing. If an expec-tant mother isn't fit enough to nourish her developing embryos, they spontaneously abort.

Birthing dens vary. Many are in enlarged muskrat dens in the side of a stream- or lake bank, some may be in hollow logs or stumps, and occa-sionally dens of gray or red foxes are appropriated, even though they might be several hundred yards from water. In a few instances, abandoned beaver lodges have also served as ideal otter dens, and these may be used year after year. Dens are lined with sticks and grasses.

Otter young are born blind but fully furred. Although parents spend most of the year together, the father is driven off by the mother just prior to denning. After 10 to 12 weeks, the mother leads her young out for a swimming lesson, during which tired babies often rest and sometimes nap atop their floating mother. At four months, young are weaned, and at six months the father is allowed to return, although he contributes little to his offspring's upbringing.

At eight months the young disperse to establish their own territories and find mates, and during this time wandering youngsters, already quite capable of fending for themselves, may be seen far from water. Males sometimes fight for females with much chittering, squealing, and snarling, but injuries are rare.

SEASONAL HABITS

In snow country, the best-known otter habit is its penchant for sliding along snow or icy surfaces on its belly. Because these highly efficient hunters have so much time on their hands, so to speak, and so many available calories to burn, sliding surely is done just for fun. Natural inclines are often used for "sledding," sometimes by groups, but level surfaces work, too. The usual procedure begins with a good running start, followed by a strong push-off with all four feet and ending with a slide, with front legs tucked under the body and hind legs trailing behind. Speeds of 15 mph can be achieved, with slide lengths reaching 20 feet or more.

Since fish make up a large part of otters' diets at all times of year, their presence in a given area often coincides with annual spawning runs: suckers in April and May, pike and some species of trout from May through June, and small salmon and fall-spawning trout from October through November.

In frozen lakes and ponds, you can sometimes detect otters by the fishing holes they make through the ice. The average diameter of these holes is about 2 feet or less, and, like seals, otters keep them open through continuous use; an active hole in ice several inches thick wasn't dug through all that ice, but simply kept clear as the ice thickened around it.

Ice holes are generally over shallow water, no more than 5 or 6 feet deep, because, although an otter can remain submerged for five minutes or more, it isn't a deep diver, and most of the fish it preys upon are shallow-water bottom feeders. (Remember, too, that otters, beavers, mink, and muskrats all use the layer of air trapped under ice to extend the time they can stay beneath it.) With their thick, oily coat of waterproof fur, otters are impervious to the effects of cold. Fish too large to be eaten in a single bite are brought onto the ice, where roving coyotes frequently do their best to appropriate them and ravens wait for scraps. Once again, following the sign and sounds of hungry winter scavengers can often prove productive for a dedicated wildlife observer.

Otters have little to fear from larger carnivores, because few would waste energy chasing such elusive prey, and fewer still are hungry enough to accept the serious bites a cornered otter will almost certainly inflict on its attacker's nose. One exception I've seen myself is the bobcat, which at least occasionally catches otters on solid ground, probably pouncing from hiding, and eats them.

With the exception of near-term mothers-to-be, otters seldom den except in the fiercest weather, or when a recently matured adolescent is on the move to establish its own territory. Acceptable sleeping places include thick branches or logs overhanging the water, secluded brush-piles, or almost any spots that are both defensible and escapable. In any season, most of a river otter's sleeping time is probably spent taking short catnaps.

Since otters can usually be counted on to relocate away from a habitat where the scent of humans becomes common, those observed in the wild may be active at any hour, and they actually seem to prefer going about their business in the daytime. In the few places where otters and people live together, mostly in national parks, the animals may become strictly nocturnal.

TRACKS

Like all members of the weasel family, river otters have five toes on each foot, but unlike land weasels, they have webbing between the toes of the hind feet. The downside of this is that webbing rarely prints, and then only in soft mud or wet, loose snow. In coastal areas where river and sea otters coexist, remember that sea otter tracks are about twice as large and shaped differently, and that the webbing of their hind feet usually registers in a track.

The front tracks of the river otter measure 3½ to 4 inches long by 3 to 3½ inches wide. All five toes normally print, arrayed in a widely spaced

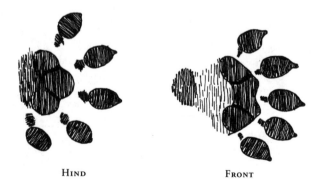

Hind   Front

River otter tracks; 3 to 4 inches long, forepaws slightly larger than hind. Note wide spacing of toes and distinctive heel pads.

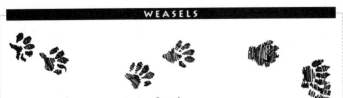

River otter track pattern, running in soft mud.

semicircle, with short claws showing. The pad behind them leaves two distinct impressions. What would be, in human terms, the ball of the foot prints with four identifiable lobes in a clear track; the heel shows as a lighter, oval-shaped mark behind it (see the illustration).

The hind tracks have generally the same dimensions as the front, but the features of the two are readily distinguishable. The pad behind the toes prints as three distinct lobes, with the largest in the center. Again, all five toes generally print, but the smallest, innermost toe prints by itself well behind the others (see the illustration). The webbing between the rear toes seldom prints definably, although a close look may reveal the curved line of the webbing's edges running between the toes.

In deep snow, the otter exhibits the humpbacked jumping gait common among long-bodied weasels (looking rather like an inchworm). Its tracks will likely be indefinable at the bottom of the trough left by its sliding body, but all four feet print together as the otter travels over snow in leaps, landing usually with its forefeet directly ahead of its hind. This produces what appear to be pairs of elongated tracks printing side by side, with the distance between each pair running between 1 and 2 feet; the tracks look as though they'd been left by a long-legged biped.

In any other medium at any other gait, expect the river otter's track patterns to be variable and always changing, with both front and hind tracks likely to print in almost any pattern imaginable. At a walk, prints tend to register individually in a staggered formation, but this doesn't occur reliably enough to be a factor in identification. Complicating matters is the otter's tendency to change gaits regularly, intermittently walking, leaping, and running. The easiest way to determine an otter's gait from its tracks is by the distance left between sets of four tracks, which averages 12 to more than 15 inches at a running gait.

SCAT

River otter scat is among the most easily identified of any animal, especially in warm weather, but many outdoorsmen see it without knowing what it is, or even that it's scat. From spring through autumn, otter scat is commonly found along trails (rarely of their own making) near the edges of riverbanks or lakeshores, and its most distinguishing feature is its slimy consistency and green color. "Shapeless" most accurately describes these semiliquid masses, which may be deposited on grass, forest humus, downed logs, or fallen trees that extend into the water. Closer inspection will reveal fragments of crayfish shells, fish scales, and a few rodent hairs.

Apparently, a mostly seafood diet is very rich and lacking in what the TV ads call "dietary fiber."

A more solid form of scat appears in winter, when otters become surprisingly efficient rodent hunters, despite their small ears and webbed hind feet. Follow any otter trail through snow and you'll likely see both the places where its maker dove under snow after a rodent (or to elude an enemy), and dark, brown-black scat deposits that are hard to miss. Scat typically contains as much hair and bone as that of the coyote, bobcat, or fox, and has generally the same physical characteristics: It's segmented in lengths of 2–6 inches, roughly cylindrical, and has a diameter of ½ inch to slightly greater than 1 inch. Tracks are always the best way to identify scat, but I've noted an occasional streak of green slime in winter scat that seems unique to otters, along with some fish scales.

SIGN

The most obvious otter sign is the slide. These troughlike depressions pushed several inches into the snow and extending up to 20 feet are common sights at otter wintering grounds. A slide in deep snow averages about 1 foot wide, and the extent to which it has been compacted by sliding bodies is an indication of how much otter activity is taking place in the area.

Snow slides also have warm-weather counterparts. River otters love to roll and slide, and if snow isn't available, grass makes an acceptable substitute. They'll slide on their bellies down grassy banks, leaving obvious trails of flattened grass, and level grassy areas frequently show flattened places where otters have been rolling from side to side. Be careful not to confuse summer slides with the wider dragging trails made by beavers hauling tree branches down to a pond or stream: Otter slides average 8 to 10 inches wide; beaver slides are more than a foot wide.

Like beavers and muskrats, river otters mark their territories, but where those aquatic rodents construct sometimes elaborate scentposts of mud, sticks, and grasses, otters use simple tufts of twisted grass marked with scent from their anal glands. These obscure scentposts are easy to miss, although their locations are fairly obvious from an otter's ground-level perspective. From a human perspective, they're often made more noticeable by nearby rolling places and slides.

VOCALIZATIONS

River otters are quite vocal and capable of a wide variety of sounds. The most common one I've heard is a repeated guttural grunting, which some have described as a "chuckle." The meaning of this sound, if it has a specific meaning, isn't clear, because it's heard among groups of otters as well as from solitary individuals talking to themselves as they meander along. A high-pitched whistle serves as a long-distance gathering call.

Mothers with young make soft clucking sounds to reassure them, but a whole range of barks, grunts, growls, and yips is also heard. Easiest to positively identify is a sharp, barking chirp—an alarm signal and a command for youngsters to gather close to the protection of Mother.

Male otters make the most and the loudest noises during the early-spring mating season. The whole spectrum of otter sounds can be heard at this time, but battle cries between mating males (which seldom actually fight), are high-pitched, prolonged chitterings that can be heard at some distance through the woods.

MINK (*MUSTELA VISION*)

No fur-bearing animal in the world is better known than the mink, and none has had greater commercial value. Its fur is long and lustrous, perhaps the silkiest in the animal world, and until recently owning a mink coat was the dream of every civilized woman.

The problem is, with an average weight of 1½ to 3½ pounds, it takes a lot of mink to make a coat. The little weasels have never been endangered, despite centuries of trapping, but difficulty in obtaining sufficient numbers of pelts has always guaranteed a premium price for mink garments. Wild mink are still trapped today and there's still a market for

Mink

pelts, regardless of antifur sentiment, but the majority of mink accessories nowadays are made from ranch-raised animals.

Adult mink have a body length of 12 to 20 inches, with a thickly furred tail 5 to 9 inches long. Fur coloring is uniform, ranging from chocolate to very dark brown, with white patches under the chin and on the chest, sometimes with spots of white on the underbelly. Two cousins are the long-tail weasel (*Mustela frenata*) and the arboreal pine marten (*Martes americana*). Differences with the long-tail weasel include the weasel's shorter body length of 8 to 15 inches; its shorter, lighter-colored fur; and its underside, white from chin to tail. The marten, or American sable, has dark brown to almost yellow fur with a darker underbelly and tail, and a distinctive patch of orange-buff fur extending from each side of its neck down over its chest. There's little danger of confusing the mink with the fisher (*Martes pennanti*), which is similar but lacks the white chin patch and may be six times larger.

HABITAT AND RANGE

Mink are creatures of the forest but, like otters, always live near water. They can climb trees, but seldom do, instead making their living on the ground near streambanks, marshes, and ponds.

Not surprisingly, mink are excellent swimmers, though not to the same degree as otters. Thick, oily fur makes them immune to the effects of cold water, and they hunt as well and as often in the water as they do on land. With such an effective coat of insulation combined with an ability to travel easily across deep snow, they're at home in virtually any environment that offers both trees and water.

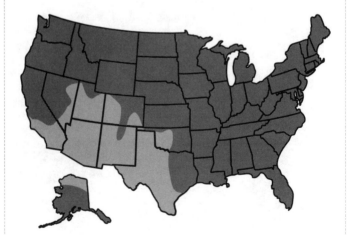

*Distribution of mink (*Mustela vision*).*

Currently mink range across all but the arid southwestern portions of the United States, habitats that lack the trees and water mink need to survive. Mink are absent from an area extending from Texas to southern California, north to Nevada, and generally eastward to Kansas. They're common throughout Canada and Alaska, ranging north to the Arctic tundra, where only a lack of forest prevents them from making a living. The species is far from endangered, despite the value of its pelt and the fact that many experienced outdoorsmen have never seen one of these elusive weasels in the wild. Mink generally avoid any chance of contact with humans, but there are always a few incidents of marauding mink snatching an easy meal of chicken, eggs, or rabbit from farmers.

FOODS

Mink are strictly carnivorous and partial to wetland habitats; crayfish, fish, and snails form much of their diets (clams appear to be too difficult for them to open). Frogs, hatchling turtles, turtle and bird eggs, and flightless waterfowl young are eaten in season, while frogs and newborn snapping turtles provide easy meals in snow country, with mink diving through maintained holes in ice-covered ponds to dig these hibernators from their muddy beds.

Mink are also efficient land predators, and no mouse, vole, shrew, or mole is safe at any time of year. Typical bundles of weasel energy, they roam constantly during their waking hours, nosing under logs, into stumps, and among brushpiles for any opportunistic meal that reveals itself by sight, sound, or scent. In deep snow, mink trails are often punctuated by the marks of sudden dives beneath the surface to pursue rodents; the mink sometimes emerges as much as 15 feet from where it went under. Mink frequently invade winter cottontail dens under brush and fallen trees and may appropriate them as their own. Red squirrels are preyed upon, but not chased above the ground unless a mink can trap them on a branch overhanging open water. Small prey is generally eaten where killed, but larger pieces are usually hauled by the neck to a nearby den, where they're cached under dirt and forest debris and eaten at leisure. Mink will eat carrion, but must relinquish any claim to foxes and coyotes—which also eat mink.

As both species are so well adapted to dual environments, it seems only natural that mink should have evolved the same predator/prey relationship with muskrats that exists between, for example, lynx and snowshoe hares. Their ability to escape into and under water keeps the 1 to 4-pound muskrats safe from most predators (otters take a few), but an adult mink can outrun them on any terrain, and taking to water is no protection against a hunter that swims and dives as well as they do. Muskrat dens in the sides of streambanks are invaded and frequently appropriated, but the species' high mortality rate to mink and other carnivores is offset by the fact that muskrat females can produce several litters of up to 11 young per year.

MATING HABITS

While the mink shares many traits with its much larger cousin, the river otter, sociability isn't one of them. Two adult mink of either sex can be counted on to scrap like prizefighters upon meeting, with males being particularly vicious toward one another in any season.

But mink must overcome this antisocial attitude to mate, and they do so in January and February. Mating is initiated by females coming into heat, and the old adage, "breeding like minks" (I'm paraphrasing), is appropriate to describe the polygamous nature of both sexes. Whereas females in most species mate with only one male per season, male and female mink alike take a number of partners in a single mating season. Some believe that males eventually settle on one mate, but the point is moot because adults have nothing to do with one another beyond the act of procreation.

Pregnant females give birth to three to six young in April or May. Birthing dens may be existing muskrat burrows, hollow logs, or even abandoned beaver lodges. Wherever they are, birthing dens are lined with a soft floor of feathers, fur, and grasses to help keep the blind and naked newborns warm during the first, critical weeks.

Suckling mink develop quickly, peeking out of the den at about one month and gradually gathering enough strength to accompany their mother on her hunts. At five to six weeks, when young have the beginnings of sharp teeth, mother weans them. They'll stay close to her throughout the summer months, learning to hunt on land and water and relying on her for protection from foxes, bobcats, and, especially, hawks and owls. Each of these predators also takes adult mink, but such a fearless and ferocious opponent is never their first choice.

In September or October, young males born the previous spring are large enough and smart enough to fend for themselves, and they strike out to establish their own territories. Males usually mate in their first year, competition permitting. Young females may remain with their mother well into winter, but will definitely be ejected before she mates again.

SEASONAL HABITS

Mink are perhaps the closest thing to perpetual motion in the animal world; they're always on the move, hunting, fishing, and apparently just playing at times. They have an otterlike tendency to slide on their bellies over ice and snow, especially down slippery slopes, but mink slides are, of course, always correspondingly smaller and shorter.

While it's true that mink tend to use dens for giving birth and laying up in a particularly good hunting spot or during an especially bad storm, it's also true that they rarely hang out in one place for more than a day or so before moving on. Since they never wander far from water, and because muskrats are their natural prey, most mink dens are repossessed muskrat homes dug into the side of a bank, with entrances 4 to 6 inches in diameter. The size of a mink's home territory depends on the availability of

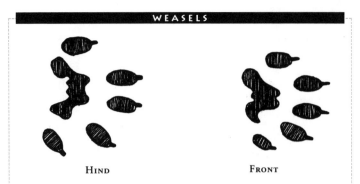

HIND   FRONT

Mink tracks, 1 to 2 inches long, front feet larger than hind. Note offset little toes, like thumbs.

prey, the number of predators, and competition from other mink, but probably never exceeds 2 square miles.

TRACKS

Like other weasels, mink have five toes on each foot, with the smallest inside toe printing lightly or not at all on firm ground. Like those of the wolverine, a mink's claws are semiretractable and usually, although not always, register in tracks. Since males are larger than females, their tracks are correspondingly larger, but the claim by some trappers that a recognizable difference exists between male and female mink tracks has never been proved to my satisfaction.

A mink's front feet are noticeably larger than its hind, averaging about 1¾ inches long for the former and 1½ inches for the latter; widths are about the same as lengths. The heel pads of the front paws leave an inverted-V impression, and the rear heel pads are also distinctive (see the illustration). Note that the inside toes of each foot are not only the smallest but also are offset below the others, like thumbs. In soft mud or snow,

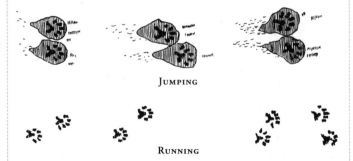

JUMPING

RUNNING

Mink track patterns. Top: normal jumping gait in light snow; note striations in snow ahead of tracks, indicating a slower pace. Bottom: running tracks in mud; note that all four feet print individually.

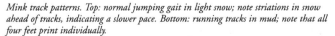

mink tracks reveal the animal's furry soles, which sometimes blur track features in winter.

In deep snow, a mink's trail shows the twin-dot pattern common among long-bodied weasels that travel atop the snow in a sort of inchworm fashion. In this gait, the front feet come down first, with the hind feet then brought forward to land mostly behind the front tracks. Their long bodies and short legs give mink the humpbacked running gait most folks associate with weasels, as well as the characteristic paired tracks that look as if they'd been left by a long-legged biped. The straddle averages 2½ to 3½ inches, with the stride, or distance between pairs, ranging from 1 to 2 feet, but adjusting with changes in terrain. The twin-dot pattern is unique to weasels, and is usually linked by a broken, troughlike depression left by the body.

At a run on more solid ground, track patterns are somewhat variable, but in every case, the hind feet land in front of forefeet, all four tracks print in some type of close group, and track sets are well separated.

Two running patterns are most common: The first is a slower run, in which all four feet print in a slightly staggered line running diagonally to its maker's direction of travel. The distance between sets is about 1 foot.

At the second, a fast run, all four feet again print independently but take on an irregular box-shaped pattern, with the forefeet registering in pairs well behind more widely spaced, paired hind tracks. The distance between track sets increases to more than two feet.

SCAT

Mink scat isn't radically different from that of other small predators, including foxes, skunks, and, sometimes, bobcats. It's usually cylindrical, 4–5 inches long, segmented, and black in color when fresh. Muskrat fur and bone fragments are predominant, along with those of smaller rodents and often fish scales and fragments of crayfish carapaces. Segments are

Weasel scat. Scat usually shows fur, hairs, and small bones. Barring differences in size and minor variations in diet, these samples are characteristic of all weasels, including skunks.

typically held together by strands of fur, and often double back on themselves in a U shape.

A lighter-colored form of mink scat exhibits the same characteristics but contains an abundance of feathers, indicating a diet of birds. Close inspection will reveal the feathers of wrens, tits, sparrows, and other plentiful swamp birds—most of them snatched from sleeping perches at night—as well as the undigested down, feathers, and bones of young ducks and geese.

It's important to remember that, although mink scat is easily confused with that of foxes and some other carnivores, the mink doesn't share their habit of staking out and patrolling a regular territory, with scentposts freshened routinely. Individual scat deposits are the norm, and likely places to find them include beaver lodges, half-submerged logs, large rocks or downed trees on shore, or other prominent landmarks.

SIGN

The most common year-round mink sign is its den, which can tell you a great deal about the owner. Mink can dig their own dens but seldom need to; instead, they set up housekeeping in existing muskrat burrows, often evicting the previous owners by eating them. Converted dens are normally found just above the waterline in stream- and lake banks, and to the untrained eye are little more than 4-inch-diameter holes. A closer look will reveal scraps of fur and bone around den mouths, most of it muskrat, but sometimes there are fish skulls, feathers, and eggshells, depending on the season.

Mink regularly dive under snow in pursuit of rodents or to elude predators, as do otters and smaller weasels. A trail that suddenly stops in deep snow will reemerge at some point within a 15-foot radius.

When ice covers lakes and slow-moving streams, mink continue to forage underwater through holes that are maintained and used repeatedly to keep them open, from the first freeze until spring. Hole diameters correspond to the little weasel's size, averaging about 4 inches, and are easily distinguished from the much larger holes (10 inches plus) of otters.

VOCALIZATIONS

As they're solitary most of the year, mink are generally silent unless fighting a rival or prey, or mating. There are no particular calls that might be considered proprietary; in fact, the sounds mink make are virtually identical to those of many other weasels. This is not to say that mink don't utter a wide variety of sounds, however; among them are birdlike screeches, hisses, snarls, and growls. Such sounds almost always mean the weasel is strongly preoccupied and thus less likely to notice the approach of a stalking human.

Another sound that mink make is a purring noise, much like a house cat, generated when the animal is content, as a mother suckling her babies. This sound is low and quiet, and usually cannot be heard in the wild.

ERMINE OR SHORT-TAIL WEASEL (*MUSTELA ERMINEA*)

Anyone who has heard of a mink coat has doubtless also heard of ermine stoles and collars. White ermine, with its distinctive black-tipped tail, is also the traditional trim for robes worn by European royalty.

This tiny weasel weighs just 1½ to about 6½ ounces, with males almost twice as large as females. Yet its thick white winter coat has known nearly the same popularity as that of the mink. Individuals of the long-tail weasel (*Mustela frenata*) species also turn white in winter, and their pelts are also known as ermine. Note, however, that neither the long-tail nor the short-tail weasels turn white in their southernmost range; this only happens in places where snow covers the ground from late autumn till spring. In summer, ermine closely resemble two of their near cousins, the least weasel (*Mustela nivalis*) and the long-tail weasel, but there are notable differences. Like ermine, least weasels have a medium brown coat, with a white underside from chin to tail, and white feet. The least weasel weighs only 1¼ to 1¾ ounces, about one-third the size of an ermine. The long-tail weasel, of course, has a longer tail—3¼ to 6½ inches compared to 1¾ to 3½ inches for the ermine—and is also about three times as large, weighing 3 to 9½ ounces. The long-tail weasel also has a medium brown coat and a white underside, but it has brown feet; its smaller cousins have white feet year-round.

Like all weasels, including skunks, ermine are tough, ferocious little fighters that most predators—and prey—quickly learn to avoid, although large owls and red-tailed hawks are always serious threats. I saw a good example of the ermine's feisty attitude one cold winter night when my six half-grown Airedales surrounded one outside my bedroom window. I

Ermine

Irene Vandermolen/Leonard Rue Enterprises

flipped on the yard light in time to see all six jump in, snarling and snapping, to kill this scrappy intruder, only to scatter yelping as the embattled weasel performed a fair imitation of the Warner Brothers Tasmanian Devil character, drawing blood from most of its attackers. The pups kept a respectful distance as the ermine faced them for a few more seconds, hissing; its mouth open to show needlelike teeth, before it scampered off into the woods.

HABITAT AND RANGE

While ermine are essentially forest dwellers, they're among the most versatile of weasels and can adapt to just about any environment that offers sufficient ground cover for them to hide and hunt. An ermine's home territory seldom spans more than 2 acres and may be in a forest, swamp, or marsh, or on a farm where corn and grains attract rodents, their primary prey. They aren't really welcome on farms, where they eat eggs, kill chickens, and even attack large livestock, but farmers who weaselproof chicken coops and outbuildings reap the benefits of having some of the most voracious rodent hunters on earth working for them.

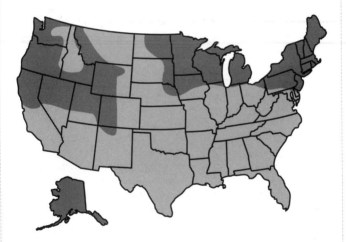

*Distribution of ermine or short-tailed weasel (*Mustela erminea*).*

Ermine have never been endangered, despite trapping and poisoning by farmers, but their range is definitely limited to northern forest regions. They cover all of Alaska and Canada except southern Alberta and Saskatchewan, and extend south through Minnesota to northern Iowa, east through Michigan to Connecticut, and north to Maine. In the West, where most nonwhite ermine live, their range extends down the Pacific Coast to northern California, east to Wyoming, and north through western Montana.

FOODS

Ermine, long-tail weasels, and least weasels are strictly carnivorous, and wherever they live, rodent numbers are kept within manageable limits. Voles, mice, rats, frogs, insects, and many kinds of small snakes are eaten, all of them killed when the ermine leaps onto their backs with all four feet, followed by a lethal bite to the base of the victim's skull.

Birds are also taken, usually at night as they roost or nest. Ermine are comfortable traveling among tree branches, and their ability to leap nearly 4 feet bodes ill for birds roosting too close to the ground. Eggs are favored when available, and most smaller birds are no match for this feisty weasel, which will happily eat them if they come within reach.

MATING HABITS

Ermine are unusual among weasels in that both parents take an active role in rearing young. Adults mate in midsummer, usually in July, but females carry fertilized eggs in stasis until January, when they either attach themselves to the uterine wall and begin developing or are aborted, depending upon the mother's health.

Three to nine young are born in March or April in a fur-, feather-, and grass-lined birthing den that may be located under a rock, in a hollow log, inside a thick brushpile, in an appropriated gopher hole, or between the walls of an outbuilding. Dens always have more than one exit and are usually equipped with several.

Ermine young are born tiny, blind, and covered only with a fine fuzz. They develop slowly compared to most small mammals, with their eyes opening at about 35 days, and are totally dependent on Mother's milk for two months. At about six weeks they venture outside the den, playing with the energy typical of their tribe, and begin eating prey brought to them by both parents. Males are probably never allowed inside the birthing den, but when the young are mature enough to roam, Mother and Father play an active role in feeding and protecting them.

Parents stay together until September, going their separate ways when the young disperse to establish their own territories. The same pair may breed again in the following mating season, but sexually mature young are ejected to avoid inbreeding.

SEASONAL HABITS

Traits common to all long-bodied weasels, from the otter to the least weasel, are superabundant energy, an insatiable appetite, and an almost frantic zest for living. The ermine exemplifies those traits, with its ceaseless wandering throughout a small home territory that seldom exceeds 2 acres. Ermine young recently ejected by the parents may be seen wandering more or less aimlessly from late summer through autumn, searching for a suitable territory to call their own. Those with established territories patrol them day and night—mostly night if humans are nearby—and, despite a fairly meandering trail, cover a lot of ground. Scampering, leaps of up to 2 feet, and dives into deep snow are punctuated by short catnaps, sometimes in one of perhaps many dens, and frequent meals of rodents that are pinned to the ground in a pounce, then dispatched with a piercing bite to the back of the skull.

Ermine and their close cousins are almost cocky at times, diving into deep snow at the approach of a human only to reappear as much as 15 feet away, regarding the intruder intently before disappearing under the snow again. Sometimes this is repeated several times, with the little ball of energy alternately disappearing and popping up again at different places until it tires of the game and leaves.

While most of their prey is captured on the ground, ermine are adept at navigating through tree branches, and sometimes take squirrel young, nestling birds or eggs, or red squirrels cornered in a tree-trunk food cache. Gray squirrel (*Sciurus carolinensis*) litters, born in spring and late summer in hollow tree trunks and leafy nests among tree limbs, are favored seasonal foods, although a much larger gray squirrel mother who stands her ground may convince a little weasel to move on to easier prey.

Like all weasels, ermine are very good swimmers, and often pursue frogs, baby ducks, or small rodents into the water. They also catch tadpoles in spring.

TRACKS

Ermine have five toes on each foot, with the smallest toes on the inside. The small toes print lightly or not at all, even on good tracking surfaces such as mud and snow, although the hind feet are likely to print the hardest. All four feet are the same size, averaging about 1¾ inches long by ¾ inch wide, with furry soles that help obscure print details, especially in winter when coats are thickest. When heel pads do print recognizably, those of the hind feet show as triangles of dots, sometimes connected in a track, with the peaks of the triangles pointing forward. The heel pads of the especially thickly furred forefeet print only lightly, appearing as a more or less shapeless dot.

In deep snow, ermine exhibit the familiar twin-dot leaping track pattern common among long-bodied weasels, where the front and hind feet

HIND   FRONT

Ermine tracks; front, 1 to 1½ inches long; hind, 1½ to 2 inches long.

LEAPING

RUNNING

Ermine track patterns. Top: leaping pattern, a slow gait; note that all four feet register individually. Bottom: running pattern showing that hind feet sometimes register in front tracks.

on each side land in the same place to leave what appear to be the paired, side-by-side tracks of a hopping biped. The distance between track sets (leaps) averages 1 to nearly 4 feet (sometimes more); the surface of fresh snow will be marked with grooves about 4 inches across left by the leaping weasel's body. The distance between shallower impressions left outside the tracks by the ermine's haunches measures about 4 inches, and the straddle between the outermost edges of hind tracks runs 2 to 3 inches. Track patterns in loose sand are similar, but typically have a much narrower straddle, with all four tracks leaving a single impression, kind of like a single row of dots.

Like the mink, ermine and other lesser weasels seldom walk, but go everywhere in leaps, bounds, and scampers. On level, solid ground, a running ermine's track pattern varies from the twin-dot pattern described above to track sets that appear as three or four individual prints. In some cases, front and hind tracks are superimposed on one side, while those on the opposite side print individually, one behind the other. At other times, all four prints may register individually, the hind tracks printing in front of and slightly wider than the tracks of the forefeet. The length of a set of all four tracks is 3 to 4 inches, with leaps between sets running about 1 foot.

SCAT

Scat of mink and lesser weasels are virtually identical except for size, because all share similar diets. Mink scat typically contains rodent hair, as well as coarser fur and bone from muskrats, which are too large for ermine to handle. Ermine scat contains a large amount of fine rodent fur at all times of year, and here there's a minor distinction between the droppings of the two weasels that share the name "ermine." Short-tail weasel scat ranges from approximately 1 to 1½ inches long by ⅛ inch in diameter at its widest, is tapered sharply at each end, and is usually curved, with longer samples having a U shape. The color is near black.

Long-tail weasel scat is generally larger, with a length of 1½ to 2 inches and a diameter of ¼ inch at the widest. Scat is always tapered at one end, but sometimes the other end is bluntly rounded. The drawback to these little differences is that they aren't always reliable, and sometimes scat from the two weasels is identical.

Ermine are more conventionally territorial than most weasels because their range is so small, and scat deposits are freshened regularly at established scentposts around its perimeter. You may also find accumulations near, but never inside, dens where ermine have holed up to wait out a blizzard or severe rainstorm. Sharp-eyed hikers often find scat left at the side of a trail or dirt road, usually beside or on a tree, stump, or rock, and these sometimes prove to be regularly used scentposts. The late Olas J. Murie noted that ermine scat is often found near coyote scat, but while this is obviously some sort of territorial behavior, its meaning isn't clear.

SIGN

It stands to reason that the smaller an animal is, the less noticeable its sign will be, and it pays to think small when looking for ermine sign. In winter, the most obvious sign is its trail, twin dots partially connected by long drag marks over the surface of the snow. At intervals along these trails you might find scat and an occasional clear track, but perhaps most notable are the "diving holes" left in fresh snow, where an ermine dove under after prey, to escape an owl or fox, or just for the fun of it. Short-tail weasel holes range from 2 to 3 inches in diameter; long-tail 3 to 4 inches.

The same measurements hold true for summer dens, whose entrances are purposely kept small to make them more defensible should the napping weasel find itself cornered by a larger predator. In such a situation, an ermine will also exude a powerful skunklike odor, making it less appetizing and helping discourage even hungry predators. Ermine dens can often be identified by this pungent aroma, as well as by scatterings of rodent fur and bones near the entrances—but not inside.

Prey or carrion that proves too large for an ermine to haul to a nearby den is cached after the animal eats its fill, and will be revisited until it has been either consumed or appropriated by a stronger carnivore. Caches are partially covered with bits of grass, leaves, sticks, and dirt, and frequently have scat deposits within a few yards of them, left as a territorial claim.

VOCALIZATIONS

Ermine are more vocal than most members of the weasel family because mates travel together for a longer time, and because both parents take part in rearing young; in a nutshell, ermine have someone to talk to more than most of their cousins.

Aside from this, ermine share pretty much the same range of calls as other weasels, including chirps, whistles, hisses, snarls, and screams. They also chatter when excited, sexually or otherwise.

You can often coax ermine (and mink) into poking their heads out of a den by making a small squeak like a rodent, and some predator calls that mimic rabbits will accomplish the same thing.

RACCOON (PROCYONIDAE)
14

RACCOON (*PROCYON LOTOR*)

When I was a boy, I hunted raccoons both to put meat on the family dinner table and for the money I got from selling the tube-skinned pelts to a local furrier. I was the oldest of six kids in a household where most processed food was labeled "USDA," so fishing and hunting had a more serious intent for me then than they do today. I had no dog and simply snuck close enough to send the coons up a tree, where my trusty Remington 580 single-shot .22 dispatched them swiftly with pelt-saving head shots. The meat, which tastes a bit like mutton, was never a favorite of mine, even after removing as much of its rancid-tasting fat as possible—a necessary step before cooking.

Leonard Lee Rue III

Raccoon

It's also necessary to understand that wild raccoons are not the cuddly critters from the TV shows, but exceptionally tough and ferocious fighters when injured or cornered. I've seen them whip game dogs twice their size, even luring hounds into deep water where the coon actively tried to drown them. I don't hunt raccoons anymore, but if I did, I'd want an autoloading .22; I had to reload that old single-shot of my boyhood too often at a fast run.

Anyone old enough to watch cartoons can recognize the raccoon's distinctive mask, short ears, and fluffy ringed tails. In real life, the raccoon weighs (officially) from 12 to 48 pounds, although I've taken two that reached nearly 60 pounds, both old females. A high-humped back and rocking run make the species recognizable even in silhouette. The body length, including the tail, runs from 2 to more than 3 feet, with a tail 7 to 16 inches long banded with four to six dark stripes. The raccoon's thick fur is typically grizzled gray with the infamous black mask around the eyes and ears, but brown and rust are also common fur colors. As is the case with many species, individuals are generally larger in the North.

Closely related to the raccoon are the coatimundi, or just coati (*Nasua nasua*), and the ringtail (*Bassariscus astutas*), both of which are much smaller and more slenderly built, and both of which occur well south of the burly raccoon's northern range.

HABITAT AND RANGE

Raccoons are generally creatures of the forest, where their ability to climb trees can be used to advantage, but a remarkable adaptability and broad diet make them at home virtually anywhere except open prairie, deep desert, and high rock. Habitat nearly always includes a slow-moving stream, pond, or lake where crustaceans, mollusks, and insects are found in abundance. Fresh, clean water is probably even more important in

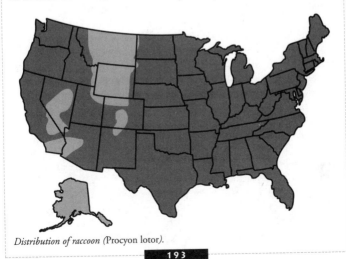

*Distribution of raccoon (*Procyon lotor*).*

determining suitable raccoon habitat than trees. Their home territory ranges from about ½ to 1 square mile, depending on the availability of food, but emancipated youngsters might wander for miles.

Raccoons are comfortable living close to humans—raiding gardens, carrying off chickens, stealing eggs, and strewing unprotected garbage everywhere. These and other social infractions make them a nuisance in rural areas, but in suburban communities they can be aggressive and dangerous when they lose their fear of humans. Even worse, when populations grow beyond manageable limits, nature culls out some of the weaker individuals with the horrible disease of rabies.

The current range of raccoons covers nearly all of the lower 48 states, except the plains of Montana, Wyoming, and parts of Kansas, and the deep deserts of Arizona and Nevada. They're common in the southernmost portions of Canada, from British Columbia through Québec, but they stop well short of Canada's northern interior, and there are no raccoons in Alaska. To the south, the species reaches far down into Mexico, seemingly as capable of living in a subtropical jungle as in northern hardwoods. From its range we can conclude that the raccoon, with its thick fur but hairless soles, is poorly adapted to extreme cold, and that a permanent water supply and trees are essential factors in its choice of habitat.

FOODS

As with bears, it would be easier to list what a raccoon won't eat than to itemize a diet that includes just about anything organic, but here are a few examples: frogs, tadpoles, crayfish, clams, snakes, insects, grubs, berries, fruits, roots, flowers, mice, rats, voles, and carrion—the latter only if food is scarce. And as many suburban- and rural-dwelling humans know, coons are also very much attracted by the spicy smells of people food, and are masters at opening garbage cans. A flexible trash can with a lockdown lid is a good defense, although they'll eventually learn to open it. Under no circumstances approach a wild raccoon; the tamer it appears, the more likely it is to attack in defense of food or young.

Probably the most common image of a feeding raccoon is of one at the waterside, "washing" its food before consuming it. Indeed, the word *lotor* in its scientific name translates to "the washer." In reality, a raccoon "washing" its food is kneading and tearing at the flesh (fruit or animal) in search of indigestible or possibly dangerous materials, such as bone fragments, pits and seeds, arrowheads, or shot pellets. Few other carnivores can do this; because they don't have the raccoon's remarkably dexterous, fingerlike toes and so must swallow small prey whole, excreting indigestible matter later. Raccoons aren't finicky eaters, as some believe, they're just utilizing their natural intelligence and tools to make life a bit easier.

Raccoons' affinity for water makes streambanks and shorelines good places to look for the mostly nocturnal animals at sunset and before sunrise. Beachcombing is a favorite way to forage for clams and crayfish, and turtle eggs or hatchlings are preferred delicacies from May to July.

Farmers often strongly dislike raccoons because they help themselves freely to chickens, rabbits, eggs, and garden produce. I dispatched one on the family farm after it had run off with 24 chickens and roosters in less than a month. A mother raccoon with young can seriously damage maturing corn crops by breaking down stalks to get at the ears; often a cornfield provides enough food and room for several individuals and families to feed in harmony. Predatorproof enclosures can protect small livestock, but crop damage continues to be a problem.

MATING HABITS

Raccoons mate from December through February, later in the North than in the South, to match the birth of one to seven kits to the onset of spring. Males seek out females, the only time these normally sedentary animals travel far—up to three to four miles—from their home territory. Competition for females is slight because they outnumber males by three or four to one in any given area, and courtship battles are pretty much limited to aggressive posturing, with a high-arched back, much hissing and chattering, and a showing of teeth. Breeding normally lasts no more than a few days; the male is then ejected to search for another mate, or, if mating season has ended, to return to his home territory.

Most young are born in April and May in a leaf-lined den, usually located in a standing hollow tree, but sometimes in a hollow log, in a dry culvert, inside the walls of an abandoned outbuilding, or in the appropriated den of a coyote, muskrat, or woodchuck. The birth weight of newborns is a tiny 2 ounces, and the blind young are totally dependent on their mother. They open their eyes at three weeks and by two months have taken to roaming about, but never far from, the den entrance. Mothers leave them for short foraging excursions at night; at these times owls, the most dangerous predators upon young raccoons, keep an eye out for wandering delinquents.

At three months the youngsters being accompanying their mother on her foraging expeditions. Few predators are willing to brave the ferocious fighting nature of a coon mother, who pushes her young up the nearest tree then turns to defend them—to the death if necessary.

By September the fast-growing young raccoons are weaned, weigh 6 to 10 pounds, and can fend for themselves. Most stay with their mother throughout autumn before dispersing, however, with males leaving earliest. Female young typically remain longer, but are forced to leave before their mother mates again. Many of these young females will become pregnant their first year and have to find their own birthing dens.

SEASONAL HABITS

Raccoons of both sexes are solitary. Because mothers spend all summer and autumn raising young, a gathering of raccoons is always a family group. In a wholly natural environment, they may be seen foraging at any time of day, but most raccoons living near humans are strictly nocturnal.

The species' common name is a distortion of the Algonquin a-roo-coon, which means "scratches with hands," and, as with most Native American names, it appropriately describes this animal's most distinguishing characteristic. Possessing nearly the same manual dexterity as monkeys, raccoons can grip and carry off items (including my binoculars, one time), or manipulate catches, locks, and doorknobs that are beyond the means of other animals. As mentioned previously, garbage cans are frequently raided, and even cabins are invaded and looted by the masked bandits.

Raccoons have permanent, year-round dens. Most are below ground, whether in a dry culvert or under the roots of a tree, and provide a cool place to sleep away the heat of a summer day. The animals never hibernate, but during particularly cold or harsh weather may lay up in a cozy den for several days at a time, until the weather improves or hunger drives them out to forage.

Although they don't sleep away the winter months, raccoons are otherwise remarkably like bears in their diets and habits. They claw open rotting wood and turn over rocks and logs to get at spiders, worms, and grubs, and the same late-summer berry patches that attract bears also draw raccoons. And, like bears, raccoons are strongly driven in late summer and autumn to put on a layer of fat against the coming of winter, gaining about 25 percent of their original body weight. August through October is a good time to observe raccoons of all ages, as their urgent need to fatten up makes them more active than at other times of year.

TRACKS

Like weasels and bears, raccoons have five toes on all four feet, each tipped with a short, sharply curved claw. And like bears, porcupines, and humans, they walk plantigrade, or flat footed, with the entire surface of each sole making contact with the earth. Contrast this with the natural tendency of deer, canids, and most four-legged animals to walk on their toes, ready to flee or give chase instantly. A flat-footed walk always indicates two things about any species: It has little fear of natural enemies, and it can't run fast. As with other flat-footed species (the exception is humans), a raccoon's smallest toes are on the inside, acting almost as thumbs and printing more lightly than the other four.

A raccoon's forefeet are nearly handlike, with long "fingers" that give each foot a length of 2 to 2½ inches. Note that the toes are visibly wider at the tips. On mud and snow in particular, toes are often widely splayed to increase the amount of surface area they cover, thus providing more support on soft surfaces. On firmer surfaces, raccoons—like most plantigrade species—exert most of their body weight downward on the outsides of the soles of all four feet, so a partial track may show only a faint outline of the outer edges.

The rear feet, which average 3 to 3½ inches long and strongly resemble our own, cover enough area by themselves to support the coon's

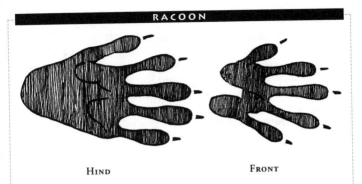

HIND   FRONT

Raccoon tracks: front, 2 to 2½ inches long; hind, 3 to 3½ inches long. Note long, finger-like toes that provide near-human manual dexterity

weight on soft surfaces, so the splayed-toe characteristic isn't as common in hind prints. The toes of a raccoon's hind foot are far longer than our own, almost qualifying as fingers, and are tipped with sharply pointed, sharply curved claws that help make it one of the best tree climbers in North America.

Raccoons have another trait common among flat-footed species, from apes and bears to humans: Their normal gait is a relatively slow, shuffling walk in which the sole of each foot skims the earth as closely as the terrain permits. Such an easy, almost lazy walk allows omnivores thoroughly to scour their territories while conserving calories, which might better be utilized as winter fat.

At a normal walk, raccoon track patterns are fairly distinctive. Aside from identifiably shaped prints and extralong toes, their most unusual feature is that the foreprint usually registers ahead of the hind track of the opposing foot, always in pairs. Changes in terrain may cause tracks to print side by side or partially to overlap one another sidewise. Also notable is the way raccoons walk in a heel-toe manner, where the toes of all four feet point directly ahead. The stride, or distance between pairs of front and hind tracks, varies considerably with the terrain and size of the animal, but may range from 6 inches to more than 2 feet. A wide straddle that averages 3 to 4 inches, but sometimes reaches more than 6 inches among large, old animals, reveals how broad and powerfully built this species is.

Raccoon walking track pattern as it might appear in mud. Note that all four feet register individually.

At a run, raccoons adopt the "rocking horse" gait common among most quadrupeds, in which hind feet land ahead and to the outside of foreprints in sets of four, usually individual, tracks. Running speeds depend on an animal's size and weight, but 15 to 18 mph is probably average, which means an adrenaline-charged human can easily outrun a coon in a fair race. The stride at a full run may reach 3 to 4 feet, but remember that this animal isn't a long-distance runner, and it will frequently slow to a walk or, if pursued, turn to fight or climb a tree.

SCAT

Raccoon scat is fairly distinctive. Deposits generally consist of two or three individual segments 1½ to 2 inches long by roughly ¾ inch in diameter. The color is dark brown to black; older deposits turn white with age. The texture is rough and irregular, showing seeds, bits of bone, some fur, parts of crayfish carapaces, and an occasional feather.

Raccoons patrol their typically small territories regularly, and, like bobcats and coyotes, they establish scat scentposts that are freshened daily at dusk and dawn.

Raccoon scat. Individual segments 1½ to 2 inches long, often showing seeds.

SIGN

The best place to begin scouting for raccoons in any habitat is at the waterside. From the first warm days of spring to the first hard freeze of winter, raccoons spend most of their waking hours at shorelines, where they dine on clams, crayfish, and an occasional spawning fish caught in the shallows. This prey, along with other food taken elsewhere, may be brought down to the water's edge to be sorted through and cleaned of indigestible materials.

In any established territory, raccoon tracks in the mud of a shoreline will always lead to a well-used trail marked by scat scentposts and an occasional track. The biggest problem for trackers is that most of this territorial route will probably be a worn deer trail, which provides easy walking for a host of other species as well. Careful study of the muddy or sandy portions of these generic trails will often reveal clear tracks, and sphagnum moss will hold the recognizable outline of a raccoon's foot for as much as a day.

When they're excavated, raccoon dens are always found on high ground, but hollow standing trees are the best places to look for active dens in any forest environment. The entrances are usually located well above ground, out of reach of larger carnivores that might eat the young while Mother is away foraging. The trunks of den trees will show many scratch marks from the claws of climbing coons; these are fairly obvious on smooth-barked beech or poplar trees but require closer inspection on rough-barked oaks or maples. The bases of den trees are usually marked by accumulations of scat around their bases.

VOCALIZATIONS

Raccoons are generally silent, but they do have a broad range of calls. No one really knows what they mean, but different sounds appear to have specific applications. Once, while lying camouflaged at the edge between forest and field, I was approached by a mother coon with three youngsters in tow. None was aware of my presence, and when they came within 10 feet I began to wonder just how the mother might react if she suddenly found herself face to face with a man. When I rose to shoo the family off with quiet hisses and hand waving, the mother, a youngster herself, sent the family up a nearby tree with a sharp, high-pitched bark, then joined them. They ruined my deer hunt, but I did get to hear a wide variety of chirps, chatterings, and sharp little barks from all four animals. I also heard a soft purring sound, much more audible than a cat's purr, that seemed the equivalent of baby talk.

Raccoons can be quite loud. One May evening, while I was observing a family out foraging, I saw another adult, probably a male, approach the group. The mother reacted with a warbling screech that was startling, followed by screams and much chattering. After a quick scuffle, the male broke and ran past my hide with the female close on his heels, both making high-pitched warbling noises punctuated by shrill screeches.

OPOSSUM
(MARSUPIALA)
17

VIRGINIA OPOSSUM
(DIDELPHIS VIRGINIANA)

Many think the all-American opossum belongs to the rodent family because of its pointed snout, beady eyes, and naked, ratlike tail. Actually, this sole North American species of marsupial is more closely related to Australia's kangaroo, wombat, and bandicoot. With adult weights reaching 14 pounds and a body length of up to 21 inches (*sans* tail), opossums are far larger than any rat, and their 50 sharp-pointed teeth—more than any other land mammal in North America—in no way resemble the gnawing incisors of rodents. Other visual differences include grayish to brownish to almost white fur, normally grizzled; an unusual pink nose; nearly naked pink-tipped ears; and a sharply pointed snout with long white whiskers. Whatever the body color, the head is always lighter colored, even white.

Leonard Lee Rue III

Virginia Opossum

Another real difference is the opossum's long, pale, prehensile tail—one that can wrap around and grip objects. This ability allows the animal to use it as a fifth "hand" to hang from tree branches, like some monkeys and unlike rodents.

HABITAT AND RANGE

When I was growing up in northern Michigan, there were no possums; it was commonly believed that the winters were too cold for them to survive. By the early 1980s, it became obvious that this theory was flawed, and as of this writing opossums are found up to the northernmost tip of Michigan's lower peninsula, despite several recent winters of record-breaking cold. As the late great Olas Murie predicted in his book, *A Field Guide to Animal Tracks*, way back in 1954, "Undoubtedly [opossums] will eventually occupy the greater part of the country, except the coldest and the most arid regions."

In fact, the opossum originally occupied only a few states in the American Southeast. It was never popular as fur or meat, although it has served as both, and this—combined with a diet that includes almost anything organic—has allowed populations to expand. The animals are not well adapted to cold weather, but in the Far North they've learned to den up during cold spells and subsist largely on the carrion of winter-killed or road-killed animals. Weather notwithstanding, possums are capable of making a living in virtually any type of habitat, from oak forest to cedar swamp to brushland, so long as the terrain provides suitably secure denning places. In most cases, their home territories are near open water.

Today, opossums occupy the eastern half of the United States from South Dakota down to Texas and well into Mexico, extending eastward to the Atlantic Coast but stopping in extreme southern Maine. Isolated

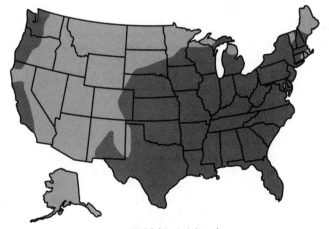

*Distribution of Virginia opossum (*Didelphis virginianus*).*

populations are also found in Wyoming, New Mexico, and along the Pacific Coast of California, Oregon, and Washington. Except for the southern peninsula of Ontario, between Michigan and New York, none are known to live in Canada. Yet.

FOODS

Opossums can and do eat almost anything digestible, which has caused humans to label them "garbage eaters." In truth, opossums do relish the spicy scraps found in garbage cans, and they frequently venture close to houses to raid these food sources under cover of darkness. Unlike the case of raccoons, however, closed trash containers are usually beyond opossums' abilities. Their weakness for garbage makes them relatively easy to bait into camera range with inexpensive table scraps.

In a more natural environment, the opossum's diet is as varied as any omnivore's, consisting of insects, bird and turtle eggs in spring, crayfish, small rodents, berries, fungi, fruits (especially apples), farm crops (especially corn), frogs, snakes, and road-killed animals not claimed by larger carnivores. In snow country, most of its diet comes from winterkills, the bodies of which it may actually inhabit, using the rib cage as a temporary den while stripping meat from the carcass.

As a hunter, the opossum is better off scavenging. Its nose is very keen, but its eyesight is poor, its hearing is only fair, and it runs too slowly to catch anything faster than a mouse or a snake.

MATING HABITS

Like rodents, opossums are prolific, with females bearing up to three litters of 11 to 14 kits per year. There's no fixed breeding season; mating is prompted by the scent of females coming into estrus. Opossum kits are born in a sheltered den just 12 to 13 days after the female becomes pregnant, but as marsupials, their birth is actually a two-stage process. Blind, hairless, and about the size of a honeybee, each of the so-called "living embryos" makes its way independently from the birth canal, climbing along the mother's fur until it reaches her belly pouch. Once there, newborn kits crawl inside and attach themselves to one of 11 to 13 nipples, where they remain for the next two months. Those that don't find a nipple, or are too weak to make the journey (mothers won't help them), die of starvation.

After about 60 days, the youngsters emerge from their mother's pouch, still smaller than newborn kittens but ready to begin eating solid foods. Helpless, they ride about on Mother's back for their first few weeks in the outside world, but development is swift thereafter, with kits striking out on their own at three to four months. The life span is thought to be about seven years.

One of the more ridiculous myths about possums is that males mate with females through their nostrils. This outlandish belief, which persists, stems from the male's unusual forked penis, but the truth is that mating occurs in a conventional manner, with males mounting receptive females from behind.

SEASONAL HABITS

Opossums are most famous for "playing possum," a surprisingly effective defense against predators more commonly seen in insects and lower animals. When a predator attacks, or sometimes even approaches, an opossum may just fall over on its side or back, tongue lolling out one side and eyes closed, and may even defecate to make itself smell dead. In some cases these feigned fatalities can last for hours.

Often, though, a surprised possum will make a show of ferocity, opening its mouth to show its many teeth, drooling, and hissing loudly. If this doesn't work, it will play dead. And if playing dead doesn't stop a predator from trying to eat it, the opossum will fight—but only as a last resort, because it can't run fast enough to escape, and even a large specimen is no match for most carnivores in a fight.

If opossums are territorial, it isn't apparent. Scat serves probably to warn intruders that an area is taken, but the meanderings of most opossums are dictated almost entirely by food, or perhaps sex, and there seems little emphasis on proprietorship of land. Like most animals, they may follow already established trails out of convenience, abandoning them at the first hint of trouble, sometimes by retreating up a tree. Roadways are frequently crossed repeatedly at the same point, and the same shorelines may be revisited often, but an opossum's travels are dictated more by its nose than by any territorial instinct.

The classic opossum image is of a nocturnal animal, but this isn't always the case. Those living in close proximity to humans, feeding not only upon our crops but also upon the rodents that plague us, may be active exclusively at night; in a wilderness setting, however, they may also move about by day, particularly in winter when food is scarce.

TRACKS

The most commonly heard description of opossum tracks is that they're "star shaped," an allusion to the extra wide spread of the animal's toes. There are five toes on each foot, front and hind, but possum tracks are unique, and there's little danger of confusing them with those of other 20-toed animals such as raccoons or weasels.

The front tracks of the opossum measure 1½ to 2 inches in length, with an average width of 2 inches, or slightly wider than they are long, because of the widely splayed toes. The three center toes are longer than the two outer toes, with both of the latter being almost identical in length and thickness (in contrast with most other four-footed animals, which feature the smallest toes on the inside). All five toes are tipped with short claws that show in tracks, though not prominently.

But the opossum's hind feet are what make identifying its tracks a sure thing. As with the forefeet, the three center toes are longer than the outer

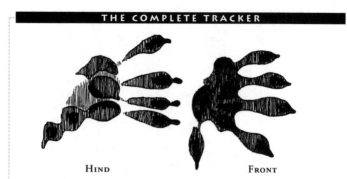

HIND   FRONT

Opossum tracks; front, 1½ to 2 inches long; hind, 2 to 3 inches long. Note thumblike toes on each foot.

toe on either side, but in this instance they print side by side, like pickets in a fence, rather than being splayed. The outermost toe is nearly as long, but it's widely separated from its neighbors. The innermost resembles a thumb, and like our own thumb, it's opposable (see the illustration), printing far to the side and sometimes pointing backward. Note also that the rounded tip of the inside hind toe has no claw, while the other four are tipped with short claws that show in a clear track.

Since opossums are slow moving by design and have little to gain from running, nearly all of their track patterns reveal a walking gait. In a normal pattern, the front and hind tracks on each side tend to register side by side in pairs, with the front track to the inside, much like the raccoon's. Depending on terrain and walking speed, tracks may be superimposed, or sometimes the forefeet print in front. The length of the stride, or distance between pairs, averages 7 inches but may range from 5 to as much as 11 inches. The stride averages about 4 inches.

Opossum walking track pattern in mud. Note long, thumblike toe of hind foot; all four feet print individually.

SCAT

Opossum scat varies with diet. Most samples are segmented, vaguely cylindrical, and irregular in shape. Segments from adults typically measure 1 to 2 inches long by ½ inch in diameter, and are sometimes connected by fur or fiber. The color and consistency also vary with diet, from soft and black with visible seeds throughout to brown and firm with

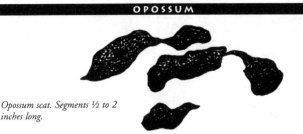

Opossum scat. Segments ½ to 2 inches long.

an abundance of rodent and animal hairs, or any combination in between. Old scat pales with age, turning white after about a week before crumbling back into the earth. Of course, this description also applies to the scat of many other species, including coyotes, bobcats, and foxes, so you should never base an identification on scat samples without additional sign to confirm it.

Unfortunately, location isn't much help, either. The trails that wandering opossums follow on their forays for food and sex are seldom of their own making—which again applies to many other species—and scat deposits might be found almost anywhere. A good strategy is to begin any search for opossum scat near favorite seasonal feeding spots, such as cornfields, streambanks, and berry patches.

SIGN

Opossums are low-profile animals in that they don't go out of their way to make their presence known to other animals, even of the same species. If they have scentposts or other territorial markings that can be detected by humans, I don't know what they are.

Nevertheless, they do leave sign, and probably the most noticeable of these are dens. With their short claws and relatively delicate "fingers," opossums are poorly equipped for digging, so in most cases dens are made from the abandoned homes of other animals, most notably the gray fox, woodchuck, and raccoon. Occasionally, porcupine dens in standing trees are appropriated, and often dry culverts, crawl spaces under abandoned outbuildings, hollow logs, or junked cars serve the purpose. Dens are lined with leaves, grass, and feathers, made as comfortable as possible because their owners spend a lot of time in them, especially during daylight. Established opossums usually have several dens, each located close to a seasonal food source.

Other sign includes crayfish carapaces, left at a shoreline, grasshopper legs, and bits of rodent fur. The problem is that all of these are common sign of a number of other animals as well.

VOCALIZATIONS

Opossums have a limited vocabulary. They're silent most of the time but, when faced with a potential enemy, hiss loudly and may emit a not-very-intimidating growl.

BEAVER
(CASTORIDAE)
16

BEAVER (CASTOR CANADENSIS)

No animal has more influenced the development of North America than the beaver. Nature's own construction worker, this large aquatic rodent changes the environment to suit its own needs, building dams to insert large ponds in the middle of small streams and, as a side effect, providing habitat for many other species. Fish that can't live in fast-moving water are brought in as eggs stuck to the feathers of waterfowl, themselves drawn to

Leonard Lee Rue III

Beaver

beaver ponds to feed on aquatic plants that live only in still waters. From these simple beginnings develops an entire habitat, complete with its own complex food chain. Mink and otters prey on muskrats (and beavers) that live there, while deer and moose feed on the lush vegetation in and around established ponds, themselves attracting larger predators, from bobcats to bears and mountain lions. Ospreys, hawks, and owls find nesting places in trees killed by flooding, and the abundance of food fish, rodents, and small birds that set up housekeeping around beaver ponds provides food for them and their young. No animal does more, or even as much, to sustain its own environment than the beaver.

Beavers have also had a real impact on the growth of civilization in North America, and some of the most powerful financial empires on the continent owe their beginnings to trading in beaver pelts. Beavers are native only to North America, and, because the first European explorers had never seen an animal that could actually build houses and forge a habitat suited to its needs, the first reports sent back home were exaggerated, to say the least. According to these often ridiculously illustrated records, beavers were intelligent, near-human bipeds living together in villages on lakes they'd created, with humanlike social structures that, according to some, included beaver chiefs wearing feather headdresses. Some of these tall tales doubtless were inspired by the beaver's large size: Adults typically weigh from 45 to 60 pounds, but in the past, weights of up to 110 pounds were fairly common.

The truth finally won out, but that spelled even more trouble for the beaver. Renaissance-era Europeans created a huge demand for its thick, lustrous pelt, while trappers and frontiersmen soon realized the practical value of warm, waterproof coats made of beaver skins. Top hats worn by Abraham Lincoln and other 19th-century notables were also called "beavers," an obvious allusion to their construction. Worse still for the big rodent, its flesh, especially the flat, fatty tail, were considered delicacies (the meat *is* very good). By the 1900s, beavers had been trapped to extinction in many areas; demand for pelts subsided only when trapping regulations were implemented to protect remaining stocks and beavers became unaffordable.

HABITAT AND RANGE

Beavers always live in some sort of flowing waterway, from small lowland creeks that can be backed up to form a pond to rivers as large as the Mississippi. But unlike the muskrat and otter—the latter is the beaver's most important enemy—a beaver also needs trees, especially poplar, aspen, and birch. These species, along with a few shrubs such as willow and viburnum, provide the food and building materials necessary for beavers to live.

Despite being driven to endangerment just a few decades ago, the beaver is now found almost everywhere in the lower 48 states except peninsular Florida, most of Nevada, and southern California. To the

*Distribution of beaver (*Castor canadensis*).*

north, beavers are at home in all but the northernmost regions of Canada, and occupy about one-third of Alaska's southwest. Today, beavers not only have made a comeback, but also have overpopulated areas where natural predators have disappeared, causing problems when their dam-building activities flood power lines and human habitats. Unfortunately, trapping is very hard work, and antifur rhetoric has damaged the pelt trade to the point that trappers themselves have become endangered. Rather than protecting the species, antifur forces have placed control of beaver numbers in the hands of government agencies, whose idea of pop-ulation control historically has been limited to poisoning and shooting, which benefits no one.

FOODS

Unlike most members of the rodent order, beavers are strict vegetarians. They eat a variety of aquatic and land plants in season—cattail shoots, pond lily roots and stems, violets, and plantains—but the beaver's main source of food is trees. Food trees, naturally, are those most often found along streambanks: poplar, aspen, cottonwood, basswood, and white, silver, or yellow birch. Aspen and poplar are mainstays all year, but shrubs such as river willow are also important, and occasionally pine, maple, or cedar is felled—the latter apparently more for construction purposes than for food.

One prevailing myth is that beavers eat wood, but a quick look at their cuttings reveals that they eat only the bark of younger, smooth-barked trees. Tree trunks too heavy to move are gnawed clean where they lie; branches are hauled to the safety of water after being cut into manageable sections of 6 to 8 feet in length, depending on their diameters. The beaver sits upright on its haunches like a prairie dog and grips a section of limb with nimble, fingerlike front toes, gnawing off bark as we eat corn from a cob. Limbs are rarely found near the tree they came from unless the owner was chased off midmeal; they're instead dragged off to be fitted into some niche in the rodent's lodge or den.

The beaver's ability to chew through wood is the stuff of legends. A typical adult can fell a 10-inch, 30-foot-tall cottonwood in about six minutes. It always uses what it cuts, however, and the trees it takes are among the fastest growing in North America. While people often regard beavers as destructive, in a natural habitat the rodents do only good, by toppling tall trees that shade out new growth and providing a valuable source of food for other herbivores that couldn't reach it otherwise.

In late autumn in snow country, beavers cut branches from food trees and anchor them solidly into the mud at the bottom of the pond. When ice covers the pond and hard weather makes land foraging difficult to impossible, beavers holed up inside a lodge make periodic trips through its underwater portal to retrieve branches from this submerged larder. Limbs are usually brought back inside the lodge, although beavers can chew under water, thanks to voluntary muscles that seal the mouth (and also the ears and nostrils) behind the incisors. Their underwater food supply can sustain an entire beaver family till spring.

MATING HABITS

Beavers mate from late January to early March at a pond new pairs established the previous summer or, in the case of older pairs, perhaps several summers before. Gestation is four months, with up to eight young, called kits, born in May and June. Litter size largely depends on the availability and quality of food, ultimately represented by the female's physical health, but four kits is average. Kits weigh about 1 pound at birth, and are born fully furred with open eyes. They can swim well but not dive at two weeks, and it may be more than a month before newborns develop the breath control necessary to swim out of the lodge. When they do, youngsters will frequently be seen hitching a ride on their mother's back when they tire of swimming. Kits are weaned at about two months and quickly learn to use their long incisors to gnaw through wood and feed themselves on bark.

Beaver families are unusually close knit. Parents mate for life unless one dies, and kits remain with them for two years before leaving to establish their own ponds. One of the species' odder traits is the way year-old youngsters not only get along with the previous generation but also actually care for and may even defend younger siblings. Because they have so many baby-sitters, newborn kits enjoy constant attention. This highly social behavior means that a given beaver pond could boast as many as 18 individuals most of the year, except for a brief period in early spring, when two-year-olds are ejected and the pond matriarch has yet to give birth to the next generation.

Males are usually the first to leave the community, in their second spring, but females follow closely behind. Newly emancipated youngsters instinctively select a place for their own pond that won't interfere with their parents' home—except where population densities are extreme. From late spring to midsummer, solitary adolescents may be seen wandering in almost any type of terrain (I've even seen them on a sandy Lake Michigan beach) as they travel 10 miles or more in search of a new home. Most find a mate along the way, almost certainly by scent, and the two work together to find a suitable location for their own pond before mating in late winter.

SEASONAL HABITS

The beaver's unusually strong social structure probably evolved as a "strength in numbers" type of natural defense. Many predators eat beaver young, among them otters, hawks, owls, alligators, bobcats, lynx, coyotes, and foxes. Adult beavers are formidable fighters when threatened; Captain Meriwether Lewis of the Lewis and Clark expedition (1803–06) nearly lost his 200-pound Newfoundland dog on that journey after a cornered beaver ripped its throat open. But few predators of any size will face an adult beaver when youngsters are available, and it seems likely that having so many potential victims could confuse an enemy long enough for all to escape.

Spring is the busiest—and most dangerous—time for members of a beaver clan. It's imperative that their lodge entrance remain at least a foot under water to help keep out predators and to keep it below the freeze line of the pond, and a torrent of melted snow or spring rain poses a serious threat to the dam. Strong as those mud-and-wood constructions are, heavy flooding can sweep them away, lowering the pond's water level dangerously. A breach in their dam creates almost feverish activity among the pond's residents, who will abandon their normally nocturnal habits to repair it in broad daylight. If flooding is too heavy, older members of the family work cooperatively to excavate a drainage ditch that circumvents the dam on one side, acting as a pressure release.

Summer is less frantic, although heavy rains are still to be reckoned with, and most attention is focused on eating and raising young. A beaver's favorite pastime is lying in the sun and combing through its thick fur with the naturally split claws on its hind feet, spreading an oily secretion called "castoreum" from glands located near the anus. Castoreum gives beaver fur its lustrous and waterproof qualities, and regular grooming is required, especially in winter. Early trappers attributed miraculous healing qualities to castoreum, and rubbing a patch of fur containing those glands over the afflicted area of a sick person's body was reputed to cure almost anything.

Beavers are relatively uneasy on land, because, although their sharp, yellow-orange incisors can inflict even fatal injury on an attacker, they know that any carnivore hungry enough to chance it can easily exceed their shambling 6- to 8-mph running speed. Individuals interrupt their chores frequently to rise up on their haunches, nose elevated, to test the air for signs of trouble—something a stalker should bear in mind.

In the water, the big rodents are far bolder, and I've had them swim by within 10 feet of my camera lens once they were convinced I posed no threat.

In winter, beavers are active as long as they have open water and sometimes even after an unbreakable layer of ice seals the pond, rising from underwater outings to breathe the 3 to 4 inches of air trapped between it and the water's surface. Cold seems not to affect them at all, and tree-toppling activity will continue so long as the animals have a way into and out of the water. Winter yards of deer, elk, and moose frequently include nearby beaver ponds to take advantage of the valuable browse beavers provide through their tree cutting.

TRACKS

Beavers are ideal training animals for the beginning wildlife observer intent on developing skills, because they're quite heavy, and so many of their tracks are pressed into soft mud that shows good detail. Like the muskrat, beavers have five toes on each foot, but in this case all are prominent enough to show in a clear track. The toes of the front tracks are normally spread widely, with the center three being longer and thicker than the outermost toe on either side. On firmer ground, the smallest, innermost toe may print lightly or not at all. The front tracks measure 2 to 3 inches, sometimes more.

The toes of the hind feet also print in a fan-shaped pattern, but in this case webbing connects each toe to its neighbor right out to the claws. On snow and mud, some portion of the webbing should print noticeably; even when it doesn't, the long toes, with their distinct outward curve and enlarged knuckle joints (see the illustration), leave clear impressions.

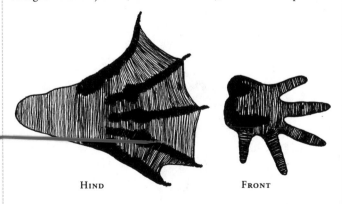

HIND   **FRONT**

Beaver tracks; front, 2 to 3 inches long; hind, 5 to 7 inches long. Note nimble "fingers" of front paws. Webbing of hind feet, shown here, seldom prints except in soft mud.

Beaver walking track pattern in mud. Note distinctive shapes of front and hind tracks and toe-in walking pattern.

Note again that the small, innermost toe prints more lightly than the other four.

Like bears, raccoons, and humans, beavers are plantigrade, or flat footed. The elongated hind feet have a distinct rounded heel and an average length of 5 to 7 inches. An extended toe spread makes them nearly as wide at the claws as they are long.

The ungainly beaver rarely travels at any gait but a walk, and its track pattern exhibits an extreme toe-in stance reminiscent of the badger. The front and hind feet of the same side print together in distinct pairs, with a stride between pairs that varies from 3 to 5 inches. On mud, the animal's flat, heavy tail sometimes leaves wide drag marks.

SCAT

Beavers are one of the few animals that regularly defecate in water, and their feces can cause a (usually) mild, flulike infection, which old trappers referred to as "beaver fever." For this reason, don't drink water anywhere downstream of a beaver pond without first purifying it.

Beaver scat found on land will almost always be at the water's edge. Segments are cylindrical, 1½ to 2½ inches long (sometimes shorter), and look as if they were formed of compressed sawdust. The diameter is an indication of the animal's size, with 1 inch being average for adults. The color of fresh deposits is dark brown, with lighter-colored bits of undigested wood, turning pale with age. Deposits more than two days old are rare, because they break down very quickly into a sawdustlike powder.

Beaver scat. Segments are 1½ to 2½ inches long. Scat is seldom found on land as beavers are one of the few animals willing to defecate in water.

SIGN

No animal leaves more obvious sign of its presence than the beaver. Most prominent is its lodge, a conical or dome-shaped construction located in deep water (3-plus feet) inside the pond. The exterior is a very thick shell of de-barked branches, mud, miscellaneous wood, even man-made debris—almost anything that can be used in its construction will be used. It may be as much as 20 feet wide at the base by nearly 10 feet high; larger lodges represent older, longer-established clans. You'll see little activity around the lodge itself, because beavers entering or exiting regularly travel 30 or more feet under water before surfacing.

Dams are also conspicuous, of course, and, once again, older dams are larger than recent constructions. Their composition is identical to that of lodges: interlocking twigs and barkless branches arranged in a strong design so intricate that human engineers have been unable to duplicate it. The water depth on the upstream side normally runs 4 to 6 feet, and some dams may be more than 5 feet wide. Length, to paraphrase the old adage, always reaches to the opposite bank, and I've seen some dams more than 80 feet long. Dams aren't watertight but have a steady flow of water running through them all the time, even though the topmost surface may be high enough to walk across without getting wet feet. In fact, surprisingly large spawning salmon and trout often get upstream through underwater holes in these seemingly impregnable walls. Contrary to what some believe, beaver dams seldom completely stop the spawning runs of fish, although they do help ensure that only the strongest get through to mate.

"Cuttings" are another obvious sign of beaver activity. Toppled trees, sometimes still attached to their stumps, may be found 50 yards or more from a stream. Trees are downed by gnawing an hourglass-shaped groove around their circumference, resulting in a conical shape at the terminal ends of both trunk and stump. Toothmarks are evident as twin grooves measuring ⅛ inch or larger individually, and an abundance of wood chips will lie on the ground around the base. Wood chips are also found at the butt ends of branches that have been gnawed off and taken to the pond. Trunks too large to be hauled off are typically stripped of bark over the course of several days, and portions left uneaten will draw the animals back to finish the job.

Beavers can bring down impressively large trees, with trunk diameters of more than 30 inches. This, combined with the fact that some trees are cut at a height of 4 to 5 feet above ground, has led to tales of giant beavers that no one actually sees. The truth is, these abnormally high grooves were cut when there was a solid layer of hardpack snow on the ground.

The last type of beaver sign is its scentpost. Scentposts are conical or dome-shaped masses of twigs, grass, and mud found around the outer perimeter of ponds. To activate them, a beaver—usually the dominant male—raises its tail, backs up to the mound, and rubs castoreum from its anal glands over the outer surface. Scented mounds are often small enough to require a bit of searching, but some may be up to 1 foot tall by 3 feet across at the base.

VOCALIZATIONS

Beavers are usually silent, but they do have a basic language of sorts. I heard one of their stranger calls early one summer morning while observing a young pair at a new dam. Whenever the two were out of sight of one another, one or other would raise its head as if sniffing the air and emit a high-pitched call I can only describe as "beeeee . . . beeeeee." This unique sound faintly resembles the alarm call of a blue jay, but with a slower pace. There's also a mallardlike quacking that I've heard from parents caring for youngsters. Except for an occasional grunt uttered while an animal is working, I've heard no other calls from adults.

Young kits are very vocal, however, making a variety of noises ranging from abbreviated whines that sound just like a puppy to calls that sound a lot like the honking of a Canada goose, and even a muted ducklike quacking.

The beaver's best-known communication, however, is its danger warning, made by slapping its wide, flat tail hard against the water's surface. Startling animals suddenly will usually precipitate an alarm slap, followed by the disappearance of all the beavers in a pond for a half hour or more. Ironically, approaching the pond slowly and in full view doesn't disturb them as much, and if you wait quietly in a secluded spot, chances are that startled beavers will reemerge within a half hour to go about their business.

NEW WORLD PORCUPINE
(*ERETHIZONTIDAE*)
17

PORCUPINE (*ERETHIZON DORSATUM*)

Every animal species, including our own, is a direct product of its environment. Most followed fairly generic patterns, the predators developing fangs, claws, and sometimes venom for preying on weaker animals, while prey animals simultaneously evolved the ability to outrun, outswim, or otherwise defeat these natural weapons.

Native only to North America, the porcupine falls into the "otherwise" category. Its common name translates to "he who rises in anger," an allusion to the animal's nearly ideal defense against predators. Instead of evolving a fight-or-flee approach, it adopted a passive stance, growing an unusual coat of stiff bristly fur interspersed with 30,000 spiked quills—which are really highly modified hairs. Each quill is a pointed spike 1 to 3½ inches long covered with microscopic barbs. Quills are concentrated along the back and especially on the tail; the head and belly are unquilled. At a full-speed run of only 3 to 4 mph, a "porky" seems easy prey for swift-moving predators, but woe to the carnivore that thinks it can kill this 8- to 40-pound herbivore with a bite to the spine or neck.

Despite the myths, porcupines cannot throw their quills, but they can detach them from the skin voluntarily as needed. When attacked, the porcupine hunches low and keeps its arched back to the attacker, not out of cowardice, but to keep its heavily armed tail in an assailant's face. As the predator circles, the porky turns with it, and when the attacker lunges forward, it's met by a hard slap and a faceful of quills. Once embedded, the hollow, airtight quills expand from the victim's own body heat, causing the barbs to dig in more firmly. The immediate result is intense pain, followed by a throbbing swelling. An unlucky carnivore with mouth and tongue bristling with porcupine quills will die slowly from infection and starvation, and those lucky enough to escape with just a few quills stuck in their flesh usually won't try attacking a porcupine again. From my own observations, quills don't actually work themselves ever deeper into the victim's flesh, as even some veterinarians believe, but are rather pushed inward as the frantic animal tries to scrape them off against trees and the ground.

Yet there are predators with the intelligence to defeat a porcupine's defenses. Coyotes, bobcats, and foxes will, if food is scarce, attempt to

Leonard Lee Rue III

Porcupine

knock the waddling pincushion onto its back to deliver a lethal bite to the underside. But by far the best porcupine hunter is the fisher (*Martes pennanti*), an 18-pound forest-dwelling weasel that has become scarce in the face of civilization. Porcupines, on the other hand, have no trouble at all coexisting with humans. Today, several times more porcupines are killed by cars than by carnivores, and rural dog owners within the porky's range have good reason to fear a population boom (most house cats are smart enough to steer clear).

Porcupines can be very destructive. They're extremely fond of salt, and often fearlessly invade outbuildings to eat perspiration-soaked wooden tool handles. They also like the varnishes used to seal wood-sided houses and buildings, and one fellow I know had a corner of his cedar cabin collapse after its wooden foundation was eaten away by porcupines.

Ironically, humans are perhaps the only predators that can kill a porcupine in complete safety—and a porcupine is just about the only prey an unarmed human can catch. A hard blow across the nose with a heavy stick will shock the animal's brain, killing it. Conversely, a porky can absorb several rounds of buckshot to the body and still climb a tree, because its very basic brain doesn't register systemic shock the way those of higher animals do. Hunters who shoot them for meat know that head shots are the order of the day. The flesh is rich and strong tasting, with a faint fishy smell, but quite palatable if cooked properly.

HABITAT AND RANGE

Porcupines need forest to live; where there are no trees, there are no porcupines. Trees provide food, dens, and escape from most predators capable of killing them, although fishers are adept at knocking treed porkies to the ground, sometimes killing them on impact. A single animal needs only a small area to support it, depending, of course, on the availability of food; a territory may encompass just a few acres.

The porcupine's original range has greatly decreased since the first Europeans landed in the New World, the sole reason being the destruction of forest habitat. In most places where porcupines still reside, their numbers have increased due to a lack of predators. Today, porcupines inhabit nearly all of the United States west of the Rockies, except for the west coast of California, and they extend north to cover all but the northernmost regions of Canada and most of Alaska (from the south), while ranging eastward through northern Minnesota, Wisconsin, and northern Michigan to the New England states. There are, of course, deforested areas within these regions where the porcupine has disappeared.

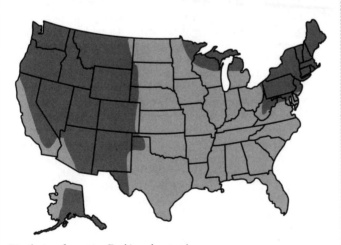

*Distribution of porcupine (*Erethizon dorsatum*).*

FOODS

The porcupine is a strict vegetarian, but its diet is varied and well suited to a four-season environment. In summer it feeds on the ground, grazing on clover, plantain, lupine, alfalfa, and even skunk cabbage. It's fond of apples at all stages of development, and will also eat buds, bark, blossoms, and small twigs from the trees, although orchard damage is typically slight.

When snow makes ground forage inaccessible, the porky's lot is much easier than that of most other herbivores, because not only can it live on the inner (cambium) layer of bark from many trees, but it can also climb to their topmost branches. Long, curved claws make it an excellent if slow climber, and it will sometimes spend several days feeding among the branches of one tree. Unfortunately, its favorite winter food is the bark of the white pine, of great value to the timber industry, and it sometimes kills trees by girdling them. For this reason porkies are considered pests in timber-producing states, and often there's no closed hunting season on them.

Favored spring foods include the first sticky buds of poplar, aspen, and birch. Here, too, an individual might spend up to a week feeding in a single large tree. Note that porcupines seldom eat the bark of these trees, but beavers, elk, and moose make it a regular winter staple.

MATING HABITS

Porcupines mate in October and November. During this time, pairs of the otherwise solitary creatures might be found clambering around the leafless branches of larger trees, grunting and whistling softly to one another. There's no ritual combat between breeding males, largely because roughly three out of four porcupines are females, but in thickly populated places I've seen as many as five adults in a single tree.

Actual mating takes place on the ground, and inane jokes aside, the act is fairly conventional. After a pair has spent a few days getting acquainted, the female becomes relaxed enough to lower her quills fully and allow the male to mount her from behind. They may remain together for several more days, mating frequently, before parting ways, the pregnant female going off to find a den while the male seeks out another mate.

Birthing dens may be in rock crevices or small caves, but in most cases are sited in standing hollow trees. Den entrances are usually on or near the ground, often gnawed to the proper size by porkies' sharp, rodentlike teeth, but resting platforms are always well above the ground. Interestingly, these platforms, horizontal ledges wedged firmly inside the hollow trunk, appear to be made entirely from the porcupine's own compacted droppings. In many cases, a second observation hole will be gnawed through the trunk at the same height, and it's fairly common in winter to see a denned mother-to-be peering down from her lofty hideout at approaching humans.

Gestation takes about seven months, extraordinarily long for a small mammal, with a single baby born in May or June. The young are born fully developed, with a coat of short but soft quills, and are delivered head-first encased in a placental sac. The newborn's quills harden immediately upon contact with air, and within 30 minutes the youngster is a virtual miniature of its mother. The baby stays with its mother until spring, nursing for the first month; the two part almost as soon as the first spring plants appear. Growth is rapid for the first year, and newborns mate the following autumn. The life span averages about eight years.

SEASONAL HABITS

Porcupines are strictly nocturnal, emerging at dusk from summer sleeping trees or winter dens to feed and returning to safety before sunrise. By day in summer they can nearly always be found sleeping high above the earth on a large, horizontal tree branch, usually with tail facing trunk and at the ready to defend against carnivores. In snowless weather, sleeping trees may be of any species so long as they're tall, have thick branches, and are well isolated. Since nearly all of a porcupine's diet consists of ground plants during the summer, its habitat may be up to a mile from the nearest conifers, but will always include open meadows and forest glades.

When snows make foraging impossible, male porcupines in particular spend up to several days at a time in a single large food tree (adult females will likely be pregnant and seek out denning trees instead). Note that in very cold or very windy weather porcupines are driven to forsake the trees and instead take refuge in rock crevices, caves, or, most often, previously established dens in standing trees, identifiable by the thick, compressed layer of scat pellets at and inside the den entrances.

TRACKS

While porkies aren't especially heavy animals (the largest I've taken hunting weighed just over 45 pounds), their tracks and trail are among the most easily identifiable in the animal world. The soles of all four feet have a bumpy, pebbled texture that leaves a distinctive impression in dusty trails and wet mud. Tracks made in tall grass will probably be too faint to read, but the furrow made by its wide, low-slung body may be more than a foot wide and remain visible for several hours after its passing.

A porcupine's feet are similar to the bear's; the hind feet are long, flat, and generally human-shaped, with five toes tipped with long, curved claws. The forefeet are also flat and elongated but have only four toes, also tipped with long, curved claws that make climbing trees almost effortless.

HIND   FRONT

Porcupine tracks: front, 2 to 3 inches long; hind, 3 to 4½ inches long. Note bumpy, pebbled soles, four toes on forefeet, five on hind feet, and claws that print well ahead of toes.

The hind feet average 3 to 4 inches long from heel to claw tips, the forefeet 2 to 2¾ inches. Because of the animal's fairly extreme toe-in walk, much like a badger's, most of a porky's weight is pressed down on the outside toe, leaving prints that are progressively lighter from the outside to the inside. And like the badger, bear, and raccoon, porcupines walk flat footed, with their soles making complete contact with the earth.

At a casual walk, the porky's usual gait, all four feet print independently, with the forefeet registering directly back of the hind feet in staggered pairs on each side. When snow or deep sand makes walking more difficult, the hind feet print in the front tracks, sometimes directly on top but usually overlapping, with the hind feet again registering slightly ahead of the front tracks. Note, however, that on loose surfaces such as snow, sand, or dust, prints may be partially or wholly obscured by broomlike diagonal sweepings of the tail.

With its wide, heavy body and short legs, a porky literally drags its belly as it walks through snow or tall grass, leaving a recognizable trough-shaped trail. In rough terrain, this trail might be masked by the animal's tendency to travel along established deer trails, where walking is less strenuous. Since the two species share similar diets, deer trails frequently lead to porcupine feeding areas as well.

Porcupine walking track pattern. Note toed-in characteristic and broomlike brushing of quilled tail, which often obscures tracks.

SCAT

As the illustration on page 221 shows, porcupine scat can be quite variable, but the form most often seen is a dark brown pellet roughly 1 inch long and slightly crescent shaped, sometimes with a narrow groove running lengthwise across its inside radius. The ends are rounded, with one end generally larger in diameter, and the texture is somewhat like compressed sawdust, showing bits of wood and plant fibers. This scat form is particularly common from autumn through early spring, when green plants are absent and the porky's diet consists of bark, twigs, and buds. Because pellets are often deposited on deer trails, which porcupines use as their own, they're often mistaken for deer scat.

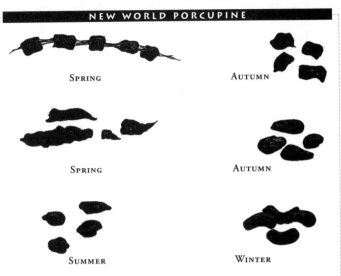

SPRING

AUTUMN

SPRING

AUTUMN

SUMMER

WINTER

Seasonal variations of porcupine scat.

From spring through summer, when the porcupine's diet changes to green plants, scat becomes more variable. Most unmistakable is a beaded form made up of small pellets attached together by grass fibers like beads on a string. Another type, common when the animal has been eating rich foods, consists of black, misshapen pellets up to 1 inch long and always tapered to a sharp point at one end.

SIGN

Although solitary and reclusive, porcupines are never inconspicuous. The most obvious sign of their presence is live trees with large patches of bark missing at heights no ground herbivore could reach. White pines are a particular favorite where available, but spruces and hemlocks are also gnawed, and young, smooth-barked maples have a strong attraction in early spring, when their sugary sap starts to flow. Occasionally you'll find dead trees as well, killed during previous winters when the porky's appetite for bark left the trunks girdled.

Another winter porcupine sign is freshly clipped twig ends lying atop the snow under a live conifer, snipped off by the animal's rodentlike incisors. Some believe that porcupines clip off the twigs then climb down to eat them, but I think these twigs were dropped accidentally because their owners never get around to recovering them. It works out, though, because hungry deer appreciate getting additional food from a source they can't reach. Note that red squirrels also bite off pine twigs, dropping them purposely to the ground, from whence seed-bearing cones are then removed for storage in their winter larders. One difference is that porcupines tend toward proportionally larger trees than do diminutive red squirrels.

The large, sticky buds of aspen and poplar are favorite porky foods in early spring, and, again, the ground under these trees will be littered with fumbled twigs and buds. Porcupines seem to regard these buds as a real treat, and often can be found foraging among the branches in broad daylight. Oddly, porcupines don't eat the smooth bark of these soft-wooded deciduous trees, although elk, moose, and beaver consider it a winter staple.

One reason that discarded deer, elk, and moose antlers are rarely found is because porcupines, squirrels, and most rodents devour them for the rich minerals they contain. But porcupines also gnaw the bones of winter-killed deer and other large animals for the same reason, and bones showing chisel-like toothmarks are definite signs of a porcupine in the area.

VOCALIZATIONS

Perhaps because of its primitive brain, the porcupine has no real language and spends most of its life in complete silence, even when mortally injured. The one exception is during the October–November mating season, when breeding pairs "communicate" with a variety of clicks, grunts, groans, and whistles. If any of these sounds has a specific meaning, it remains undiscovered.

HARES AND RABBITS
(*LEPORIDAE*)
18

I N NATURE, AS IN CIVILIZATION, the most effective and adaptable designs are also the most imitated and enduring. For example, members of the cat, dog, and human families have successfully adapted to virtually every habitat on earth. And since nature left to itself maintains balance in all things, it follows that such remarkably adaptable predators forced the evolution of equally remarkable prey animals—not to mention the extinction of less adaptable species.

Rabbits and hares are perhaps nature's ideal prey. Countering the swiftness and cunning of more powerful predators such as the coyote and bobcat with razor-sharp senses, effective camouflage, and greasy-fast running speed, these relatively defenseless herbivores prove that ferocity isn't necessarily the most effective defense. As proof of their success, rabbits and hares exist in nearly every part of the world.

Hares are generally larger than rabbits, with longer ears and longer legs that allow them to detect enemies at a distance and outrun them in open country. Rabbits prefer thick country, where they can hide or, if pursued, vanish among the thickets with a burst of incredible agility. A substantial difference between the families is that rabbit females (called does; males are called bucks) give birth to blind, hairless young that require considerable attention for their first two weeks of life. Hare young are born fully furred with their eyes open, and can hop about within hours of their birth. Members of both families are good swimmers, but hares often take to the water when pursued, even crossing rivers, while rabbits avoid swimming unless pressed hard.

Similarities include a reproductive rate best described as astonishing, an adaptation against being preyed upon by so many carnivores, including most birds of prey; few hares or rabbits live longer than one year in the wild. Both species are extremely sensitive to ground vibrations, and both may drum a hind leg rapidly against the earth to warn their fellows of approaching danger. Neither species is a long-distance runner, especially not the rabbit.

Despite their ratlike incisors, rabbits and hares are not rodents but lagomorphs. Rodents have a single row of incisors, while lagomorphs are distinguished by a double row of upper incisors, with smaller secondary teeth directly in back of the main incisors.

Adequate coverage of each of North America's eight native rabbits and three native hares would require a volume in itself, but those in this chapter, the snowshoe hare and the cottontail rabbit, cover the greatest range and are for the most part representative of all rabbits and hares.

SNOWSHOE HARE OR VARYING HARE (*LEPUS AMERICANUS*)

The snowshoe is the smallest American hare, with the shortest ears, and an adult weight of 2 to just over 4 pounds, compared to as much as 15 pounds for the arctic hare and 9½ pounds for the whitetailed jackrabbit. Jackrabbits were originally called "jackass rabbits" because of their long, mulish ears, and snowshoes share this common name even though their ears are nearly as short as a rabbit's. Their lower surface area decreases the amount of body heat lost in the snowshoe's often bitterly cold habitat.

The name "snowshoe" is derived from the hare's oversize hind feet, which are covered with thick fur in winter, giving it an ability to run atop deep snow that only the lynx, its most serious enemy, can match. Its other common name, varying hare, refers to the seasonal color changes of individuals living in snow country. In late autumn, snowshoes develop a thick white coat that keeps them warm and hard to see, changing back to an equally well-camouflaged mottled-brown-and-black coat in spring. Where winters include little or no snow, namely Oregon and Washington, snowshoes remain brown all year. A black subspecies in New York's Adirondack Mountains also retains its color year-round.

Len Rue, Jr.

Snowshoe Hare

HABITAT AND RANGE

Generally considered a creature of the northern forests, the snowshoe is as much at home in swamps, thickets, and clear-cuts as the cottontail rabbit, which shares part of its southern range. While the snowshoe runs faster than the shorter-legged rabbits, it too needs cover to elude coyotes and lynx, which can run it to exhaustion in a flat-out race. An old Native American trick was to chase a hare from one hiding place to another until it just gave up from exhaustion, a technique I've tried myself, although only once successfully.

Snowshoes are the most widely distributed hares in North America, although, as their common name implies, most of that range is to the north. In the lower 48 they're found throughout the northern Atlantic coast from Maine to New Jersey, with a few extending southward to North Carolina. To the west they range from northern Pennsylvania through all of Michigan, most of Wisconsin, northern Minnesota, and northern North Dakota. Strong populations are found along the Rocky Mountain range from Montana through northern New Mexico, across through Washington and Oregon, and southward into California and Nevada. To the north, snowshoe hares are common throughout Canada and all but the northernmost tip of Alaska.

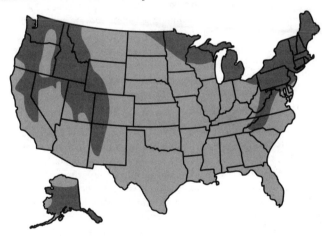

*Distribution of snowshoe hare (*Lepus americanus*).*

FOODS

Every species of hare or rabbit has evolved physical characteristics that fine-tune it to a specific habitat—the whitetailed jackrabbit of the open plains, for example, has a steady run of 36 mph, blazing short-distance sprints of 45 mph, and a thinner coat than the snowshoe hare. But all species share an ability to digest almost any vegetable matter short of solid wood, and it's doubtful that any would go hungry if displaced to another's environment. Every species eats the ubiquitous clovers, plantains, and grasses in summer, and few smooth-barked shrubs or their buds are off-limits as winter fare. Unlike our own atrophied nub, the appendix of a hare or rabbit is a large and vital organ that serves as an efficient predigestion chamber, helping reduce tough vegetation to usable proteins.

The snowshoe is no less specialized in its environmental adaptations, but, like its cousins, it does eat foods that are also more or less specialized to the same habitat. Summer is the season of plenty, with the only worries mating, raising young, and avoiding predators, this being the biggest worry. Violets, sedges, cresses, and mushrooms are just a portion of this hare's summer menu, while the buds of young northern pines and firs are nibbled at year-round, probably for their raw sugars.

Unlike most animals, snowshoes don't bother to put on a layer of fat as insurance against the coming winter. Early mountain men who relied upon them as winter fare soon discovered "rabbit starvation," caused by a serious lack of fat in their diets, which could be debilitating or even fatal. This lack of fat is the result of a highly efficient digestive system that can directly metabolize needed nutrients from the roughest roughage, allowing the hare to survive comfortably eating vegetation on which other herbivores can barely subsist. Snowshoes eat bark, buds, and twigs of many trees and shrubs, including staghorn sumacs, pines, willows, young birches, cherries, aspens, and, especially, raspberries.

An apparently unique characteristic of the snowshoe hare is its willingness to eat meat. When available, carrion is nibbled on, and more than a few trappers have cursed the hare's habit of raiding traps baited with meat meant for carnivorous furbearers.

MATING HABITS

Snowshoes mate individually every month of the year, another example of the hare's extraordinary abilities to survive almost anything. Does outnumber bucks by five or six to one, but mating battles are fairly common among breeding males, which impregnate one doe then immediately move on to find another. Combat between rivals resembles a boxing match, with both contestants sitting upright on their haunches, heads far back to protect their eyes, batting at one another with needle-sharp front claws and occasionally inflicting a painful bite. Fur is torn out and blood will likely be drawn, but mating battles generally end without serious injury to either party.

Snowshoe does produce two or three litters per year, with as many as six young in each litter, although four is the norm. Since hare young are born fully furred with open eyes, and can run by the end of their first day, the doe makes no great effort to fashion a birthing den. In summer, dens consist of simple saucer-shaped depressions, 8 to 10 inches in diameter and 4 inches deep at the center, lined with grass and fur bitten from the mother's underbelly as insulation and to expose her nipples. In winter, birthing dens are more protected, often located among the branches of a snow-covered fallen tree or sometimes in a hollow log, stump, or culvert.

The young nurse for about a month, growing rapidly, but they also begin eating vegetation soon after birth. Does typically mate again immediately after giving birth, nursing one generation while pregnant with the next. At four months, the young are ready to produce their own offspring and leave to find mates. A single pair of snowshoes and their offspring could produce more than 3,000 rabbits in a year, so predators are vital to the species' health.

SEASONAL HABITS

The snowshoe's best-known seasonal change comes in winter, when its mottled-brown-and-black fur is replaced by a thick coat of white-tipped hairs that make it very hard to see against a background of snow. The color change doesn't occur among hares living where snow is uncommon, but in snow country it begins as early as October, requiring about three months for complete transformation. Before the color change is complete in either direction—brown to white in fall, white to brown in late winter—a hare's coat will be a mottled mixture of both. Color changes are photoperiodic—that is, prompted by lengthening or shortening days—and sometimes hares are surprised by an unusually snowless winter and an unseasonably early spring, either of which leaves it starkly white against a dark environment. When this happens, hares hide more and move about less, apparently aware of their vulnerability.

Snowshoes aren't very territorial under normal conditions, when food and mates are in good supply, but neither can they be called social. Each adult needs about 1 acre to live, depending on terrain and weather, but individuals trespass freely. Inbreeding is probably common, and this might be a contributing factor in the species' 10-year population cycles: Their populations build to a peak then experience a sudden and severe die-off every decade. Lynx populations are so tightly and exclusively intertwined with those of snowshoe hares that they, too, experience cyclical fluctuations, lagging one year behind the hares.

Like most animals, snowshoes make use of regular trails for convenience when traveling to or from feeding or breeding areas. And, as with most small animals, the trails they employ during the summer months aren't usually their own, but were made by deer.

In winter, snowshoe trails become more exclusively their own; deer have yarded up in one spot and move little in the deepening snows, while the aptly named snowshoe travels about unhindered. Yet despite its excellent mobility, the snowshoe establishes regular packed trails, 8 to 10 inches wide and up to 1 foot deep, for convenience and to facilitate full-speed flight from potential predators.

Snowshoes are active at night, but I don't consider them nocturnal because they go about their business at any hour of the day, laying up for short catnaps in secluded spots that offer easy escape from predators. In winter these places are usually near a well-packed trail, and usually in the same bushy environment where they feed.

TRACKS

Snowshoe hares have large feet for their size, with the hind feet measuring 4 to nearly 6 inches long and having a wide toe spread of 3 to 4½ inches. The forefeet are nearly round, with a length of 1½ to 2 inches. The soles are heavily furred, especially in winter, leaving tracks that are blurred and often featureless. Snowshoes have four toes on each foot, with the center toes being noticeably longer than those on either side, although not to the extent of the eastern cottontail, which is about the same size but has smaller feet.

TRACKS IN SNOW   RIGHT HIND FOOT

Snowshoe hare tracks. Shaded areas of tracks indicate portions of feet pressed most heavily against the ground. Prints in snow are often obscured by furry soles. Note widely spread toes of hind foot, shown here with most fur omitted to show detail.

Snowshoe track patterns are typical of hares and rabbits, with the forefeet printing 5 to 8 inches behind the hind feet in the sets of all four tracks. The hind feet normally print side by side at any speed, with the forefeet sometimes printing side by side to the rear in a pattern resembling double exclamation marks (!!), but often one forefoot registers diagonally behind the other. The length of a set measures about 10 inches in the former case, 16 inches in the latter.

This same pattern applies at most gaits, but you can get an idea of the hare's speed by the distance between its track sets. At a casual hop, this distance runs approximately 10 inches; it increases to about 20 inches at an easy traveling speed and spreads to 20 feet or more when the hare is pursued. When you're tracking any hare or rabbit, remember that they all can instantly change direction. If a trail seems to disappear, look closely at the last tracks for indications that the hind feet were twisted; the direction of the twist will be the new direction of travel.

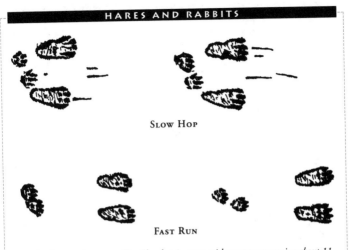

SLOW HOP

FAST RUN

Snowshoe hare track patterns. Top: Slow hop in snow, with patterns measuring about 11 inches in length, with roughly 14 inches between patterns. Bottom: Fast run in snow or wet mud, patterns measuring 20–24 inches long, front feet farther behind back feet, leaps between patterns, 40–70 inches. Note striated marks ahead of hind feet in slow hopping gait; not present in running gait, where animal is clearing the ground completely.

SCAT

Hare and rabbit scat is easy to identify in any season. All is generally spherical, sometimes slightly oblong or irregular but never acorn- or capsule-shaped as a deer's is. The size varies with the species and individual, but snowshoe pellets usually range from ⅜ inch to ½ inch, noticeably larger than a rabbit's scat but slightly smaller than those of most other hares. Scat tends to be softer in summer when the diet consists of green plants, and may be flattened or disk shaped.

Snowshoe pellets are fairly smooth, but a close-up look reveals a fibrous consistency formed of compacted plant matter. The color ranges from dark brown to almost black in winter, brown to dark green in summer.

Rabbit and hare scat. Samples shown apply to all types of rabbits and hares, with cottontail pellets averaging ¼ to ⅜ of an inch in diameter, snowshoe hare pellets measuring ⅜ to ½ of an inch. The fact that rabbit and hare scat is rarely soft indicates an extremely efficient digestive system.

Like deer, snowshoes deposit scat wherever they happen to be, but most will be found in small accumulations on trails. Average deposits are eight to twelve pellets; smaller accumulations are indicative of smaller individuals. No apparent effort is made to defecate repeatedly in the same place, which implies no real territorial instinct.

SIGN

The most important signs left by hares and rabbits are the neatly clipped diagonal cuts made by the animals' incisors while nipping off plant stalks, twigs, or buds. Unlike the stepped cut made by porcupines, a hare's bite is smoother and more scissorslike, quite different from the ragged tears left by deer.

Mating places or, more precisely, the places where battles between rival males took place are usually defined by disturbed vegetation or snow and marked by bits of fur. There are no specific sites or types of terrain where these ritual fights take place, but most I've found were in the rough grasses of a deep swamp.

Birthing beds can be found any time of year. In summer they're most often found within secluded thickets, in the form of packed-down, saucer-shaped depressions lined with leaves, grasses, and telltale fur. Winter birthing beds are normally out of sight under snow-covered fallen trees, brushpiles, or even under barns or cabins. Winter birthing beds also serve as dens during harsh weather, and can be identified by their packed, round entrances, about 6 inches in diameter, usually with obvious tracks leading to them and often with scat deposits around the perimeters.

VOCALIZATIONS

Snowshoe hares are normally silent, but they do have a limited range of calls. Mothers purr softly while nursing their young, and the young emit high-pitched whimpers and whines. Most notable is the alarm call, a prolonged squeal often called a "death cry," because it's most often heard when the hare is pinned and being killed by a predator. Note that hares have a much lower-pitched alarm cry than rabbits do.

EASTERN COTTONTAIL RABBIT (*SYLVILAGUS FLORIDANUS*)

Cottontails are often confused with snowshoe hares when the latter is wearing its brown-and-black summer coat, but several physical characteristics can help you distinguish between them. Rabbits are generally smaller than hares, with cottontails weighing 2 to 4 pounds (which in this instance is nearly identical to the weight of a snowshoe hare). Cottontails remain the same color year-round, having a grizzled coat of gray, brown, and white, with a rust-brown patch at the nape of the neck. Their ears and legs are shorter than those of the snowshoe hare, but not obviously so, and some individuals wear a white blaze on their foreheads.

Eastern Cottontail

HABITAT AND RANGE

The habitat of the eastern cottontail, and related cottontails, consists of thick brushlands, where its very fast but short-range sprinting speed can put enough territory between it and a predator to allow it to hide again. In such thick territory, its grizzled coat provides effective camouflage in any season. As with other thick-country animals, cottontails have weak eyesight; in these habitats, good vision is less valuable than keen hearing

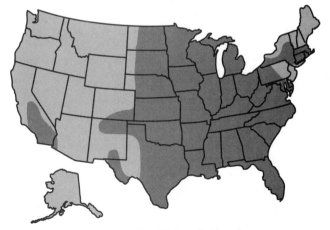

*Distribution of eastern cottontail rabbit (*Sylvilagus fioridanus*).*

Leonard Lee Rue III

and an excellent sense of smell, both of which are found among all rabbits and hares.

Eastern cottontails are the most common rabbit in North America. Excepting Maine, they cover the entire eastern half of the lower 48 states, from North Dakota south through Texas and into northern Mexico. Populations are also found in the brushlands of Arizona and Nevada, the southern peninsula of Ontario between Michigan and New York, and parts of southern Manitoba.

FOODS

The diet of the eastern cottontail is nearly identical to that of the snowshoe hare and other rabbits and hares, depending, of course, on available vegetation. In a nutshell, the cottontail can subsist on almost any vegetable matter. In summer, the most commonly consumed plants include clovers, plantains, grasses, and cresses. The leaves and buds of aspen, poplar, willow, and other shrubs are eaten as well.

When snow covers ground forage, a cottontail's diet becomes rougher, consisting largely of bark from young poplars, cherries, sumacs, and raspberries. Small twigs are also eaten, because rabbits and hares can efficiently digest and metabolize anything short of solid wood. In any season, this rabbit's diet consists of vegetation that grows in or near thick cover.

MATING HABITS

Eastern cottontails breed from February through the following September, and females, which may breed as early as eight months of age, can produce three to four litters of seven or more young each year. New mothers usually mate again immediately after giving birth. Unlike hares, whose young can run when just a day old, rabbit young are born naked and helpless, requiring considerable care for about their first two weeks. There's no bond between mating pairs, and as soon as receptive does become pregnant, bucks move on to find another mate.

Because of their helplessness, rabbit young need more shelter than do hare young. Birthing dens are found in dense brushpiles, under stacks of old lumber or abandoned timber, inside hollow logs, occasionally in groundhog burrows, and sometimes in the crawl spaces of cabins or outbuildings. Mothers leave their babies periodically to feed, and most nursing takes place at dawn and dusk.

Because cottontail does normally outnumber bucks by about five to one, mating battles between rival males are rarely serious, although they do occur. More serious but less frequent are fights between females, which are more territorial than males.

SEASONAL HABITS

Cottontails aren't normally gregarious and might even be categorized as solitary except when mating. One exception is following a prolonged period of harsh weather that forced them to hole up in a protected den.

After several days of inactivity, these athletic animals seem driven to gather in small groups of perhaps a dozen individuals, which can often be seen frolicking in open spaces, usually near feeding areas.

While eastern cottontails are averse to swimming unless actively pursued, they do enjoy a summer dust bath and are seen frequently on the shoulders of dusty or sandy roads, where they roll around to dislodge excess fur and parasites. Most of this activity occurs at night, but dusk and dawn are good times to watch them bathe.

One of the eastern cottontail's better-known habits, especially among hunters, is its tendency to run when pursued in a circle 50 to 100 yards in diameter, depending on the thickness of the terrain and the proximity of the pursuer. If it can, the rabbit will make for the closest brush and freeze, relying on its effective four-season camouflage to conceal it, because most four-legged carnivores can catch it in a flat-out race. But if the pursuit is too close, the cottontail will return to its own trail in an attempt to confuse an enemy into taking the wrong path.

TRACKS

Like all rabbits and hares, eastern cottontails have four toes on each foot. Foreprints average 1 to 1½ inches long and about 1 inch wide. When they print clearly, toes appear pointed, without obvious claw marks. The two center toes are longer than the outer two, with the inside toe being the smallest and set farthest to the rear.

The hind feet are elongated in typical rabbit fashion, averaging 3 to 4 inches in length by 1¼ to 1½ inches at their widest. Again, the toes register as pointed impressions, with the two center toes being much longer than the outside toes. The smallest toe is on the inside of the foot, but this difference isn't always discernible, especially on snow, where front tracks appear as round holes, hind tracks as oblong impressions.

The track patterns of the eastern cottontail are identical to those of other rabbits and very similar to those of hares, which are, of course, larger, with much larger hind feet. When the rabbit is sitting, as it might be while nibbling on food plants, its front feet print side by side ahead of

HIND   FRONT

Eastern cottontail tracks: front, 1 to 1½ inches long; hind, 3 to 4 inches long. Shaded areas indicate portions of foot pressed hardest against the ground. Claws generally more prominent than those of the snowshoe hare.

HOPPING

RUNNING

Eastern cottontail track patterns in shallow snow. Note that foreprints in running pattern register one behind the other, while those created by a steady hop are side by side.

and between the hind tracks. The straddle ranges from 4 to 6 inches, growing wider with speed.

Rabbits aren't designed for walking; their normal mode of travel is a series of hops. This track pattern registers as the hind feet ahead and to either side of the forefeet; slower hops sometimes show the forefeet printing directly behind the hind feet, like two exclamation points (!!). The animal's speed can be estimated by the distance between sets of four tracks, which might be as much as 15 feet. Another indication of speed is the length of a rabbit's tracks, which grow shorter as it leans forward on its toes to run faster.

SCAT

Eastern cottontail scat is similar to that of other species of rabbits and hares: typically spherical and firm, sometimes resembling a thick, flattened disk when forage has been especially green and rich. One fairly reliable difference, however, is size; cottontail pellets are smaller than those of any of the hare species, measuring ¼ inch to ⅜ inch in diameter. The color is brown to dark brown, becoming lighter with age, with a generally smooth texture that usually shows traces of plant fibers.

SIGN

Their characteristic gnawing is the most obvious distinguishing sign left by eastern (and other) cottontails. While hares typically leave a single slanted cut on plants and twigs they've fed upon, rabbits are more delicate eaters, leaving several small, rodentlike toothmarks on all but the smallest plant stems. Individual toothmarks are roughly ⅛ inch across, larger than those of most rodents and smaller than beaver or porcupine gnawings.

Young trees and shrubs stripped of bark from ground level to a height of about 4 inches—higher if the gnawing occurred with hardpack snow underfoot—are another sign of cottontail work. But, once again, hares also eat bark in winter, and the surest way to tell the difference between the two sign is to find identifiable tracks or teethmarks.

VOCALIZATIONS

Like hares, rabbit mothers sometimes purr or call in soft, almost inaudible squeaks to their suckling young. Youngsters themselves emit high-pitched squeaks that are also barely audible.

Aside from this, cottontails are nearly always silent except when being physically mauled by predators, in which case they squeal loudly in a voice higher pitched than that of hares.

SQUIRRELS
(SCIURIDAE)
19

THIS IS A LARGE and diverse family of the order Rodentia, a group whose members are distinguished by one pair of upper and one pair of lower incisors, with no canines, leaving a wide gap between cutting incisors and chewing molar teeth. More important to a tracker, all squirrels are distinguished by having five toes on the hind feet but only four toes on the forefeet.

Beyond these common factors lies extreme diversity; some squirrels are as small as a 4-ounce chipmunk, others as large as a 14-pound marmot. Some live in trees, some in underground dens, and many occupy either, routinely or seasonally. All are vegetarians, although a few, such as the red squirrel, frequently eat insects or bird eggs. The family name translates to "shade tail," but while this description is accurate for tree squirrels, it hardly applies to the nearly tailless prairie dog or woodchuck. Some hibernate through winter; some estivate, laying up in warm dens for more than a week at a time during harsh weather; many, though, are active year-round. Some of them, namely the flying squirrels (*Glaucomys*), were the world's first hang gliders.

Complete coverage of the nine genera and 63 species of North American squirrels is far beyond the scope of this book. Those selected for this chapter aren't always representative of all squirrels, but they are among the most common throughout North America, and all have certain common behaviors.

FOX SQUIRREL (*SCIURUS NIGER*) AND GRAY SQUIRREL (*SCIURUS CAROLINENSIS*)

Fox squirrels are the largest of tree squirrels, weighing from 1 to 2½ pounds. There are three fairly distinct color phases: Those in the North are generally grizzled gray-rust above and yellow-orange below; those in the South are black with a white-tipped tail and sometimes a white blaze on the face; those west of the Rockies are generally rust colored.

Since there are so many similarities between the fox squirrel and its smaller cousin, the gray squirrel, information in this section applies to either except where noted. Obvious differences between the two include

Fox Squirrel

Gray Squirrel

size and color: Gray squirrels are usually gray above and white below, but a black phase with white-tipped hairs is common in their northern range. As might be expected, the gray variety occurs most often in beech forests, where their coats provide excellent camouflage against the trees' smooth gray bark; blacks are more often found among maples and oaks, where black fur against rough black bark accomplishes the same thing. Also, gray squirrels are about half the size of fox squirrels, weighing 1 to 1½ pounds. I've also noticed that the black phase has a thinner, less fluffy tail than its gray counterparts, and where hunting regulations are concerned, the two color phases are sometimes regarded as separate species.

HABITAT AND RANGE

Fox squirrels are tree squirrels; hardwood forests provide nearly all their food. As such, they're well adapted to a life far above the ground, eluding enemies simply by running up the trunk of any nearby tree with unmatched ease and, if necessary, leaping from one lofty branch to another with an agility that makes even primates look clumsy.

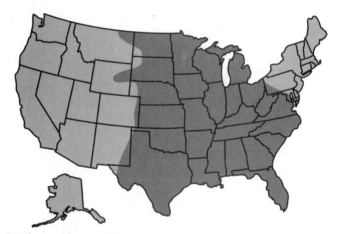

*Distribution of fox squirrel (*Sciurus niger*).*

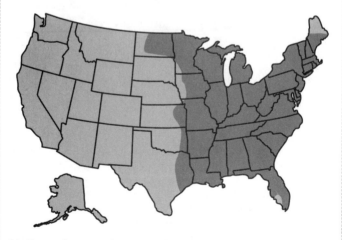

*Distribution of gray squirrel (*Sciurus carolinensis*).*

Fox squirrels are also equipped with superb senses. Their sense of smell appears at least as keen as a whitetail's, and, whereas most forest dwellers have better hearing than vision, tree squirrels—as most hunters can attest—have keen eyesight. Their hearing is fair, but they can be stalked more easily in noisy, dry-leaf country than can large-eared animals. Another chink in the squirrel's armor that hunters use to good effect is the animal's short attention span; even after shooting one, a hunter need only sit quietly for about 15 minutes before other squirrels forget about him and return to their normal activities.

The range of the fox and gray squirrels in their various color phases covers most hardwood (oak, maple, beech) forests in the lower 48 states. Population maps in this section show only the range of eastern subspecies, but close relatives occur throughout the continental United States.

FOODS

Fox and gray squirrels are almost strictly vegetarians, more so than some close relatives such as the red squirrel and flying squirrel. Favorite foods are nuts of every kind, because nuts are rich in fatty oils, proteins, and other essential nutrients. As Olas Murie once noted, squirrels will freely eat nuts they've never seen before—such as macadamia and Brazil nuts—apparently being able to discern the food value of these strange fruits by their odor.

Most of the squirrel's nut diet consists of less exotic types: acorns, beechnuts, hazelnuts, walnuts, and hard-shelled hickory nuts. Maple nuts, or samaras, are an important food throughout most of the animal's range, as are many other types of buds and seeds. Many kinds of fungi are also eaten, but rarely in great quantities. Raspberries and other berries are eaten in season, when foxes, coyotes, and bears allow it, and the tender bark of many types of sapling trees is eaten as well.

While squirrels are known for caching food in preparation for winter, fox and gray squirrels don't hoard nuts as does the red squirrel, instead burying them individually 2 to 4 inches beneath loose forest humus near the places where they were found. Legend has it that squirrels can remember where every nut is buried, but the truth is that they locate such caches by smell, often through more than a foot of snow, then tunnel down to retrieve them. In fact, squirrels probably miss as many nuts as they find, inadvertently replanting the forest by placing seeds out of reach of deer or other animals that might eat them.

Squirrels are also known for raiding ripened cornfields. A bushel of field corn dumped in hardwood forest is guaranteed to attract every fox or gray squirrel for hundreds of yards, and unharvested fields of standing field corn left as fodder are sometimes the best places to set up a photography blind. Here there are notable differences between foxes and grays. Being larger, fox squirrels typically leave the dangerous openness of cornfield or bait pile carrying entire ears in their mouths, taking them to a favorite eating log or stump inside a tree line, where they consume every kernel. Grays must remove kernels one at a time, sometimes stuffing several into their cheeks before retreating to the trees, but often eating corn where they find it. Note also that fox squirrels eat the entire kernel, while grays eat only the germ from its inner (pointed) end.

If hauling bait to a squirrel area isn't feasible, you can often entice the animals into the open by using scents. Acorn scent from Buck Stop, Inc. (designed to lure deer), has worked well for me, especially during poor acorn harvests, and walnut concentrate from the supermarket is also a powerful attractant.

MATING HABITS

Mating times for both fox and gray squirrels appear to vary, but both usually mate from October through late November, sometimes into December; matings occur earlier in northern than in southern climes. Males come into heat before females (September–October), and battles between rival males are sometimes vicious, with much biting, wrestling, and a great deal of frantic chattering. By my own estimation, females in either species outnumber males by about two or three to one, a rather low ratio that probably explains why mating battles occur perhaps a month before actual mating takes place.

In the case of gray squirrels, breeding normally occurs twice a year, and new mothers mate again from April to June. Fox squirrels aren't as likely to produce a second litter, but some two-year-old females may if food is abundant. Gestation time is three months, with litters of two to three gray squirrels or two to four fox squirrels born in February and March and again in August and September. Winter young are born in enclosed dens in hollow trees, usually with entrances too small to admit most predators, while late-summer young are born in cup-shaped leaf nests wedged into the crotches of tree branches high above the ground.

Squirrel young are born partially furred but with their eyes closed, and nurse for about three months, leaving their mothers just before the next litter is born. Males take no part in the rearing of the young.

SEASONAL HABITS

Excepting the nocturnal flying squirrels, tree squirrels are active by day and sleep at night in cup-shaped nests or less elaborate loafing platforms high above the ground. Since their most important predators, the weasels, bobcats, and foxes, are mostly nocturnal, these working hours are probably an adaptation designed to avoid them. Squirrels of both species are most active at dawn and dusk, but a sharp eye and good binocular can find them moving among the treetops at any hour of the day (optics are necessary for detecting hidden squirrels among backlighted branches). On very hot summer days, both species are understandably less active; squirrels remain motionless on branches or loafing platforms to enjoy whatever breeze is available.

Autumn is the best time to observe tree squirrels, because that's when they're most active, harvesting and caching nuts in preparation for the coming winter, and, of course, mating. Again, the most active times are at dawn and dusk, but the drive to stash food keeps them busy throughout the day. A quiet observer can watch them leaping among tree branches, nipping off nut-bearing twigs, then descending to earth to bury or sometimes eat them on the spot.

A notable difference exists between the feeding habits of fox and gray squirrels: Grays normally eat food where they find it, sometimes carrying individual nuts into a tree where they can feast in safety, while fox squirrels employ regular feeding platforms. These platforms may take the form of flat-topped stumps, large fallen logs, or sometimes the moss-covered humps left by decayed fallen trees. In every case, these places will be littered with nutshell pieces, stripped pinecones, corncobs when available, and other food debris.

TRACKS

All members of the squirrel family have four toes on the forefeet and five toes on the hind feet. Moreover, the tracks of all tree squirrels are virtually identical except for size, and distinguishing the identity of fox or gray squirrels by their tracks alone is likely to be impossible.

The forefeet of the gray squirrel average 1 inch long, the forefeet of fox squirrels about 1½ inches, and in both cases tracks are nearly round. The hind tracks measure 2 to 2½ inches for fox squirrels, 1½ to 2 inches for gray squirrels. On firm ground or when running, the heels of the hind

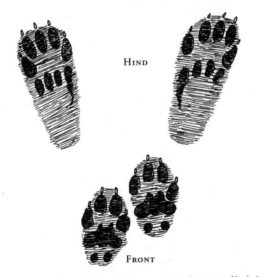

Hind

Front

Fox and gray squirrel tracks in snow, showing typical track pattern of both: hind feet, 2 to 2½ inches long; forefeet, 1½ to 2 inches long. Shaded areas indicate portions of foot most likely to print.

Fox and gray squirrel running track patterns. Note that all four feet print independently, front feet printing almost directly behind hind feet to form twin exclamation points (!!).

feet may not register, leaving an abbreviated track that's shorter but wider than front tracks. One interesting trait among fox, gray, and red squirrels is the way the toes of all four feet are usually splayed wide in shallow mud yet print close together in deeper mud and snow.

At a glance, both the tracks and the track patterns of tree squirrels might be mistaken for those of a very small rabbit or hare, especially on snow, where the entire sole of each hind foot leaves an impression. Like rabbits, tree squirrels generally move from place to place with hops that place foreprints to the rear of hind prints, looking like dual exclamation points (!!). While this pattern is typical, expect to find the same variations common to rabbit trails, where the forefeet sometimes print between and slightly rearward of the hind feet, sometimes side by side, and sometimes with one forefoot behind the other. The forefeet rarely print ahead of or even with the hind feet, but terrain and an animal's gait produce many variations.

The length of a track set (all four feet) varies with its owner's size, but a workable rule of thumb is 7 to 8 inches for grays and 8 to 9 inches for foxes. A good estimation of an individual's speed and attitude can be made from leaps between tracks sets: 8 to 12 inches indicates casual meandering, 18 to 24 inches is an easy bounding run, and leaps of 30 to 36 inches or more tell of a squirrel in a hurry. The straddle is roughly 4 to 5 inches for both foxes and grays.

SCAT

You have to look for squirrel scat, because it's almost never obvious among the deep leaf humus and other debris of a hardwood forest floor, and on snow the small segments are likely to melt out of sight. Most of the deposits I've found have been within a few yards of the base of a usually large tree, which helps to narrow the search area.

Winter scat closely resembles tiny deer scat. The usual form is pellet shaped, dark brown to black in color and having a rough but fairly regular surface. Pellets are typically narrower at one end than the other, and deposits may contain 8 to 12 of them. The length runs from ⅛ inch to ¼ inch, perhaps longer for large fox squirrels.

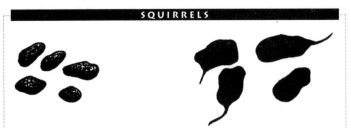

Fox and gray squirrel scat. Pellets (left) ⅛ to ¼ of an inch long, typical of a dry, fibrous winter diet. Summer droppings (right) are ¼ to ½ inch long, with stringy plant fibers indicating a more succulent diet.

In summer, when the diets of gray and fox squirrels switch from dry foods to more succulent buds and fruits, scat segments become more stringy and fibrous, and may be up to twice the size of winter pellets, at ¼ inch to ½ inch long. The color ranges from dark green-brown to brown to black, when ripened berries are in good supply. Segments are usually deposited in clusters of 6 to 10 pellets, and many segments exhibit a "tail" of plant fibers extending about ¼ inch from one end.

SIGN

The most obvious gray and fox squirrel sign from August through October are oak tree "cuttings." Acorns grow in clusters at the end of fragile, easily broken twigs, and squirrels have found that the easiest method of harvesting acorns is to nip these twigs off the parent branch, then climb down and dispose of each nut individually. Where acorns are plentiful, squirrels go into a kind of frenzy, cutting nut-bearing twigs in great quantities and littering the forest floor with conspicuous green oak leaves. Those not collected by squirrels add valuable fatty foods to the diets of whitetails and a few other animals.

The same types of cuttings are occasionally found in maple or beech forests, but more often these smaller prizes are simply nipped off and carried away. In either case, the work can be identified as a squirrel's by a stepped cut, made by the overbite between its upper and lower incisors.

When enough nut-bearing twigs have been cut to satisfy the industrious squirrel, it descends and nips off individual acorns, eating some right there and burying others individually in shallow holes dug with the forefeet, then covered and tamped down with the nose and forefeet. Caches are noticeable as small disturbances in the humus, seldom more than a few yards from the parent tree's base.

Also noticeable in winter are the tunnels made by squirrels burrowing through hardpack snow to reach cached nuts. These tunnels are generally round, with diameters of 3 to 4 inches and sprays of loose snow around their mouths. In several inches of snow, tunnels rarely go straight down but descend at an angle to the earth.

Nutshells on the forest floor are another sure squirrel sign, and I've noticed that, with acorns, the more open the shell, the larger the squirrel.

Smaller squirrels tend to nibble small holes and remove the nut meat in pieces, while larger individuals expose and remove the entire fruit, leaving large chunks of shell nearby. Empty beechnut shells and maple samaras are also left by foraging squirrels, but chipmunks, marmots, and ground squirrels eat them as well.

An obvious sign of gray or fox squirrel habitation, especially in leafless winter trees, are the cup-shaped leaf-and-twig nests they build into the crotches of more or less horizontal branches 15 to 50 feet above the ground. Identifiable as clumps among the upper branches, these are summer nests and probably won't be occupied in winter.

Loafing platforms are even more common in summer, but these are almost flat and much less elaborate than nests, although construction of both is the same. Note that with either nest or loafing platform, haphazard construction is a sign that adolescents did the work.

VOCALIZATIONS

If language is an indication of intelligence, then gray and fox squirrels fit into the category of higher animals. They may have a short attention span, but the range of identifiable calls they use to communicate is more elaborate than that of most small animals. Here are a few:

A sharp, high-pitched "kik-kik-kik" chattered in rapid succession means potential danger is approaching. If you're an experienced hiker, you've doubtless heard this call often.

A prolonged "ki-i-kik" emitted in intervals of about two seconds is also an alarm call, but of a less urgent nature—a fox trotting by, for instance.

The "kik . . . kik . . . kik" call is an all-clear signal, telling other squirrels that whatever initially caused the alarm has passed on.

Barking is another call used by gray and especially by fox squirrels. As the term implies, it sounds like the shorter, high-pitched bark of a small dog, emitted individually or in a series with several seconds between each. This seems primarily a mating call, and males in particular will perch on a low horizontal branch, barking out what appear to be challenges, which may be answered by several other males (possibly females, too) in the area.

RED SQUIRREL
(*TAMIASCIURUS HUDSONICUS*)

The red squirrel is our smallest and most colorful tree squirrel. Also known as the pine squirrel and chickaree, this feisty little bundle of energy weighs just ½ pound at maturity. The closely related Douglas squirrel (*Tamiasciurus douglasii*) of the Pacific coastal region weighs just a bit more, 10 to 11 ounces.

Size aside, red squirrels look like other tree squirrels, but can be further distinguished by a brown to bright rust coat and tail contrasting with a white underbelly. The tail is tipped with black and seems to be held aloft more than those of other tree squirrels. A wide white ring around each eye contrasts sharply with the head.

Leonard Lee Rue III

Red Squirrel

HABITAT AND RANGE

Red squirrels are tenacious enough to survive in almost any forested environment, but in my own experience they're never far from pines, hemlocks, or other conifers, whose seed-bearing cones constitute a vital part of red squirrels' diets. Mixed forests with beech, oak, or maple are also appreciated as food sources, but rare is the red squirrel whose territory excludes conifers. Likewise, fox and gray squirrels won't live in a forest made up exclusively of pines, although either species might enjoy an occasional pine nut.

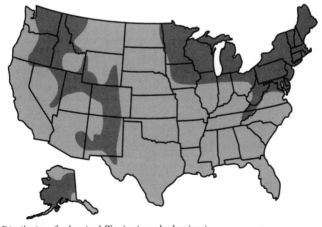

*Distribution of red squirrel (*Tamiasciurus hudsonicus*).*

To the east, red squirrels range from the Appalachian Mountains to northern Québec south of the Arctic tundra. From eastern Minnesota, the range covers northern Canada, skipping the plains of North Dakota and Manitoba, and extending southward along the Rockies into Arizona and New Mexico. From there they range will inland along the northern Pacific Coast to cover most of Alaska. The closely related Douglas squirrel occupies most of the southern Pacific Coast where the red squirrel leaves off.

FOODS

Red squirrels are the most omnivorous of tree squirrels. Buds, nuts of all kinds, grasses and forbs (ground plants), and, of course, pine seeds, are eaten. Unlike grays and foxes, whose main food is acorns, red squirrels can subsist entirely on pinecone fruits, a natural way to prevent competition between them and their larger cousins, but animal proteins are also welcome fare. Beetles, grubs, bird eggs, hatchlings, and frogs are eaten frequently on an opportunistic basis, and even mushrooms dangerous to man (the amanitas) are regularly nibbled.

Red squirrels are also the only tree squirrels that cache large amounts of food in one place. Several caches might be scattered around in hollow stumps and trees and revisited daily throughout the winter.

Red squirrels are very aggressive, and many a suburban or rural bird feeder has become their exclusive domain. Sunflower seeds make excellent bait for attracting camera-shy red squirrels, as well as larger squirrels of all types.

MATING HABITS

Red squirrels mate from late December through January, and perhaps again in July or August if food is abundant. Mating rituals are preceded by energetic chases and fights in treetops and on the ground, mostly between rival males. Reds are the most aggressive and territorial of the tree squirrels, and females may also fight violently among themselves if a claimant's territory is challenged or her young threatened. Females outnumber males by about four to one, so mating competition isn't serious.

Birthing dens are generally found well above the ground in cracks and holes in hollow standing trees, their interiors lined with grass, leaves, pine needles, and maybe bird feathers. The young are born from late February through April, in litters of three to seven, and they suckle for more than two months. By the time they're weaned, red squirrel young are completely self-sufficient.

SEASONAL HABITS

Like other tree squirrels (flying squirrels being an exception), red squirrels are diurnal, or active during daylight. The times of greatest activity at any time of year occur at dusk and dawn, and legend has it that you can gauge the severity of a winter by how frantic red squirrels are in their foraging and caching activities.

While red squirrels are most often found around conifers, where cones provide a reliable staple food, autumn food caches may be anywhere near these trees. Hollow tree trunks, large stumps, and appropriated woodchuck dens are common cache sites, but almost any enclosed places—including the exhausts and interiors of abandoned vehicles—might be employed as stash spots if their locations are convenient to the squirrels' natural habitat.

Black bears looking to put on weight before denning for the winter are adept at finding and consuming every scrap of food the little squirrels work so diligently to cache. One of the forest's best intruder alerts, the chattering and screeching of antagonized red squirrels tells a tracker that something large or dangerous (to the squirrels) is moving nearby—a valuable clue to the presence of other species.

TRACKS

Red squirrel tracks are virtually identical to the tracks of fox or gray squirrels, with four toes on the forefeet, five on the hind feet, and prominent toe tips with claws that show in a clear track. One difference is that neither gray nor fox squirrels live in exclusively coniferous habitats, while red squirrels can subsist on a diet composed entirely of pine nuts.

Another difference, of course, is track size. Fox and gray squirrels may be more than twice the size and weight of an adult red squirrel, and this disparity is reflected in the size and depth of tracks. Foreprints run ½ inch to ¾ inch long; hind prints ¾ inch to more than 1 inch—up to 2 inches if the entire foot prints.

Note also the red squirrel's tendency to lean forward onto its toes as it hops forward in typical squirrel fashion. Like those of foxes and grays, a red squirrel's hind feet are elongated with a distorted resemblance to the human foot; unlike them, however, it doesn't usually stand or land flat

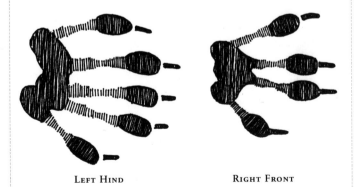

LEFT HIND   RIGHT FRONT

Red squirrel tracks: front, ½ to ¾ of an inch long; hind, ¾ to 1 inch long. Tracks shown are as they might appear in soft mud, and show greater detail than is normally found.

Red squirrel track pattern on snow or loose soil. Shaded portions indicate areas pressed hardest downward. Note that track pattern is typical of tree squirrels, but red squirrel is the smallest of these and is always found with pine trees.

footed. In loose snow, the outline of its entire hind foot prints, but on firmer ground its heels-up stance denotes a very alert animal with the reflexes to disappear in a flash.

Like those of its larger cousins, the red squirrel's track pattern strongly resembles that of a very small rabbit. Moving about in hops, forefeet print close together in sometimes staggered pairs, with hind feet registering just ahead and to the outside of them on each side. The straddle averages 3 to 3½ inches, the track sets are about 1 foot in length, and the distance between track sets is an indication of the animal's speed. Short hops of 8 to 14 inches denote a steady but unhurried gait. Longer leaps, ranging from 2 to more than 3 feet, tell of greater urgency, such as might be provoked by a hungry bobcat or red fox.

SCAT

Red squirrel scat is similar to that of other tree squirrels, and identical to the scat of flying squirrels. Usually it's segmented, ¼ inch to ½ inch long, and roughly cylindrical, with an irregular surface. Summer scat is dark brown to black, soft, and usually deposited at the base of a den tree.

Winter scat is similar but drier and more fibrous, reflecting the change in diet from green plants to stored foods.

SIGN

The most prominent red squirrel sign is its summer nest, which resembles the cup-shaped nests of other tree squirrels in shape, but not in the materials used. Fox and gray squirrels use leaves and twigs from the hardwoods of their habitat, but red squirrel nests are made of pine needles and strips of bark. Pines are the preferred nesting trees, but nearby witch hazels or willows are also used, and small trees are sometimes chosen. I've noticed that red squirrels prefer to nest closer to the earth than larger tree squirrels do, typically within 15 feet of the ground.

A common winter sign are the cuttings left below spruce and hemlock trees, as the red squirrels nip off cone-bearing twigs then climb down to eat the cones or carry them off to a cache site. Where red squirrels coexist with porcupines, which leave the same types of clippings, remember that porkies prefer white pines to all others as winter food, and seldom dine on hemlocks or spruces if these are available. Of course the toothmarks of squirrels are smaller, and the squirrels, being interested only in the cones, leave more cuttings on the ground than do the twig-eating porcupines. Fortunately, the red squirrel's discards serve as welcome winter fare for deer.

VOCALIZATIONS

The most obvious red squirrel vocalization is often described as a high-pitched "chirrrrrrrrr," a staccato call resembling the sound made by cicadas on a hot day, but louder and with a lower tone. This call is usually heard morning and evening, seldom at midday, and it seems to be a territorial claim, because other red squirrels will answer but won't approach.

Also heard is a sharp bark, similar to the sound a human might make when sucking the cheek against the molars then releasing it quickly. These barks are an alarm call; a fast series of them indicates immediate danger, a slower series less urgent danger. With a bit of listening and practice, most people can learn to imitate red squirrel barks, and sometimes the little animals will approach out of curiosity—of which they have an abundance.

WOODCHUCK OR GROUNDHOG (MARMOTA MONAX)

An old myth has it that this marmot (a family of oversize ground squirrels) emerges from its hibernation burrow every year on Candlemas Day, February 2, to check the weather. If it sees its own shadow, goes the legend, the rodent returns to its burrow to sleep for another six weeks, because it knows that's when spring will arrive. In fact, there's often a one-to two-week thaw at about this time in southern snow country, and marmots, like bears, sometimes wake up briefly to stretch their legs during unseasonably warm spells.

Close relatives of the woodchuck include the yellow-bellied marmot (*Marmota flaviventris*) of the western United States and the hoary marmot (*Marmota caligata*) of the Pacific Northwest, from Montana up through Alaska. The ranges of these rodents overlap in only a few places, but different species are easily distinguishable. The yellow-bellied marmot, or rockchuck, is the smallest marmot at 5 to 10 pounds, and can

Leonard Lee Rue III

Woodchuck

Leonard Lee Rue III

Yellow-bellied Marmot

be identified by its grizzled brown coat with yellow-orange chest and feet, and the distinctive "collar" of the same color around its neck. The hoary marmot, so called because of its frosted-looking grizzled coat and white face, is the largest marmot at 8 to 20 pounds (discounting the larger but rare Olympic marmot). Woodchucks, the most widespread of marmots, weigh 5 to 14 pounds and have predominantly brown coats with grizzled shoulders, a bushy tail 4 to 10 inches long, and dark brown or black feet. Also, the woodchuck is the only marmot that doesn't live in mountainous country, instead keeping to open but dry lowlands.

The woodchuck's common name stems from a generic name, *woochuk,* used by the Cree tribe to describe all marmots. The name has nothing to do with eating or chucking wood, or even with the fact that woodchucks normally live at the edges of forested areas.

HABITAT AND RANGE

In a sense, woodchucks are the northern woodlands version of prairie dogs, except in this case the plains are fields or meadows, and the forests provide a wider variety of food options. Dens are permanent and fairly elaborate, with 8- to 12-inch entrances that belie sometimes vast interiors. Entrance tunnels may reach depths of 5 feet and sometimes extend 30 feet or more, with an enlarged sleeping chamber, an adjoining defecation chamber (yes, indoor plumbing), and one or more emergency exits. When scouting possible woodchuck habitats, bear in mind that the animals require at least 3 feet of high-and-dry ground to live, so open swamps and bottomlands with a high water table are not good places to look. Dry, open woods bordering open areas are the best places to find dens, which are frequently dug under large rotting logs, or deadfall timber.

The range of the woodchuck extends from Tennessee to Delaware, northward through Maine, and across Québec and Ontario. To the west it runs from Arkansas and Kansas north through Minnesota and eastern North Dakota, as well as throughout the northern halves of Manitoba, Saskatchewan, Alberta, and British Columbia, reaching well into the

*Distribution of eastern woodchuck or groundhog (*Marmota monax*).*

center of Alaska. Apparently, the only factor limiting woodchuck expansion is the availability of suitable habitat. The species coexists well with humans; despite having once been considered fine table fare, it has never been endangered.

FOODS

Most of a woodchuck's diet consists of meadow plants such as clovers, alfalfa, plantains, dandelions, cresses, and violets, but it also eats raspberries, blueberries, and beechnuts along with a variety of grasses and their roots. I also suspect that many types of mushrooms and other fungi are eaten, but so many chisel-toothed rodents nibble on these that I'd have to catch one in the act to be sure.

Fruit trees are also fair game. Although the stocky, squat woodchuck is a ground dweller, its squirrel bloodlines are apparent in its ability to climb trees. Serviceberries and wild cherries are eaten, along with apples and other orchard fruits, but woodchucks appear nervous among the branches of a tree and prefer foraging on the ground.

The woodchuck's willingness to live in close proximity to humans, its voracious appetite, and its need to dig holes that can break the legs of livestock made it a pest in farming areas. An overpopulation can seriously damage corn, beans, and other crops, or even wipe out a family garden. In the woodchuck's defense, its digging habits help aerate the soil, making it better for growing crops, and concentrated scat deposits are very good fertilizer.

MATING HABITS

When male woodchucks emerge from hibernation burrows in February or March—as late as April in the Far North—they begin fighting one another for territory and females almost immediately. Battles are noisy and sometimes violent, with much biting, wrestling, squealing, whistling, and rapid chattering of teeth. Sharp, chisel-like incisors can make these battles bloody, but weaker contenders rarely continue after first blood is drawn.

Once territory has been established, the dominant male is entitled to mate with any adult females in it; aside from rejecting immediate family members, females seem not to care which male impregnates them. After a brief courtship, the male moves into a female's burrow and stays for about a week, the only time these normally solitary animals actually live together. No other bond is formed between pairs, and males take no part in rearing the young.

Gestation time is four weeks, with four or five blind, hairless young born in a deep, subterranean chamber lined with soft grasses in April and May, earlier in the South than in the North. Newborn 'chucks require almost constant care, and females may not leave their dens for up to a week after giving birth.

At one month the youngsters open their eyes and begin to crawl about the birthing chamber. At about six weeks they emerge from the den to forage for solid foods with Mother, and they quickly learn to keep an eye eternally skyward for birds of prey, the woodchuck's most dangerous enemy. Like beavers, woodchucks are ferocious fighters when cornered or when young are threatened, but red foxes, coyotes, and badgers sometimes feel up to the challenge, often appropriating and enlarging the victim's den for their own use. At two months the youngsters disperse to establish their own territories.

SEASONAL HABITS

Woodchucks are diurnal, or active by day, and left unmolested will indulge in a fair imitation of sunbathing on warm days, but always with a surprisingly sharp eye out for danger. If a dangerous predator is sighted or scented, a woodchuck typically raises itself erect on its haunches to get a better look and smell, sometimes climbing onto a downed log or even climbing a tree to enhance the view. If approached, a mother sends her young scurrying for the safety of the burrow with a sharp, abrupt whistle, then follows herself. Once inside, they're safe from air attacks, and few land predators can reach them. Those that can are eluded by escaping through one of perhaps many escape tunnels and perhaps up a nearby tree, out of reach of their most dangerous land enemies, the red fox, coyote, and wolf.

The territory claimed by an adult woodchuck is always small, usually no more than 3 acres, but size is ultimately determined by available foods. Adults might have more than one burrow, seldom more than two, and the species' slow, waddling gait ensures that those venturing too far from the den lead abbreviated lives.

Autumn is when 'chucks are most active, because, like other true hibernators, they need to put on as much as 25 percent of their body weight in fat reserves for the coming long winter sleep. Hibernation begins in November or December, when green food plants disappear, and the sleeping animals undergo remarkable metabolic changes. The body temperature drops from 97°F to about 40°F, respiration slows to one breath each six minutes, and the heart rate decreases from 110 beats per minute to about 4.

TRACKS

As members of the squirrel family, woodchucks have four toes on the forefeet and five on the hind feet, with toes not quite as long as a tree squirrel's but ending in the same enlarged "fingertips." In fact, except for the obvious difference in size, woodchuck tracks might easily be mistaken for those of a giant tree squirrel. Forefeet average 1½ to 2 inches long, hind feet 2 to 2½ inches. Yellow-bellied marmot tracks are slightly smaller and hoary marmot tracks larger, but all marmot tracks are otherwise indistinguishable from one another.

Although woodchucks walk flat footed on level surfaces most of the time, there's a tendency toward walking on the balls of the hind feet only,

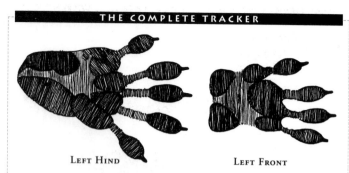

LEFT HIND   **LEFT FRONT**

Marmot tracks (all species); front, about 2 inches long; hind, about 2½ inches long. Rearmost half of hind heel pad seldom prints, leaving a partial track smaller than front tracks.

keeping the heels airborne and printing an abbreviated track that averages 1 to 1½ inches long—shorter than the foreprints. A clear track will show this with a deep impression at the toes, ascending gradually farther back until merging indistinctly with the surface. Note that, unlike many pawed animals that walk with most of their body weight on the outer big toe, marmots exert a fairly even amount of pressure against all four or five toes, so in a typical track all the toes and claws show.

Woodchucks rarely run unless frightened, but meander about with a slow, shambling pace in keeping with their stout bodies. In this track pattern, the hind feet print directly onto or heavily overlap the foreprints, in staggered pairs on each side. The stride, or distance between pairs, is 3 to 4 inches, the straddle 3½ to more than 6 inches. Note the similarities and differences between marmot and porcupine tracks, both of which walk flat footed and have the same number and arrangement of toes on all four feet.

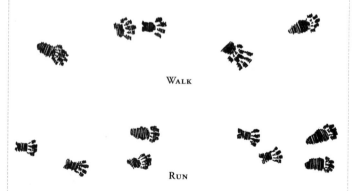

WALK

RUN

Track patterns of eastern woodchuck and yellow bellied marmot. Top: walk, with hind feet frequently overlapping front tracks. Bottom: run, with all four feet printing independently, front feet registering behind rear tracks.

Scat samples, eastern woodchuck and yellow bellied marmot. Length varies, with scat lengths running from 2 inches to more than 4 inches. The two samples at left have faded with age.

SCAT

Scat of woodchucks and other marmots is extremely variable due to the animals' broad vegetarian diet, which changes with the availability of seasonal plants, berries, and fruits. When feeding heavily on green grasses, a 'chucks scat may measure more than 4 inches long and be held together by long, undigested fibers that produce a very irregular strand, often larger at one or both ends. Fibers will be visible, with colors ranging from brown to black (remember, scat samples lighten with age).

More typically, marmot scat resembles that of an adult house cat in size and general configuration. Scat is generally cylindrical and consists of several connected segments that measure 2 to 2½ inches long by ½ to more than 1 inch in diameter, irregularly shaped, and usually brown or black in color. Plant fibers are usually evident.

When scouting for marmots, remember that most scat is deposited inside the den in a special defecation chamber. This habit probably evolved as a means of minimizing scent that might attract predators, but it also identifies the marmot as a homebody that spends much time indoors.

SIGN

The most obvious woodchuck sign is the one most hated by ranchers, farmers, and horseback riders: its burrow. The main entrances run 8 to 12 inches across and open onto tunnels that are always deep enough to break a hoofed animal's leg. The danger is multiplied by one or more less conspicuous escape tunnels excavated to a radius of 15 feet or more.

Recently dug dens are evidenced by piles of fresh, loose dirt about their entrances, but older dens that have been occupied for a couple of years will have blended back into the landscape, the loose soil washed into the earth by rain and melting snow. When freshly dug soil is present, the animal can usually be identified by clear tracks left in it.

Note that coyotes, badgers, and, especially, gray foxes may convert marmot dens to their own use, sometimes after eating the original occupant. The entrance to a coyote den will be enlarged to 1 or 2 feet across. Badger holes are distinctly elliptical, with a width of 8 to 12 inches. Fox den entrances are also 8 to 12 inches in diameter, but are more rounded and open onto an enlarged chamber just below the surface.

Feeding sign left by marmots is inconspicuous and easily mistaken for sign left by rabbits, porcupines, and various chisel-toothed rodents. But in tall grass, woodchucks can often be backtracked to their dens along a well-packed trail, which branches into lesser used trails leading to favorite feeding areas.

VOCALIZATIONS

Most often heard is the woodchuck's alarm whistle, an abrupt, high-pitched "tweeeet" that sounds much like a person whistling through his teeth. This whistle is also heard from other marmots, but it's usually louder and more prolonged, especially from the hoary marmot. Youngsters respond to it by scurrying for their den, and any other marmots in the area will be instantly alert for danger upon hearing an alarm whistle. A softer series of whistles is uttered by alarmed adults running for the den.

Occasionally, woodchucks also "sing." I've never heard this call, at least not up close, but it has been described as a sharp whistle followed by a softer tone and ending with a rapid series of even softer notes. From a distance, only the first two whistles are audible.

A loud, fast chattering of teeth is also a sign of alarm and a warning that the animal is ready to stand its ground and fight—so beware of chattering marmots. Other sounds of agitation or aggression include hissing, growling, and squealing.

NEW WORLD RATS
AND MICE (*CRICETIDAE*)
20

TO COVER COMPLETELY OR even adequately the more than 70 native North American rodents is beyond the scope of this book. That I've elected to cover just one species in this section belies the critical role rodents play in every terrestrial ecosystem on the planet. Voles, mice, squirrels, and other rodents are a critical food source for predators ranging from snakes and birds to weasels and wolves. Because they have so many natural enemies, all species are prolific, with some producing several litters per year and most breeding year-round.

Further complicating things, our most abundant species of rats and mice, the Norway rat (*Rattus norvegicus*), black rat (*Rattus rattus*), and house mouse (*Mus musculus*) are really invaders brought from Europe by ship centuries ago. Virtually everywhere on the continent, these aggressive immigrants, which have adapted to life in close proximity to humans, have permanently upset the natural balance by displacing wild native species, making themselves a staple food of native carnivores. By destroying predators (especially snakes), humans have frequently caused themselves real grief; in the mid-1920s, for instance, parts of California were literally overrun by house mice, which had reached dangerous concentrations of roughly 82,000 individuals per acre.

COMMON MUSKRAT
(*ONDATRA ZIBETHICUS*)

Although many equate the muskrat with urban rats, this New World rodent is more closely related to voles. Names such as "marsh rat," "swamp rat," and even its common name all contribute to the misperception of this harmless rodent. Like all New World rodents and unlike those of the Old World, muskrats are not parasitic on humans, nor do they carry the deadly, highly contagious diseases attributed in particular to the Norway rat.

Muskrats differ from rats of any species in several ways. The most obvious is size; the dreaded Norway rat, that bane of civilization throughout recorded history, is the largest rat in North America, yet averages only a quarter the size of the 1½- to 4-pound muskrat. The muskrat tail is also different, being triangular instead of round, with a flat bottom and black,

Muskrat

scaly texture. Most striking, in my opinion, is the muskrat's face, which is more squared, blunt, and squirrel-like than the faces of sharp-featured rats.

Another closely related immigrant, this one brought here intentionally, is the nutria, or coypus (*Myocastor coypus*), of South America. Like muskrats, the nutria wears a rich coat of thick brown fur of great value to the fur trade—except in this instance there's more of it, because nutrias weigh from 2 to 25 pounds. Nutrias have escaped captivity and established isolated populations in the southern half of the United States, sometimes driving out the less aggressive muskrats. Aside from size, the most obvious difference between muskrats and nutrias is the latter's round, sparsely haired tail. Even with nutria pelts taking up the slack, approximately 10 million muskrat pelts are sold in the United States each year.

In days past, muskrats also had commercial value as food, although they were sold under the more acceptable name "marsh rabbit." Today, few people have ever tasted muskrat, which is too bad, because the meat is very good.

HABITAT AND RANGE

Like beavers, another distant cousin, muskrats are aquatic rodents that never live far from water. They can live on practically any freshwater lakeshore, wet marsh, or riverbank, but beaver ponds provide deep, still water for these superb swimmers, as well as a lush environment for the grasses, cattails, and sedges they need to live on. Mink, otters, skunks, raccoons, and bobcats pose the greatest danger to adults, while many carnivores regularly invade nests to eat muskrat young.

Despite centuries of trapping, muskrats have never been endangered, although immigrant nutrias have almost entirely displaced them in Texas, Louisiana, and Florida. The species is found rarely or not at all in New

*Distribution of common muskrat (*Ondatra zibethicus*).*

Mexico, Arizona, Utah, Nevada, and California, primarily because these states don't provide the wetlands muskrats require. With these exceptions, muskrats are common through the remainder of the lower 48 states, nearly all of Canada, and all but the northernmost tip of Alaska.

FOODS

Muskrats are primarily vegetarians, living on a wide variety of wetland plants, such as cattail shoots, grass stems, sedge roots, and an occasional pond lily root in summer. Parts of these and other food plants floating on the surface are a sure indication of muskrat activity. Terrestrial food plants include plantains, violets, and dandelions, and the animals will sometimes venture 100 yards or more inland to get them.

In winter they eat willow and other buds as well as watercress, the latter being the only green plant in the water in snow country. Access beneath the ice is usually gained by short underground tunnels leading from the shoreline and entering the water several inches below its surface. Mink, a muskrat's most serious predators, usually have their own "plunge holes," but they frequently appropriate muskrat tunnels as their own.

Like most rodents (beavers are one exception), muskrats also include at least some animal flesh in their diets. Clams, crayfish, and frogs are eaten as are some insects. Preferred feeding spots on shore or sometimes in shallow water are selected to provide as much security from predators as possible, and these places will be littered with clamshells, crayfish carapaces, and frog parts. Favorite feeding spots are used regularly, and are good places for you to set up an observation blind.

Floating mats, or "rafts" of rushes, reeds, grass, and sticks, also serve as feeding platforms, and are constructed specifically for their maker to rest upon while feeding. Rafts are always right up against a bank, never in a current, and in water deep enough to allow a fast plunge to escape predators.

MATING HABITS

Muskrats breed prolifically, like the proverbial rodent, because so many predators from air, land, and water eat them regularly. There's no fixed mating season, and females may become pregnant in any month, producing up to five litters per year. Breeding is prompted by the scent of females coming into heat, and since females are in the majority by about a four-to-one margin, males rarely fight over mating rights and in fact seem pressed to keep up with demand in some areas.

Gestation from pregnancy to birth takes a very short three to four weeks, with differences in duration probably due to the physical health of the mother. Litters may be as large as 11 young if conditions are ideal, but generally run about 7. The young are born naked and blind in "houses," which very much resemble beaver lodges but are constructed mostly of cattails, or in excavated dens in the sides of streambanks, close to the high-water line.

After two weeks, young are fully furred and can swim and dive with their mother, but they continue nursing for one month, during which the female will probably mate again. After weaning, the mother drives them away, but if the population isn't too dense the youngsters probably won't travel far. If the opposite is true, adults competing for food will fight until weaker or smaller individuals relocate, sometimes traveling several miles to establish new territories.

SEASONAL HABITS

As might be expected from their environment, muskrats are superb swimmers, able to swim backward or forward with equal ease, although not quite with the expertise of otters, which prey on them at all ages. Since much of their food is obtained under water, and because water is a means to escape land predators, they also dive well and can remain submerged for more than 15 minutes. Even more impressive, they can return to the surface after such a long period, take a few quick breaths, and submerge again for an equal amount of time.

Muskrats are also pretty good tunnelers. In nature they use this digging ability to excavate dens and tunnels into streambanks and lakeshores, but they apparently see no difference between these places and man-made dikes or dams. Bottomland crops planted close to water (the flatland farms of northern Ohio are a good example) are also considered fair game, and no tuber or taprootlike vegetable is beyond their reach.

In areas where humans are present, muskrats are likely to go about the business of living during darkness, although it isn't unusual to see one during daylight. In more remote habitats, they're not only active during the day but also seem to prefer daylight hours, which makes them good, easy subjects for beginning observers and photographers.

TRACKS

Muskrats have five toes on each foot, front and back, but the innermost toes of the front feet are so tiny that they rarely register, even in clear tracks. The toes are always widely splayed in tracks of both front and hind feet, but only the hind feet are partially webbed. If webbing ever shows in hind tracks, I haven't seen it, even in mud. Fortunately, track configurations are sufficiently distinctive to make a positive identification without it.

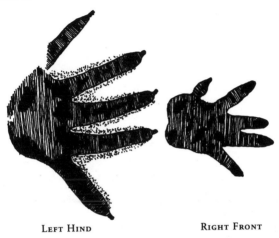

LEFT HIND   RIGHT FRONT

Muskrat tracks: front, 1 inch to 1½ inches long. Note vestigial "thumb," which rarely prints. Hind, 2 to 3 inches long. Rear feet are webbed slightly.

The hind feet of the muskrat are much larger than the forefeet, so you should have no trouble telling them apart. The length of the hind tracks runs 2 to 3 inches, of the front tracks 1 to 1½ inches. The innermost toe of the hind foot prints faintly most of the time (see the illustration), making tracks look four toed.

Muskrats seldom run, as they're designed neither for pursuit nor for flight on land. At a normal walk on muddy ground, most of an animal's track patterns show the forefeet printing in front of the hind feet of the same side in pairs, occasionally overlapping or printing side by side. The stride, or distance between track pairs, averages 3 to 4 inches.

On snow, where walking is more difficult for the short-legged rodent, tracks tend to register as a zigzag line, with the front and hind feet on each side registering in the same holes. The stride averages 3 inches or longer, with a distinctive serpentine trail left between tracks by the dragging tail.

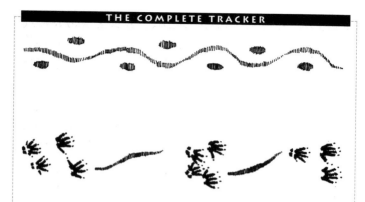

Muskrat track patterns. Top: walk in snow, showing serpentine trail left by dragging tail. Bottom: run in mud. Note that all four feet print individually, forefeet behind hind feet, with tail dragging between leaps.

SCAT

Muskrat scat is usually deposited in pellet form, or sometimes as a softer green mass. Deposits have a unique configuration in which most pellets are stuck together lengthwise, a pattern I haven't seen in any other species. Pellets average ⅛ to ¾ inch long, are generally green in color when fresh, growing darker with age, and contain mostly plant fibers.

Like nearly all territorial mammals, muskrats use their own scat as scentposts to help mark their territorial boundaries. A favorite place is on a natural bridge formed by downed trees that span a stream, or sometimes on large branches or trunks that extend out over the water at ground level. In established territories, these scentposts exhibit an accumulation of scat pellets of varying ages, showing that the scentpost is active and freshened regularly. Scentposts are good places to set up a camera or blind, particularly in more remote habitats, but bear in mind that

Muskrat scat; pellets ⅛ to ¾ of an inch long. Often deposited as a territorial mark on logs and other prominent landmarks in the rodent's swampy domain. Note crescent shapes and the way pellets lay side by side, a pattern unique to the muskrat.

muskrats are comparatively shy animals. Disturbing a scentpost in any way, or leaving human scent anywhere in the area, is often sufficient to cause its owner to abandon it.

SIGN

Muskrat sign is varied and obvious once you know what to look for. Remember that these rodents seldom venture far from water unless seeking out a new territory, so any search for sign can be narrowed down to shorelines and streambanks.

The best indication of a muskrat population comes from their sloppy eating habits. Cut green grass stems floating atop water prove that a muskrat recently stopped there to have a meal, and a really sharp eye can detect the places where those stems were cut. Also look for floating rafts of rushes, grass, cattail leaves, and sticks pressed against the shore, again with fresh grass stems floating nearby. Rafts are created to give the animals feeding places out of reach of most land predators, allowing instant escape into the water.

Muskrat "houses" are definite indications of an active population. These hollow structures are typically located at the shoreline, but always in water deep enough to allow their owners to come and go without leaving the water or even surfacing. They closely resemble the conical- or dome-shaped beaver lodge, except that they're constructed entirely of cattails, grasses, and mud, whereas the hatchet-toothed beaver has the tools to fashion its own from sturdier wood.

Some muskrat houses are small, beginning at less than 3 feet in diameter at the base; these are most likely feeding stations for solitary adults. Others may be as wide as 8 feet across the base and usually contain a mother with young. In winter, houses also provide convenient access to the water below them, even though on the surface there might be a layer of ice several inches thick. What with a layer of snow as insulation, the dead-air space inside, and the animal's own body heat, the water beneath a muskrat house never freezes.

Other muskrat dens are excavated into the side of a shoreline high and dry enough to permit such digging. This type of den is probably preferred, although of course its construction is impossible in marshlands, where most muskrats live. Where excavated dens are found, entrances average 4 to 5 inches in diameter, and lead into a larger chamber. Scatterings of crayfish and clam shells may be around the doorway, but remember that mink regularly take up residence in muskrat burrows after eating the residents and their sign is similar, except that it typically includes small bones and fur. Note that muskrats are truly fastidious rodents, with dens, feeding houses, and rafts kept immaculately clean.

Finally, there are muskrat scentposts formed by small clusters of grasses, leaves, and mud ashore that are scented by the animals' perineal (anal) glands. This type of scentpost is small, consisting of little more than a handful of material.

VOCALIZATIONS

I wish I could be more thorough in this section, but if muskrats have anything approaching a language, neither my experience nor my research has discovered it. A cornered muskrat—which with its sharp teeth can be surprisingly formidable—makes a loud squeaking sound, sometimes accompanied by chattering and sharp squeals. Unfortunately, this description applies more or less to calls between a mother and her young, fighting adults, and muskrats involved in every other activity I've witnessed.

INDEX